D0801845

Organizations
and Chaos

ORGANIZATIONS AND CHAOS

Defining the Methods of Nonlinear Management

H. RICHARD PRIESMEYER

Q QUORUM BOOKS
Westport, Connecticut · London

Library of Congress Cataloging-in-Publication Data

Priesmeyer, Henry Richard.
    Organizations and chaos : defining the methods of nonlinear
management / H. Richard Priesmeyer.
        p.   cm.
    Includes index.
    ISBN 0–89930–630–6 (alk. paper)
    1. Management.   2. Industrial management.   3. Organization.
    4. Chaotic behavior in systems.   I. Title.
    HD31.P727   1992
    658—dc20   92–7486

British Library Cataloguing in Publication Data is available.

Library of Congress Catalog Card Number: 92–7486
ISBN: 0–89930–630–6

First published in 1992

Quorum Books, 88 Post Road West, Westport, CT 06881
An imprint of Greenwood Publishing Group, Inc.

Printed in the United States of America

The paper used in this book complies with the
Permanent Paper Standard issued by the National
Information Standards Organization (Z39.48–1984).

10 9 8 7 6 5 4 3 2 1

To Margaret

Contents

Tables and Figures

Preface

Organizations *are* nonlinear systems and they should be managed using the tools provided by chaos theory. That is the central theme of this book. Here is an explanation of how chaos theory can be made practical for managers in boardrooms, marketing departments, and production. Here is a discussion of chaos theory that directly relates its implications to business. It answers the question "How can you apply chaos theory to business?"

There seems to be at least three fundamental approaches to the study of chaos. The most common one is to take some mathematical equation and use it to generate interesting fractal patterns. A second approach is to explore the purely mathematical questions chaos theory provides. A third approach, and the one taken in this book, is a practical one—it takes real corporate performance data and reveals the underlying chaotic behavior. The images offered in the text provide the substance necessary for meaningful discussions on chaos in organizations.

The text is divided into three parts. Three chapters in Part I provide an introduction to chaos theory, a discussion of the methodology used throughout the book, and a discussion on interpreting phase planes and marginal history charts—the products of this analysis. Part II takes a functional approach to business applications. There are chapters of marketing, finance, production, and human resources. In each of these functional chapters you will find examples on how chaos theory can be applied to common ideas in the field. For example, the chapter on marketing applies chaos theory to product life cycles, distribution, and market share analysis. The chapter on production shows how chaos theory can be used to improve quality.

Part III applies chaos theory to decision-making in an organization. A chapter on forecasting introduces the reader to a concept called *visioning*, while the other chapters in Part III deal with strategic management issues, how one can establish a "Center of Chaos" within an organization, and how one can begin to see the myriad of chaotic systems around us. There is also a short chapter of closing thoughts.

Throughout the book I have provided *propositions,* 34 in all, which define succinctly the key ideas in the discussion. These propositions are collected in the appendix according to the functional areas they address. They provide a starting point for those interested in advancing what I have done here.

Somewhere, about one-third of the way through the manuscript, I realized how easy this book was to write. There was never a shortage of material to discuss, never a shortage of implications to describe. Unlike some new ideas, which would have played out after so much mining, this idea—to apply chaos theory in business—kept providing diamonds.

CORPORATE CHAOS THEORY: CONCEPTS AND METHODS

1

From Theory to Application: An Introduction to Organizational Chaos Theory

Consider change: the management of it, the forecasting of it, the predictability of it, the expectation of it, the reliability of it, the surprise of it, and, most interesting of all, the structure of it. Change is what makes life interesting. It's what makes thinking necessary; change in our world provides the substance of life—without it we would face only continued constancy—an endless sameness that would fail to challenge us and teach us how to manage our world.

Still, with change all around us, we insist on focusing on snapshot pictures of our world. We are like two-dimensional flatlanders in a three-dimensional world. We record our corporate performance with audited reports that disregard the transitions in our organizations. We capture measures such as on-hand inventories and budgeted expenses as singular quantities and record them with precision, believing that greater accuracy will somehow provide greater truth. We don't seem to mind that those measures don't reveal the dynamics of the continually changing organization they represent. Even stock prices are quoted as a single price with only a mention of their latest change. No one seems to be concerned about the patterns and structures of change.

This is not a world of constants that can be captured with measures of singular, static performance like total sales, total profits, and daily production quantities; it is a world of dynamics. Using measures of static performance is like listening to a symphony one note at a time; any harmony or discord becomes apparent only when the notes are combined into a rhythm, a pattern of change. We are resolute in our commitment to measures of static performance; we are trained in them, we feel comfortable with them, and, in some cases, we are legally obligated to them. But our commitment is mostly the result of knowing no alternative. We've been studying the notes and have not yet heard a symphony.

Even the most fundamental ideas in our world are subject to change. Europeans believed that their known world was the only world until adventurers discovered great new lands beyond the horizons. Those discoveries forced us to abandon the idea that the world was flat and to accept a new reality that the world is a sphere. We gave up a false view for an apparently correct one. That was not always the case. Attached to the new understanding of the world as a sphere was the mistaken belief that Earth must be the center of the universe. That belief was supported by elaborate theories, models, and machines, which provided proof with clocklike precision; never mind that some of the movements of the clock were unnatural and unexplained. Those aberrant movements, however, could not be ignored by some, and eventually, after an accumulation of evidence, Nicolaus Copernicus wrote to Pope Paul III in 1543:

I can easily conceive, most Holy Father, that as soon as some people learn that in this book which I have written concerning the revolutions of the heavenly bodies, I ascribe certain motions to the Earth, they will cry out at once that I and my theory be rejected.

Those words, along with the rest of Copernicus' argument, broke open the door to modern astronomy. It established the heliocentric theory, a newer, more correct understanding of reality.

This new view eventually was accepted and included with other beliefs, some of which will later be proved incorrect. For example, if evidence of intelligent life is discovered elsewhere in this universe, it will force us to abandon the idea that we are alone and will create a significant transition in our understanding of who we are.

Our understanding of this world evolves haltingly over time as the implications of one change accumulate until the weight of evidence they present is too great for flawed notions to stand. Then, almost spontaneously, one paradigm falls and a new one that is somewhat closer to reality is adopted.

CHAOS THEORY

We currently are in transition to a new paradigm that has enormous implications for every science. Like previous discoveries, it comes with accumulated evidence that is sufficient to force a rejection of long-standing beliefs. Chaos theory, also called nonlinear systems theory, has been rapidly gathering substance and support for the past twenty years. It has evolved beyond development and has now found practical applications. It has already found applications in the fields of hydrodynamics, meteorology, biology, chemistry, physics, astronomy, and cardiology, displacing old beliefs with new ones. It is now time for chaos theory to change the way we think about organizations and how we manage them.

A new theory may not seem as profound as the discovery that Earth is not the center of the universe, but remember that at one time, Copernicus had only a heliocentric theory. Also note that Copernicus' discovery affected primarily astrophysics; it didn't force wholesale revision of virtually every science. Chaos theory is profoundly important stuff.

Chaos theory is pervasively important because it attacks fundamental beliefs that we hold about our world and puts them in question. Specifically, it suggests that nothing in this world is random, and that all the disorder and apparent unpredictability about us are natural products of entirely deterministic processes. Consider the implications. Sales forecasts may not need to be forecasts at all; they may be values that are entirely knowable. Major environmental disruptions to a business may not be unpredictable. Disorder that results from a merger or an acquisition may be understandable in advance. Most important, if nothing in this world is random, then why do we use statistical methods that discard as error so much valuable information about our businesses?

If you own, manage, or work for any organization, you may already be affected by changes related to chaos theory. An entomologist uses chaos theory to study the balance of competing insects in a farmer's field. As the population of one species of insect declines, the population of another soars; the pattern reverses itself repeatedly, with each species first enjoying growth in numbers and then decline. The entomologist knows that destroying one species will leave the others unchecked. He also knows when all species can be destroyed with a minimum of insecticide and with proper timing. All this may not seem important to you unless you're the farmer or expect to make a living supplying the farmer with insecticide. Large structures such as buildings, bridges, and aircraft are known to be affected by nonlinear forces that can cause destructive vibrations. Chaos theory is used to identify and manage these forces. That is important to anyone who builds large structures, maintains them, finances them, or insures them. Cardiologists have learned that our hearts adhere to nonlinear patterns of performance. With that knowledge they can more effectively treat cardiac anomalies and identify patients who have an increased risk of recurring cardiac problems. That is important to the hospital, the insurance company, and the supplier of cardiac pacemakers (not to mention the patient). Chaos theory has directly affected these sciences, resulting in important implications for business. However, we have not brought the theory to bear directly on the behavior of our own organizations. Therein lies the purpose of this effort. Here is an explanation and illustration of how to use chaos theory to manage organizations.

DEFINING CHAOS

Chaos traditionally is defined as disorder, turmoil, or total confusion. It is supposedly the amorphous, lifeless void from which Earth emerged at creation. Chaos means a lack of any structure or order. For an example of chaotic behavior one would probably point to a waterfall or the weather. The definition begins to take on new meaning, however, when we begin to study chaotic systems. Instead of total disorder, structure is found. It seems that waterfalls are not at all disordered; they are entirely deterministic, albeit enormously complex. Similarly, the prediction of weather, although surely deterministic, involves so many complex patterns that we must now consider long-term weather prediction impossible. Yet hydrodynamics and meteorology have been advanced by chaos theory because it has revealed structures or patterns of behavior in systems that were thought to be driven by random processes. The new definition of chaos recognizes that disorder may be simply a high order of complexity that can emerge from entirely deterministic processes. Chaos now refers to the range of behaviors that deterministic processes can adopt.

Determinism

Consider loading a dozen golf balls into a cannon and firing them all at once from the first tee at your local golf course. Can you predict the destination of each ball? Are their destinations random, or are they determined by all the forces that interact on each ball? If they are randomly determined, what is the source of this randomness? It is entirely believable that the destinations are determined by the myriad of physical forces involved, including the weather. Just because we don't understand these forces and their interaction doesn't mean that any random process is at work. Complexity is not the same as randomness. Ignorance is not the same as randomness. Our inability to know the final placement of each golf ball is not due to randomness; it is only the result of complexity and ignorance. If we learn more about the complex forces involved, or if we reduce the complexity of the forces, we increase our ability to know each ball's final position.

Fortunately, when we play golf we hit only one ball at a time, thereby reducing the complexity considerably. We are, therefore, more able to know the destination of the ball. Its future locale is determined by its current position and all the forces acting on it, just as the weather is determined by its current position and all the forces that act on it. Nothing in golf is random.

Sensitivity to Initial Condition

How a chaotic system behaves is highly dependent on its initial condition, since each new position is based on a movement from the previous one. To use the golf analogy, the position of your ball after two strokes is highly dependent on its position after the first stroke. Similarly, the trajectory and ultimate destination of a bullet or a baseball are highly dependent on the initial condition. Sensitivity to initial condition results because the position of these projectiles at any moment is determined by their position at the previous moment.

Consider for a moment the type of computation necessary to forecast the destination of an object such as a baseball. Is it an average of all positions? Should we measure its position throughout the trajectory and disregard, as error, any values above or below some line of best fit? Is its position somehow determined by the median, mode, or standard deviation of the positions? Or should we assume that there is no randomness, there are no errors, and compute the future position at each moment given the position at the previous moment to ultimately determine a final destination? Dependence on initial conditions requires that we adopt a new method of computation, one that extends computation into the future by building on the results of the past. It also places new demands on us, since any error in measuring the initial condition is compounded prodigiously as we build on that measurement to compute a final position. Clearly, dependence on initial conditions also requires that we break with traditional statistical approaches that accommodate any concept of error.

Dependence on initial conditions is what makes accurate long-term weather forecasting impossible. Even if we fully understood the forces at work, we would never know the initial conditions with sufficient accuracy to correctly compute a prediction of the long-term future. We may be hesitant to believe such an emphatic statement of impossibility, but the more we learn about this world, the more we discover what nature permits and what it denies us. Long-term forecasting of chaotic systems cannot be achieved; that is the bad news. The good news is that understanding chaotic systems forces us to reexamine the concept of forecasting; why is it necessary to forecast anything that is entirely determined?

Period Doubling

It seems that chaos is not a condition, but rather a continuum of conditions ranging from absolute stability to patterns of activity that are incomprehensibly complex. Low-order chaos is understandable and predictable. High-order chaos appears random only because we do not understand it. With this view, chaos can be taken to define any activity we do not understand. What is chaotic, therefore, is not determined by the nature of the activity we are studying, but by our own level of understanding. What is chaotic to some is orderly and predictable to others.

Our cocker spaniel can never anticipate the trajectory of a tennis ball as it rolls off the inclined metal roof over our garage. The predictability of its bounce eludes him. Where it lands and where it goes after each bounce must seem chaotic to him. Our kids catch it easily and throw it back onto the roof.

Our cocker can, however, intercept the tennis ball if we roll it along the driveway. That is a lower level of disorder that he can understand; to him, it is a predictable trajectory. If we throw the tennis ball into the garage, however, none of us can determine its trajectory, so we call its behavior chaotic. Some would be tempted to call its trajectory random, but that would be wrong.

This example illustrates that there are specific levels of chaotic behavior. At the lowest level we find constancy. At a higher level we find periodic oscillation, and at still higher levels we find patterns we do not understand but that are nonetheless completely deterministic. Perhaps these patterns would be predictable if we better understood the process involved. Perhaps they would be more understandable if we used the appropriate quantitative tools.

The continuum of chaos is marked with specific positions where disorder changes from one level to another. These transitions are called bifurcation, meaning to divide into two parts or branches. The term is appropriate because bifurcation points are those levels of disorder at which the complexity of behavior doubles.

Consider a scientist studying the population of rabbits in an isolated ecological system. Specifically, the researcher is interested in computing the survival rate of rabbits in the area. He knows that the survival rates of rabbits each season are at least partially determined by the survival rates of the previous season. If the population is large in one season, it is likely to be smaller the next season as a result of the ecological system's inability to sustain the higher population. Similarly, a small population in one season may help the area support a larger population the next season. Ecologists now know that this situation is defined by the logistic equation $X_{next} = CX(1 - X)$, where X_{next} is the survival rate in the next season and C is a parameter that describes characteristics of the ecological system. The equation can be described in word form as follows: The survival rate in any season (X_{next}) is determined by the characteristics of the ecological system (C) and by the percentage of the population that survived (X) and did not survive $(1 - X)$ during the previous season.

So what will be the survival rate for rabbits in the area? That depends on the characteristics of the ecological system (C). At low values of C we will find stability, constancy. At higher values we will find oscillation, and at still higher values we will find more complex patterns and perhaps patterns so disordered that they appear random. Figure 1.1 provides some examples of what will happen. In each case the initial survival rate (X_0) is established at 50 percent. Subsequent values for twenty seasons are computed by iterating the equation, taking the solution from the first computation (X_1) to compute a solution for the next season (X_2).

In Figure 1.1a the parameter C is established at .8, resulting in a continuous decline in the population that stabilizes at zero survival. Even if C is set to 1.00, there is a gradual decline in the survival rate. As C is increased above 1.00, however, the ecological conditions improve until, at $C = 1.50$, we find a stable survival rate of 33 percent, shown in Figure 1.1b. Both these figures are examples of low-order chaos. They are stable and predictable. No bifurcation (period doubling) has taken place. At higher levels of C, however, we discover more complex patterns.

At $C = 3.00$, shown in Figure 1.1c, we find a pattern that settles down to a stable and continuous oscillation that periodically visits 63 percent and 70 percent. Somewhere between $C = 1.5$ and $C = 3.0$ there is a bifurcation; the pattern of performance splits, and transits from continuous to oscillation. As C is increased further there is another bifurcation, resulting in a more complex oscillation, one that repeats only every fourth season. Figure 1.1d may, at first glance, appear random, but it is a reliable, continuous series of survival rates: 88 percent, 37 percent, 83 percent, and 51 percent. The complex pattern emerges directly from a completely deterministic equation; it is not random.

MANAGERIAL IMPLICATIONS

There are enormous implications here for management. The logistic equation described above is just one of an unlimited set of nonlinear expressions that describe patterns of behavior under some specified set of conditions. Consider for a moment that our survival rates for rabbits might instead be annual market share percentages. Figure 1.1a would then describe a continuous decline in market share, Figure 1.1b would illustrate stable market share, and Figures 1.1c and 1.1d would provide examples of complex changes in market share. Just as the logistic equation describes the structural relation between rabbits and their environment, so it might explain the structural relation between your firm and the economic, competitive, and social environment in which it operates. And this example addresses only market share. What about profit margins, inventory turnover, collection rates, and employee productivity? What can chaos theory tell us about mergers, acquisitions, and divestitures. What are the implications for forecasting?

Figure 1.1
Survival Rates in the Rabbit Study

C=.80

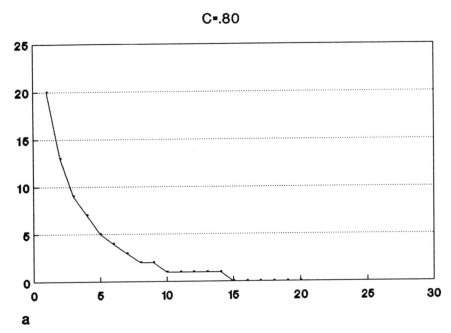

a

C=1.50

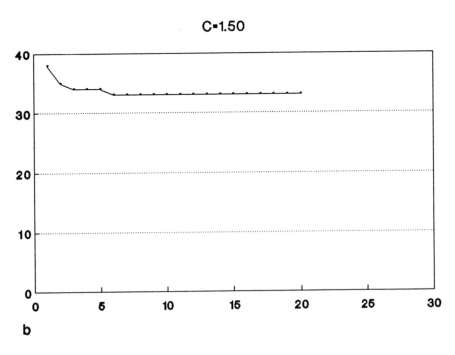

b

Figure 1.1 (Continued)

C=3.00

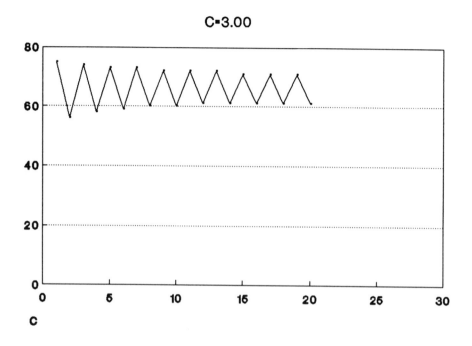

c

C=3.55

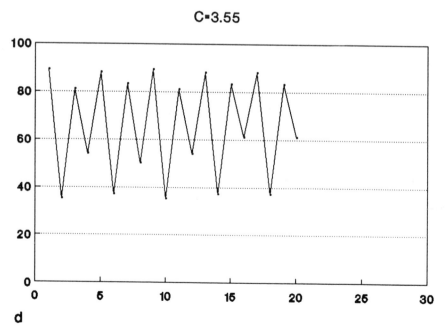

d

Figure 1.2
Stability of Market Share

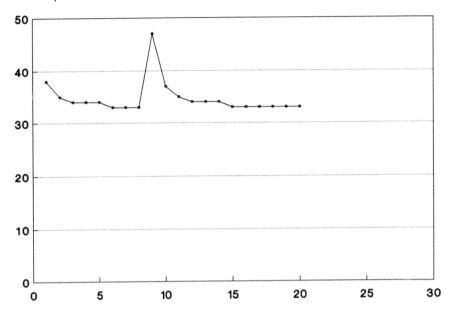

Structural Stability

The performance patterns in Figure 1.1 are structurally stable, meaning that even if you were able to alter the survival rate by a moderate amount it would not make any difference after several seasons. If market share were described by the same logistic equation, we might discover a pattern of performance like that given in Figure 1.2.

The implications are profound. They suggest that even if we used promotions to increase market share from a steady 33 percent to 45 percent, we would inevitably return to our 33 percent share; the relationship between the firm and its environment is stable only at that level. This view suggests that the only way market share can be changed in the long run is by changing the nature of the relationship between the firm and its environment. In this example that relationship is described by the parameter C.[1]

The presence of structural relationships between a firm and its environment suggests that many of the actions we take as managers are wholly ineffective in the long term. If we decide to retain some employees that we intended to terminate, it may make no substantive difference in our employee turnover rate. If we push for additional sales in the second quarter of the year, the effort may simply result in reduced sales during subsequent quarters, giving the same year-end total. If we buy more now, we buy less later. If we expand more rapidly now, we expand less rapidly later. If we fail to innovate now, we are forced to innovate later. Chaos theory allows us to enter a new domain of analysis that examines the structural relationships that bind our businesses to specific patterns of performance. It gives us a new perspective from which we can see the fundamental constraints that restrict us. And chaos theory provides a rich collection of relatively simple, quantitative tools that we can put to work in our businesses.

Conventional Techniques

To appreciate chaos theory one must first understand conventional statistics. Why do we compute means and standard deviations? What's wrong with regression, ANOVA, or time series analysis? These are the current business analysis tools. What, if anything, is wrong with them?

The tools we design and use are a function of our beliefs. If we wanted to hunt antelope and we believed that antelope cannot see red, then we would develop red clothing and red weapons and use them when hunting. If we believed that the earth is the center of the universe, then we would develop tools based on that belief that would help us understand the orbits of other celestial bodies. We generally believe that this world operates with some degree of randomness; therefore, we have developed statistical tools that simplify activity into central themes and, thus, have discarded the inaccuracy of our computations as meaningless error. We compute means and regression lines to find the common themes. We then compute standard error and perform analysis of variance, never realizing that intricate patterns of behavior may exist in those "errors." We even apply time series analysis and consolidate seasonal indexes, failing to recognize the functional relationships each observation has to its previous one. Worse yet, we focus on what we have explained and ignore the fact that we have left a large percentage of the behavior unexplained. Conventional statistics are constructed on the premise that this world is so complicated that, at best, we will understand only part of it. Chaos theory demonstrates that simple, deterministic processes such as the logistic equation can generate complex patterns of behavior. If we thought that the pattern in Figure 1.1d. was random, we might apply regression analysis to predict it. We would compute an equation for the line ($Y = b_0 + b_1 X_1$) and coefficients of determination (the R^2 statistic). We would compute standard error and then we would compute a p value to determine the probability (the chances) that there *might* be a relationship.

Chaos theory demonstrates that the pattern in Figure 1.1d is determined by a simple equation with only one parameter (C) and one variable (X). There is no error, and there is no reason to forecast future values of X; if we want to know any future value, all we have to do is compute it. If we believe that the world is random, then we build and use analytical tools that allow for randomness. If we believe that the world is deterministic, then we strive to develop analytical tools that do not allow for randomness.

Predetermination

Does chaos theory suggest that everything that happens is predetermined? No. Somehow, as events unfold, there is an allowance for freedom of choice, for a freedom to act or not to act. We still make decisions that change the nature of the processes at work. We still control activities. Chaos theory, however, is able to trace the effect of those decisions, and it may be able to direct us to make more effective decisions.

Everything is predetermined unless acted on by some other force. Sales will continue to climb unless our competitor acts to reverse the process. Cash flow will continue to decline unless we make changes in the budgeting process. Instead of suggesting that we have less control over events, chaos theory uncovers sensitive points of control where slight intervention can yield significant results.

Chaos theory increases our understanding of events and processes, thereby decreasing the level of ignorance. I am reminded of the magician who was able to flip a coin and reliably determine whether it was going to land with heads or tails up. No trick coins, no slight of hand. Was it luck? No, he had practiced by attaching a ribbon to the coin and counting the number of rotations the coin made in the air. He eventually had replaced all randomness, all luck, with a deterministic process simply by learning more about that process. Luck fills in where knowledge ends. Similarly, the methods described in this book reveal underlying patterns of activity that our current analytical methods discard as error. Those new patterns will replace some of our ignorance with understanding; they will make us a little less lucky and a lot more deterministic.

NEW CONCEPTS AND TERMINOLOGY

New sciences develop because old theories need improvement. The inefficiencies of current ideas sometimes reveal themselves as subtle, but persistent phenomenon. Like cold fusion and the theory that a meteor impact precipitated the extinction of the dinosaurs, mounting evidence gradually erodes our trust in previous beliefs and provides assurance that we are closer to the truth. Sometimes new theories present themselves with catastrophic clarity when a bridge collapses or an aircraft disintegrates. Other times simple human curiosity tempts us to look into the forgotten corners of science, and there we find wondrous surprises. The emergence of chaos theory has been marked by all these things. As the new science developed, so did new concepts and a new vocabulary.

Lorenz's Error

The term nonlinear has become associated with chaotic behavior and deserves a definition. We are all familiar with linear relationships that relate two or more variables, such that as an independent variable changes, the dependent variable responds by increasing or decreasing by some proportion. Linear relationships include quadratic (i.e., curvilinear) functions such as $Y = ax^2 + bx + c$, since these also provide functionally proportional responses to changes in the independent variable.

Nonlinear refers to a relationship that allows for a disproportionate response to changes in the independent variable. In nonlinear systems a very small change in the independent variable can result in a very large—even infinitely large—response in the dependent variable.

The term *system* refers here to any pattern of activity. A population of rabbits, their activities, and their relationships with their environment constitute a system. The manufacturing activity of a firm constitutes a system. An entire organization can be viewed as a system operating within an environment of economic, legal, and competitive forces. Organizations are nonlinear systems.

Sensitivity to Initial Conditions

In 1961 Edward Lorenz discovered one of the cornerstones of chaos theory. In his efforts to model the weather he established a set of equations to compute the interaction of atmospheric forces. He iterated the equations so that their solution at any moment was taken as the initial condition for the next set of computations. Programmed into a computer, Lorenz's equations provided a graphic plot of solutions that meandered down a paper printout. Although the computer maintained accuracy to six places behind the decimal, the associated quantitative solutions were formatted to be printed with accuracy to only three places behind the decimal.[2]

At one point, Lorenz restarted the program, using as the initial condition one of the interim solutions reported on a previous printout. The resulting graph of solutions remained faithful to the earlier solutions but only for a while. Then they began to diverge from the original forecast and soon the program was tracing a new prediction of the future. The major differences in the forecasts were the results of the difference between .506127 and .506; a difference of only .000127 had changed everything. The implications for Lorenz and all of meteorology were profound; the experiment suggested that accurate long-term weather forecasting would be impossible without knowing current weather conditions with absolute precision.

If we apply Lorenz's procedure to our market share example, we discover the same phenomenon. The heavy line in Figure 1.3 shows the so-

Figure 1.3
Sensitivity to Initial Conditions

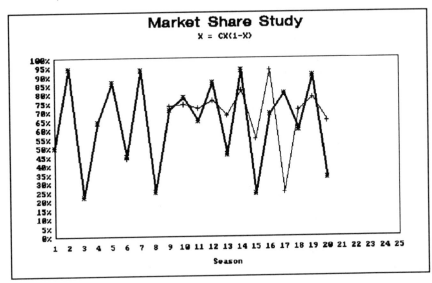

lutions that appear from our market share equation $X_{next} = CX(1-X)$ when $C = 3.75$ and $X = .50$.

When iterating the equation, X equals .45 in the sixth season. If we substitute .44 for the sixth season, we see that the solutions are similar for three more seasons but then begin to differ considerably until the two sets of solutions are entirely different. Future performance is highly sensitive to the initial conditions that, in this case, differ by only 1 percent.

Does this mean that long-term business forecasting is no more possible than long-term weather forecasting? Not necessarily. There are important differences between business and the weather, and those difference make chaos theory even more valuable to the business analyst than to the meteorologist.

Recall that the original market share example (Figure 1.2) showed that a significant change in market share may have no long-term effect. Figure 1.3 demonstrates that a change in market share of only 1 percent can have a significant effect. Both are based on the same equation. How can both be true?

Levels of Chaos

Ten years after Lorenz's discovery Robert May, a theoretical-physicist-turned-biologist, was exploring the behavior of this same logistic equation. He discovered that at lower values of C the solution would either drop to zero or stabilize at some singular positive value. At higher values it would oscillate periodically with two stable solutions, and at still higher values the oscillations would split again to provide four stable solutions. He devised a program to generate the solutions to the equation, given increasing values of the C, and he then plotted the stable solutions.[3]

May had discovered the inherent tendency of a nonlinear system to go through period doubling. He called the process bifurcation, since the solution split and diverged like branches on a tree. The diagram of solutions he produced serves as a road map to chaos, and it demonstrates that deterministic systems can decline to extinction (a solution of zero), assume a constant level of performance (a single solution), or stabilize at an oscillating level of performance (four, eight, or more solutions). At first the oscillations are understandable, having predictable cycles of solutions. But after two or three bifurcations the solutions provided by this simple equation appear random, even though they are not.

The pattern of performance given by the bold line in Figure 1.3 differs from the patterns in Figures 1.1 and 1.2 only because of increases in the parameter C. In Figure 1.3, C equals 3.75, and that raises the level of disorder to such complexity that it appears random. It also increases the sensitivity to initial conditions. If the solutions are constant (Figure 1.2) or oscillating with regular, periodic solutions (Figure 1.1c and 1.1d), then they are more capable of reestablishing that regularity after being drawn away from their regular pattern. At one level we find predictability and a tendency to return to predictability; at another we find a tendency toward disorder. All the patterns of performance can be considered chaotic but ranging from low order to high order, since they all result from the same deterministic equation.

The difference between the meteorologist and the business analyst centers around the level of chaos each confronts. The meteorologist deals with a system that is in high-order chaos; it tends to become unstable rather than assuming some regular, periodic cycle. The business analyst is fortunate to deal with chaotic systems that are typically of a lower order, although they can go chaotic. Further, in business, we are more able to alter the initial conditions and characteristics of the systems at work; we are able to change the parameters in the equations, which is something the meteorologist cannot do. Lorenz's discovery was bad news for meteorologists; it is great news for business.

Phase Space

The emerging science of chaos was beginning to reveal that the future performance of a system was often a complex, repeated pattern rather than a one-way trip into the unknown. Traditional methods such as time series failed to illustrate the complex cyclic patterns that were being found;

Figure 1.4
Phase Plane for a Market Share Study

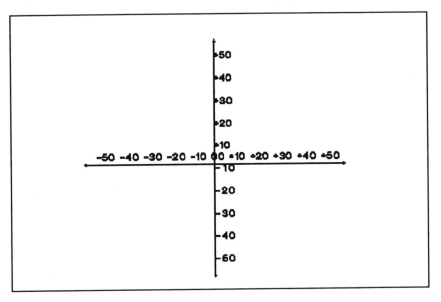

a phase plane offered the needed framework for mapping nonlinear system performance.

A phase plane refers to the domain in which a system operates. It provides an arena for the system's performance; it is the home of a system's attractor. For example, when studying market share there may be only two essential characteristics to the system, our share (X) and the share of a major competitor $(1 - X)$. Each of the characteristics is represented by a separate axis. An appropriate phase plane for a market share study, therefore, is given by two perpendicular axes (see Figure 1.4). Using Cartesian plane conventions we can define the horizontal axis as an independent variable (x); it can represent our market share. The vertical axis can represent a dependent variable (y), which is the market share of our competitor.

Focusing on Changes

One of Stephen Smale's many contributions to this field stems from his decision to map the *changes* a system undergoes rather than plot the system's status over time. A phase plane is scaled, therefore, to reflect the changes in each variable rather than the actual values of the variable. For our market share application, therefore, we will label one axis *changes in our market share* and the other axis *changes in our competitor's market share*. Because change can be either positive or negative, each axis provides both positive and negative values. It is appropriate, therefore, to center the phase space at the 0,0 intersection of the two axes.

The decision to study changes in a system opened the door to nonlinear analysis. The intricate patterns of nonlinear behavior were discovered in the changes to a system, not in the momentary status of the system. Consider for a moment a common financial measure like "total sales." What does the word total mean? What, precisely, is the intent of such a measure? Total suggests that the value represents accumulated sales of all products and services of the firm. We add up all the individual product and service sales to get total sales. Any manager knows that vastly more information about the business is available if we look at the individual product sales; we all know that considerable information is lost when we consolidate the individual contributions into a single total.

But total also refers to the total of all accumulated sales over time; it typically refers to sales over a standard accounting period. Consider that at the first hour on the first day of that accounting period total sales were zero. At the end of that first day they had changed from zero to some higher value, and each hour and each day throughout the accounting period changes were added to changes that can be accumulated into a total for the period. But should they be totaled? When we quote a total sales figure for the period we throw away all the intricate, dynamic information that describes the trajectory from zero to that total. That trajectory details the behavior of the system; it is the behavior of the system. The total is only an artifact that we commonly use.[4]

If we expect to manage sales, we must manage the trajectory. We don't go to the moon by noting its location and shooting at it. We go to the moon by first understanding the complex forces that determine our trajectory and then managing the changes in that trajectory to arrive at the moon. In business we are attempting to manage evolving patterns of performance in complex systems. To do that we should use tools that focus on the changing performance trajectories of those systems.

Fixed Points and Limit Cycles

David Ruelle provided much of the mathematical argument to support the existence of attractors. He reasoned that much of the behavior in natural systems could be explained by the tendency of the system to move toward some underlying pattern of behavior as energy is lost. For example, a swinging pendulum moves from oscillation to a fixed point as energy is lost. It also moves from a fixed point to oscillation as energy is gained. The pendulum is attracted to the fixed point; it is its point of stability at low levels of energy, just as it is attracted to two points when it is oscillating.

On a phase plane fixed points are identified as singular points. Consider our market share study again. Imagine that our company has maintained constant market share of 33 percent and that the share of the market for our competitor has been constant at the remaining 67 percent. On the phase plane our relation would be plotted as a single point in the center of phase space at the coordinates 0,0, since constant market shares would have no changes. If 0,0 is a fixed point attractor, any gains in market share that would be plotted as a move off of coordinate 0,0 will be eroded as the relation is drawn back to the fixed point. This is precisely the situation described in Figure 1.2, when market share is temporarily increased to 45 percent.

Fixed points represent constancy of change. Coordinate 0,0 represents changes in market share that are constantly zero. If we were constantly gaining 10 percent market share, then the fixed point could be plotted as a single point at coordinate $+10, -10$ in the lower right quadrant to reflect the stability of this position. Fixed point attractors can exist at any point on the phase plane. They are positions of stability, the lowest order of chaos.

Imagine the industry conditions that must exist to provide such a stable, reliable market share. There must be an absence of major forces affecting the firms, since such forces would raise the level of disorder to an oscillating level. Such stability may be found in industries that are heavily regulated and protected from price changes or new competition. For example, the airline industry before regulations and the telecommunications industry before its deregulation demonstrate industries that could count on a stable market share.

As the complexity of the market share relationship increases, other patterns will appear. These may take the form of an oscillation, which, on a phase plane, would be plotted as a line extending from one extreme in the relationship to another. Other, more complex limit cycles are common. The trajectory of these changing relations is plotted on a phase plane to produce a limit cycle, which maps the geometry of the system over time.

Limit cycles are not necessarily accurate reflections of the underlying attractors; it depends on how the limit cycle is derived. The complex pattern shown in Figure 1.5 can be generated by iterating a particular nonlinear equation, given specific starting values. This is the theorist's approach: Start with an equation and some initial parameters and iterate the equation to produce a limit cycle that illustrates the underlying attractor. One can learn much about dynamical systems that way.

Alternatively, one can take an empirical approach. By collecting data relating to a system's actual performance and performing some simple computation on that data, one can produce a limit cycle that accurately reflects the system behavior and closely approximates the attractor. It is not, however, that actual attractor, and further, there is no way to derive that actual attractor from observed data. Consider the implications of that

Figure 1.5
A Limit Cycle

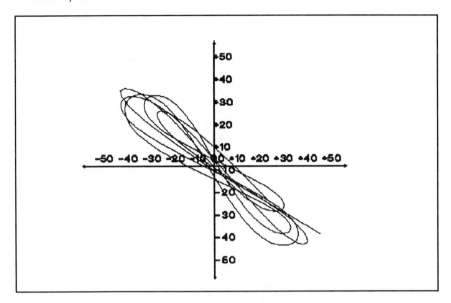

fact. If we knew with precision the equation behind the market share attractor, then we could accurately compute all future values of market share by simply iterating the equation. We could forecast the future. Our inability to forecast with precision comes from our ignorance of the attractors, not from some inherent randomness or error in nature.

Limit cycles are to chaos theory as bar charts are to conventional statistics; they describe performance over time. Like bar charts, they capture all the data involved. They are not a statistical simplification of the data.

Henri Poincaré provided a concept that is important to our effort here. In an attempt to understand the trajectory of an attractor he mathematically sliced through its orbit. Like putting a piece of paper into the traversing limit cycle, each orbit of the cycle marked the paper, forming a pattern of dots. The resulting Poincaré map substantiates the validity of capturing data about a limit cycle periodically, something we will do extensively in the chapters ahead. Although Poincaré maps plot the position of the limit cycle once in each orbit, we will typically capture the trajectory four times in each orbit.

Basins of Attraction

It is disappointing to learn that we will never know, with precision, the attractors that define the future. Chaos offers some good news, however, to offset this harsh reality. Around each attractor lies a basin of attraction, a region in which any level of performance will be drawn to follow the attractor. This means that we don't need to know the attractor exactly to use our knowledge of its existence.

The outer limit of the basin of attraction defines the threshold between a return to established patterns and an escape to uncharted territory. Any position on a phase plane that lies inside the basin of attraction will be drawn to follow the attractor; any position outside the basin will escape the attractor. If the attractor is known with precision, then the limits of the basin of attraction could be known with equal precision.

The basin of attraction permits each orbit to have a unique trajectory and still be defined by the attractor. Failure to recognize this has caused us to see randomness when there is none. It has caused us to see errors in our regression analysis and time series studies.

Attractors abound because this is a nonlinear world. We are drawn to our chairs by Earth's gravitational attractor. Our coffee settles in its cup for the same reason. In fact, all systems approach such stability unless some form of energy acts on them. The energy from a light wind pushes sailing ships steadily across the lake; the ships are attracted to a new steady state. They have to change their configuration fundamentally to go faster or slower; they are drawn to the new level of stability. A small, but steady push to a clock's pendulum is enough to change the system's attractor from one of stability to one of oscillation. Even the circuitous flight of birds has been found to follow an attractor. Those birds remaining inside the basin of attraction ultimately land with all the rest in a tree or at a pond. A few birds depart the congregation and go elsewhere; although they may have appeared to be part of the flock, they were drawn to a different attractor. If the behavior of birds is known to be nonlinear and driven by attractors, what are the implications regarding behavior in an organization? Are patterns of behavior on the job driven by the existence of attractors? Are employees actually drawn to the break room? What can chaos theory teach us about subtler behaviors that might influence absenteeism or safety?

Attractors come in some very mechanical forms also. Even machines, which we consider linear in design, can act as attractors that control other processes. Consider a soda bottling machine with a fixed processing speed. Such a machine can act as an attractor for the processing rate of an entire plant, since all other related processes will be drawn to follow that machine's processing speed. An acceleration in any other part of the processing operation—labeling, for example—will ultimately have to be slowed to accommodate the bottling machine. Even the frequency with which supplies are ordered will be controlled by the bottling machine. Consider the impact it has on scheduling routes and, ultimately, on the frequency with which money goes into the bank; all these activities will be obliged to follow a pattern established by that humble bottling machine.

Figure 1.6
The Limit Cycle of a Strange Attractor

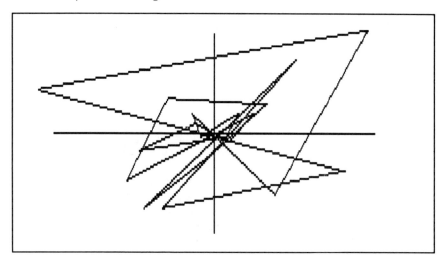

The bottling machine is just a single example of the multitude of constraints that bind an organization to certain limits. These constraints, be they mechanical or human, create functional limits and a pattern of activity with specific bounds. The structural characteristics within the firm and the competitive, economic, and legal characteristics of the firm's environment interact to form an organizational attractor, a specific pattern of performance as unique as a person's fingerprint.

Strange Attractors

Low-level chaos emerges when a system adheres to a simple attractor; low-level chaos is constancy, stability. Higher-order chaos follows a more complex attractor, resulting in some form of periodic oscillation. What must be the nature of an attractor that is capable of producing random-appearing behavior? It must be strange. Although Lorenz exposed the first such attractor by sketching just a few data points from his weather simulation, Benoit Mandelbrot provided us with the first view of their enormous intricacy. Strange attractors are intricate mathematical patterns of measureless complexity; they weave, fold, and spiral in beautiful ways to profoundly confirm that disorder is structured.

The combination of forces within a firm and outside it can easily create patterns so complex that the overall performance of the firm is unpredictable; it is high-order chaos controlled by a strange attractor, and it provides limit cycle trajectories like that shown in Figure 1.6.

In that image, which provides a limit cycle for Thiokol Corporation

(NYSE-TKC), changes in quarterly sales are on the horizontal axis and changes in quarterly earnings per share are on the vertical axis. Although we will never know the precise nature of the attractor shown, we now know that such patterns are driven by many more systematic processes of lower-order chaos within the firm. In general, all complex patterns of organizational activity appear to be driven by simpler, lower-order attractors.

NOTES

1. This discussion is not meant to imply that the logistic equation presented describes market share relations. Some other nonlinear equation probably does describe market share.

2. Much of this discussion regarding contributions to chaos theory is based on James Gleick's book *Chaos: Making a New Science* (New York: Viking, 1987).

3. Those who would like to experiment with the logistic equation on a home computer can use the algorithm below. Supply values of C between 0 and 4 and values of LastX between 0 and 1. Be sure to try values for C of .8, 1.00, 2.00, 3.20, and 3.5 with LastX equal to .50.

```
100 INPUT "C   ";C
110 INPUT "LastX"; LastX
120 FOR N = 1 TO 100
130     NextX = C * LastX * (1 − LastX)
140     PRINT NextX;
150     LastX = NextX
160 NEXT N
170 END
```

4. Consider how much additional information is lost if we compute "average sales" or if we use some conventional statistical approach that discards much of the trajectory information as error. Such computations may simplify the data, but they provide us with less information, not more.

2

Methods and Concepts: Chaos Theory and Organizational Analysis

What is the procedure for extracting an organizational limit cycle? How is it derived? What other measures capture the nonlinear trajectory of organizational activity? The previous discussion describes a limit cycle as a reflection of the changes in a system over time; this chapter details a methodology for plotting an organizational limit cycle. It also provides a discussion of related measures, concepts, and terms that form a foundation for business analysis.

THE ORGANIZATIONAL LIMIT CYCLE

Although limit cycles can be derived for virtually any organizational activity, here we will develop our methodology by discussing the interaction of two common measures of business performance—sales and profits. These two variables provided the first evidence that organizations are nonlinear systems; further, the data needed are readily available for most firms.[1]

Data Requirements and Adjustments

Our example here, and many of the later applications, focuses on the use of quarterly data. We are given, therefore, four measurements to define each annual limit cycle and four Poincaré maps of the trajectory for the entire period under analysis.

Chaos theory applications in other disciplines rely on the availability of hundreds or thousands of observations. When the study involves iterating a known formula or focuses on observations from a process with cycles of short duration, such a large number of observations is possible, resulting in limit cycle trajectories of fine detail. Here our purpose is to display a pattern that reflects the underlying attractor. Whereas the mathematician can start with a formula and iterate it to generate a precise image of the attractor, we must start with observed data and use it to suggest the form of the underlying attractor.

The type of data we choose to analyze should be determined by the level of the oscillations we want to observe. Much like an astronomer peering through a telescope, we can establish fields of view either too small or too large. If we focus too narrowly, we see details, like weekly sales patterns, that obscure more important annual patterns. If we focus too broadly, observing only annual performance data, we fail to see any of the detail in an annual pattern. For our purposes, the appropriate level of analysis is one that provides multiple observations of the expected limit cycle without detailing lesser important patterns. For studies of limit cycles at the strategic planning level, quarterly data are appropriate, sufficient, and convenient. For studies that focus on more short-term, operational processes, monthly or weekly data more clearly show the relevant limit cycles. Studies of specific processes, such as the activities on an assembly line, may require daily or perhaps even hourly measures.

Traditional statistical studies frequently adjust raw data for seasonality or inflation. Clearly the seasonality of a company's sales will be reflected in the quarterly data, which forms an annual limit cycle. If we take the traditional statistician's view, we would consider such forces distortions of the true organizational limit cycle, and we would adjust for them. Alternatively, we can consider such forces an integral part of the organization's limit cycle, and reason that removing them would only distort the true pattern of organizational performance. Seasonality reflects patterns of change in the external environment. Seasonality, like many other external environmental forces, adheres to a nonlinear attractor, and its influence can certainly be identified in the performance patterns of many companies. However, when seasonality is removed by seasonally adjusting the data, another organizational limit cycle emerges. Seasonality is just one of many forces that shape the limit cycle. Stripping off the seasonal effect is like opening the first of many nested packages; one sees what is underneath but learns nothing more about the truth that still lies hidden. There are two ways to view the resulting cycle. It can be considered a more accurate picture of the organization's pattern of performance, something closer to the truth; or it may be viewed as a useless artifact that results from applying estimates of seasonality. Note that time series approaches introduce a statistical process that makes estimates and allows for error. Avoiding such approaches allows us to avoid introducing any such estimating techniques. For these reasons, data will not be seasonally adjusted for the applications provided here.

Financial data often is adjusted to compensate for inflation. Inflation typically causes financial accounts to expand and makes performance appear better than real-dollar levels. Growth in the financial measures, whether real or caused by inflation, causes *hypertrophy,* an expansion or strengthening of the limit cycle. Even so, the effect may not justify an adjustment. When examining limit cycle patterns, it seems more convenient to retain actual values so that they may be directly related to current performance levels. Further, adjusting for inflation requires the adoption of one of many possible price indexes, all of which are estimates based on traditional statistical approaches. Working with the unadjusted data ensures that no additional errors have been introduced by such approaches.

The procedure for computing an organizational limit cycle and its related measures is surprisingly simple; the following math is all that is needed to apply the technique.

Marginal Measures

The first step toward deriving an organizational limit cycle involves computing the marginal values for each of two related variables. A marginal value is simply the difference between the value of the variable at each observation and its value at the previous observation. Algebraically, the marginal values ($m_{i,j}$) for the jth variable can be expressed as:

$$m_{i-1,j} = x_{i,j} - x_{i-1,j}$$

for $i = 2$ to n, where n equals the number of observations and $x_{i,j}$ equals the observed values.

The marginal values report the changes in the data over time; they always reflect the interval between one measurement and another; therefore, there is always one fewer observation compared with the number of original data items. For example, if we intend to analyze data from quarter 1 of 1985 through quarter 4 of 1992 inclusive, we will have thirty-two observed values (eight years times four quarters per year) and thirty-one marginal values. The first marginal value will reflect the difference between quarter 2, 1985, and the conditions at the end of quarter 1, 1985. If the variable of interest is sales, then our first marginal value would report the change in sales from quarter 1 to quarter 2, 1985.

Because marginal values reflect the dynamic evolution of a process, they provide a wealth of insight not available in a series of cumulative subtotals. We are accustomed to hearing the latest change when current performance is reported. We frequently hear statements like "Sales were up 8 percent compared with last year." Rarely, though, do we see a full set of marginal values that might reveal an underlying pattern in the changes. Even the practice of reporting rates of change as percentages only distorts the patterns of change, since each percentage is based on a different denominator. For our purposes, a simple computation of the differences is all that is needed.

Table 2.1
Sample Data Sets

Year/	Observed Values			Marginal Values		
Qtr	A	B	C	A′	B′	C′
1/1	100	100	100			
1/2	110	110	110	+10	+10	+10
1/3	120	100	120	+10	-10	+10
1/4	130	110	110	+10	+10	-10
2/1	140	100	100	+10	-10	-10
2/2	150	110	110	+10	+10	+10
2/3	160	100	120	+10	-10	+10
2/4	170	110	110	+10	+10	-10
3/1	180	100	100	+10	-10	-10

Table 2.1 provides some sample data that we can use to develop various limit cycles. Note that for each variable (A, B, and C), marginal values (A′, B′, and C′) have been computed. Take a moment to study the values in the table.

The observed values in Table 2.1 are theoretically "pure" series that we will use as examples of sales or profits for a firm. Data set "A" describes sales that constantly increase each quarter. Although we would not expect to find a company with precisely the same increase from quarter to quarter, a constant growth is common in business. Note that "A′" shows the constant rate of growth. Data set "B" describes an oscillating sales figure; it is up one quarter and then down to its initial value the next. Data set "B′" clearly shows the oscillation. Finally, "C" represents a situation in which sales climb for two quarters and then decline for the next two quarters. Such a pattern is common for companies with strong seasonal effect, such as those in the building trades, which have strong sales in quarters 2 and 3. Retailing businesses have a similar pattern, with strong sales in quarters 3 and 4. Note that each of these patterns of performance can be generated using the logistic equation presented in Chapter 1.[2]

Plotting the Trajectories

The coordinates of the Cartesian plane representing the phase plane are based on the values of the marginal values. The center coordinate is always 0,0 indicating no change in either the X or the Y variable. The axes are scaled to accommodate the range of each variable. The quadrants of the phase plane can be identified in the traditional manner with the upper right quadrant labeled 1, the upper left quadrant labeled 2, the lower left quadrant labeled 3, and the lower right quadrant labeled 4.

Each quadrant, therefore, reflects a unique combination of positive and

Figure 2.1
Phase Plane Quadrants

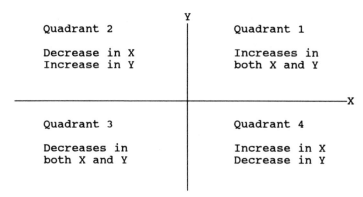

negative values for each variable. Quadrant 1, for example, reflects positive marginal values in both the X and the Y variable. It is an important quadrant to watch because it represents that moment when both variables increase simultaneously; in our example, it will reflect positive changes in both sales and profits. Similarly, quadrant 3 (lower left) reflects simultaneous decreases in both sales and profits, and quadrants 2 (upper left) and 4 (lower right) reflect decreases in sales with increasing profits and increases in sales with decreasing profits, respectively. Figure 2.1 shows the conditions of each quadrant in phase space.

As each observation is plotted, a line is drawn to attach the position of the previous observation to the coordinate of the new observation. Doing so traces the evolution of the system over time and highlights the consistency or evolving transitions in the system. Strictly speaking, each quadrant is a Poincaré map—a slice through the limit cycle—and each plotted observation is a point on one of the four Poincaré maps. Attaching the points allows one to trace the limit cycle and plot the behavior of the system over time.

Just as Poincaré maps reduce the behavior of a system by one dimension, so, too, the limit cycles reflect three dimensions of behavior on a two-dimensional grid. The three dimensions are changes in X, changes in Y, and time that is represented in the tracing of the trajectory from one point to the next.

Period 1 Limit Cycles

Let's examine the types of limit cycles that emerge if we plot the trajectories of various combinations in our sample data set. Consider the resulting limit cycle if two series of data like that in "A" are combined; let one variable be sales and the other, profits. Because profits usually are deter-

Figure 2.2
Theoretic Limit Cycles

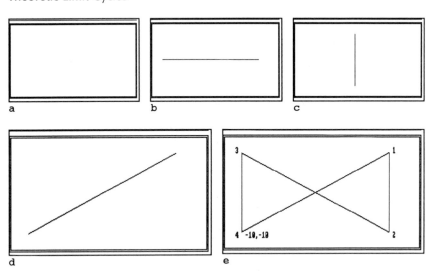

mined by sales, make sales the independent variable on the horizontal X axis and profits the dependent variable plotted on the vertical Y axis.

Because marginal values of "A" are a constant +10 a plot of the limit cycle trajectory is a single dot; Figure 2.2a reflects this situation.

Note that if sales were increasing at a steady rate of +20 instead of +10, the limit cycle would still be a single point. In fact, either variable can be constant or changing at a constant rate and the limit cycle will remain a single dot on the phase plane. Because the limit cycle visits only one position on the plane, it can be considered a Period 1 limit cycle. It reflects a system that adheres to a single-point attractor; it tends toward, it is attracted to, constancy.

Consider the managerial implications of this type of organizational performance. Forecasting sales and profits would require only an extrapolation of the latest changes. The use of linear regression techniques may actually be appropriate in this case because any difference between the linear regression line and the observed values will settle out as the system returns to its Period 1 attractor.[3] The system may behave in much the same way as the market share example in Figure 1.2. It restabilized after being temporarily influenced.

The consistency of a Period 1 behavior should improve asset utilization. Plant capacity can be matched to the consistently changing sales demand. Equipment downtime can be minimized because there is no periodic off-season. Human resources can be hired and trained and retained with no seasonal layoffs. Accounts receivable, accounts payable, and cash flow in general would be predictable because of the constancy of change. Period 1 may seem to be an ideal pattern of corporate performance; it is the farthest from any type of disruptive and unpredictable behavior. It is the easiest condition to manage; however, few companies present a Period 1 limit cycle. Further, Period 1 is not necessarily a *preferred* pattern; a company may want a periodic cycle to capture seasonal market opportunities.

Period 2 Limit Cycles

What if one of the two variables, sales or profits, is not constant? The next highest level of disorder is a simple oscillation. If one of the variables adopts an annual oscillation and the other remains constant, a plot of the trajectory will draw a vertical or horizontal line. If sales were represented by data like that in "B" and plotted on the X axis, and profits continued to be represented with consistently changing data like that in "A," we would find the limit cycle repeatedly tracing a horizontal line on the X axis. There would be no vertical changes because the marginal values of "A" are constant. However, sales would oscillate between +10 and −10, and when these Poincaré map positions are attached to one another, they trace a horizontal line centered on the 0, +10 coordinate. Because this type of trajectory visits two points on the phase plane, it is considered Period 2; the trajectory is shown in Figure 2.2b. If we reverse the data sets and let sales be represented by the data in "A" and profits be represented by "B," we will trace a trajectory like that in Figure 2.2c, which oscillates between +10 and −10 on the Y axis. Both of these examples are not uncommon in industry. For example, it is not unusual for a company to be able to maintain profits at a steady rate while sales oscillate during the year. Similarly, it is entirely possible to experience periodic changes in profits while maintaining steady increases in sales.

A more common Period 2 attractor emerges when both sales and profits oscillate proportionately. If the data in "B" is used for both variables, the resulting limit cycle forms a diagonal that oscillates between quadrants 1 and 3. Both sales and profits increase proportionately to coordinate +10, +10 and then decline proportionately to coordinate −10, −10. Figure 2.2d provides an example of this type of cycle, which is so common we will consider it a standard Period 2.

Consider the angle of the trajectory in quadrant 1. Because each axis is scaled according to the range of each variable's marginal values, the angle of the trajectory will be precisely 45 degrees if the marginal values are proportional to each other. For example, if sales were oscillating with difference scores of +10 and −10 and profits were oscillating with difference scores of +5 and −5, then we would still obtain a standard Period 2 limit cycle. The angle of the limit cycle trajectory would be 45 degrees because Y would be reproportioned to a scale from +5 to −5. Changes on the Y axis would then correspond to proportional changes on the X axis, which has a scale from +10 to −10. It follows that the horizontal and vertical limit cycles in Figure 2.2b and 2.2c correspond to angles of 0 degrees and 90 degrees. The angle that a limit cycle exhibits in quadrant 1 determines its axis, an important diagnostic measure that is discussed in greater detail and in Chapter 3.

The variety of possible Period 2 limit cycles constitutes a class of trajectories with a level of disorder greater than the constancy associated with Period 1. They reflect a level of stability, however, representing organizations or processes that have, *because of structural characteristics,* adopted a proportional oscillation in either one or both performance measures. Oscillation of only one of the variables results in either a vertical or a horizontal trajectory. Oscillations in both variables result in a standard Period 2 limit cycle that visits quadrants 1 and 3 periodically.

It is possible for limit cycles to present a downward sloping trajectory that visits quadrants 2 and 4. These are rare because they represent a decrease in one variable that corresponds to an increase in the related variable. In business, most measures such as sales, profits, inventory, cash flow, and payroll increase and decline together. One might, however, expect to find these off-axis limit cycles when studying competitive interactions in which increased activities of one firm may be associated with decreased activities of a competitor.

Proper management of the activities that create these cycles can result in lowering the oscillation from Period 2 to Period 1. For example, if the primary oscillating variable is sales on the horizontal axis (like Figure 2.2b), then the cycle can be reduced to Period 1 by either raising sales in the quarters associated with quadrants on the left side of the vertical axis or redistributing sales from the quarters associated with quadrants on the right side of the vertical axis. The result is a transition from Period 2 to Period 1—a reduction in the disorder, or chaos, of the performance. The choice is important. Raising the sales in the off quarters will not result in a Period 1 condition until the weaker quarters equal the stronger quarters' sales. To do this, the company may have to diversify by entering a countercyclical industry and may need to add significant new production capacity. The other choice, which calls for redistributing sales, merely trades off the timing of the sales volume. Creative use of trade credits, warehousing, shipping, and promotion may be all that is needed to make the trade-offs that create a Period 1 limit cycle.

If the trajectory is a vertical limit cycle, then the appropriate strategies will change to ones that attempt to stabilize oscillating profits without affecting sales. The appropriate strategies may relate to the timing of purchasing, production, or marketing campaigns. If attempts to raise profits in the weaker quarters have any effect on the consistency of the quarterly sales, the limit cycle will rotate from its vertical position and will transit toward a more standard Period 2. If the strategies used result in any disproportionality between sales and profits, then the limit cycle will split and form an off-diagonal figure eight orbit. Disproportionality results in a Period 4 limit cycle that is one step farther away from constancy and one step closer to high-order chaos.

Period 4 Limit Cycles

When a change in sales is not matched with a proportional change in profits, off-diagonal coordinates will emerge; the limit cycle bifurcates from Period 2 to Period 4. Figure 2.2e provides an illustration. Figure 2.2e was created by combining data from variables "B" and "C" in Table 2.1. Specifically, sales on the horizontal axis are represented by "C"; they increase consistently for two quarters and then decrease consistently for two quarters. Profits are represented by the data from "B," which oscillate each quarter.

The trajectory for a limit cycle like that in Figure 2.2e can follow either of two routes. Sales and profits can increase to a coordinate in quadrant 1 labeled (1). In the subsequent quarter sales continue to increase at the same rate as in the previous quarter; however, profits decline, resulting in the coordinate labeled (2) in quadrant 4. In the next quarter sales decline and profits rebound, resulting in position (3). In the fourth quarter sales continue their decline and profits drop to position the limit cycle at coordinate $-10, -10$ in quadrant 3. The orbit then repeats itself as it returns to position (1) during the first quarter of the next year.

Alternatively, the trajectory can follow the orbit in reverse through quadrants 4, 1, 3, and 2. Such is the case in the building supply industry. High inventory and payroll costs during the second-quarter building season combine to lower profits even while sales increase. The result is a position near that labeled (2) in Figure 2.2e. Sales continue to increase into the third quarter and profits rebound sharply; the result is a move into quadrant 1 to a position near that labeled (1). The fourth quarter of the year sees a decrease in both sales and profits as the business enters its off-season. Finally, decreasing costs in quarter 1 bring in improved profits while sales continue to decline; the result is a move to a coordinate in quadrant 2 (the improvement in profits, which are still weak, due primarily to comparison with the poor quarter 4 performance). The cycle then repeats itself as it moves to a position near that labeled (2) during the second quarter of the next year. In either of these possible trajectories, sales change direction every two quarters and profits change direction each quarter. The result is a pattern that lingers for two quarters, maintaining its rate of change at each of the horizontal positions, while profits continuously oscillate.[4]

Figure 2.3 provides the limit cycle for Hechinger's, a major chain of building supply and home improvement stores based in Hanover, Maryland. The Period 4 limit cycle is apparent as the trajectory orbits through

Figure 2.3
Hechinger's Period 4 Limit Cycle

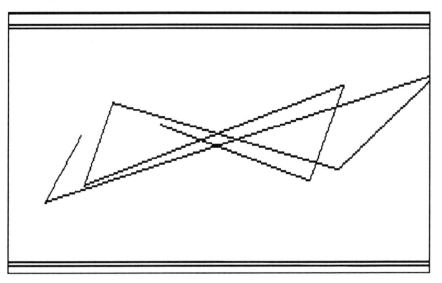

quadrants 1, 4, 2, and 3. Although each annual orbit fails to retrace precisely the previous one, the company is bound to a Period 4 attractor.

The Period 4 butterfly usually emerges when structural limitations, or "blocks," prevent adequate scaling of costs to maintain proportional profits. It represents increasing disorder over that found in Period 2, but it is still a stable, repeatable orbit. Like each of the lower-order limit cycles previously described, it is the natural result of the firm's external environment and the structural characteristics, strategies, and management decisions of the firm. It may be quite robust and capable of reestablishing itself if disturbed, or it may be sensitive and on the brink of transition to the next highest level. In either case, it is pleasingly consistent compared with what comes next on the continuum of chaotic behavior.

Period 8 Limit Cycles: High-Order Chaos

What happens next? What happens when a Period 4 limit cycle bifurcates to Period 8? Period 8 would require that the limit cycle retrace its trajectory every two years rather than annually. Although it is not rare for businesses to have some kind of two-year cycle for planning or budgeting, it is highly unlikely any two-year cycle would dominate the pattern of annual performance.

For all practical purposes, Period 8 means chaos in business. Period 8 is used to describe any limit cycle that adheres to an attractor of Period 8 or higher; we are unable to discern any repeatable pattern (see Figure 2.4).[5]

Figure 2.4
Whirlpool Corporation's Period 8 Limit Cycle

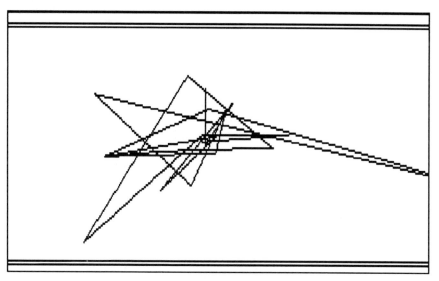

Although we are unable to understand the trajectory, it is not random; it is only too complex to predict. Further, although a firm may display a Period 8 limit cycle at this macro level, a nonlinear analysis of more specific operational activities within the firm would reveal a myriad of lower-order cycles that combine to form the observed Period 8 trajectory. Period 8 limit cycles are common in business. They result from turbulent external environments and management decisions made without knowledge of the structural patterns of change that bind the organization. From a management view, they are the most difficult to predict and control. The limit cycle, although complex, provides a new perspective of organizational performance. Being able to see the historical development of change and its recent evolution offers an opportunity to control its future.

-Being able to see the results of any intervention provides understanding of the organizational characteristics that create the limit cycle pattern.

The path from Period 1 to Period 8 also leads back again. At Period 8 we know that Period 4 provides the next lower level of chaotic behavior. We can, therefore, seek to reinforce activities that support Period 4 and thus moderate those forces that disrupt it. By proper timing of managerial intervention we can create more systematic oscillations that will lower risk, increase asset utilization, and improve our ability to forecast performance of the firm.

Similarly, Period 4 limit cycles can be reduced to Period 2 by eliminating the disproportionality that results in off-axis visits to quadrants 2 and 4.

For example, the Hechinger's limit cycle in Figure 2.3 can be moved to a Period 2 limit cycle by taking actions that increase profitability during quarter 1. Doing so eliminates the off-axis visit into quadrant 2. Trading off profits during quarter 3 for improved profits during quarter 1 would also help create a Period 2 cycle for Hechinger's. Although overall profitability will not be as great as would be possible if only quarter 1 profits are raised, the trade-off still provides the resources utilization advantages associated with a lower-order limit cycle.

Reducing a Period 2 limit cycle to Period 1 requires a proportional improvement in both sales and profits during the visit to quadrant 3. Doing so reduces the downward oscillation of both X and Y. The result is a decrease of all marginal values, resulting in a collapse of the linear oscillation to a single point. Alternatively, it may be possible to trade off sales and profits that result in the quadrant 1 visit for improved profits in the quarters associated with the quadrant 3 visit. The trade-off would reduce the oscillations of both variables, resulting in a Period 1 limit cycle.

Note the nature of these general intervention strategies; they call for timing, balancing, and trading off one objective for another. Unlike conventional strategies, these suggestions emerge from an examination of the deterministic forces, both known and unknown, that shape organizational performance. To understand organizations as chaotic systems we must accept the fact that performance is the result of existing organizational design and resources. We must understand that objectives don't create success; it flows naturally by managing changes to the structural characteristics of the firm. As managers, we will achieve more if we add intelligence and finesse to our current effort and determination.

OTHER MEASURES AND CONCEPTS

The organizational limit cycle provides a new view of corporate performance. What related measures are there to help us describe and understand the cycle?

Marginal history charts show us more about the limit cycle trajectories we display. They decompose the cycle into its two contributing variables and form a chronological record of its regularity and evolution. A marginal history chart provides a record of organizational function in much the same way an electrocardiogram records the function of a human heart. The analogy is so close that many of the terms, analytical techniques, and pathologies of cardiac medicine can be used in relation to organizational function. The similarity is not coincidental, since both organizations and human hearts are nonlinear, chaotic systems and modern cardiac medicine applies nonlinear chaos theory techniques. Chapter 3 examines the analogy in detail and provides some examples of organizational pathologies and organizational "heart attacks."

Figure 2.5
Marginal History Charts

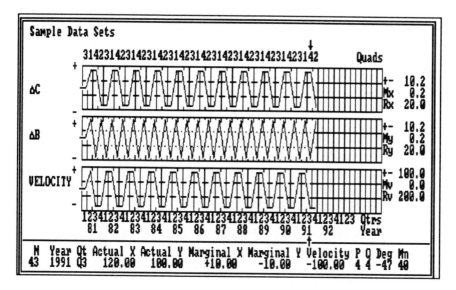

Marginal History Charts

Figure 2.5 provides a display from the Chaos System Software, developed to facilitate this analysis. It shows three marginal history charts of the standard Period 4 limit cycle presented in Figure 2.2e. The report shows a plot of the two marginal values that form the limit cycle and a new measure called "velocity."

Note that the horizontal axis of all the marginal history charts is *time* marked in quarters and years below the bottom chart. The vertical axis of each chart is centered on the mean of the marginal values of each variable, which is noted as M_x, M_y, and M_v, with, "+" and "−" indicating the direction of change for each variable. The scale of the vertical axis is determined by the range of each variable, which is reported as R_x, R_y, and R_v on the display. The scale at the top of the charts reports the quadrant visited during each quarter (quads). Finally, the arrows at the top and bottom scales highlight a particular quarter as it relates to the values provided at the bottom of the display.

The independent variable X appears on the top marginal history chart; specifically, it plots the marginal values for variable "C." Upward and downward movements on the chart correspond to marginal increases and decreases in the variable, just as a flat line would indicate no change. The upper and lower bounds of the chart are given by the variable labeled

"+ −"; the upper bound of variable "C" is +10.2, and the lower bound is −10.2.

Recall that a combination of variables "C" and "B" creates a Period 4 limit cycle, so Figure 2.5 provides marginal history charts for a standard Period 4 limit cycle. In the figure we can see that the marginal value of "C" increases and continues to increase for two quarters before it decreases for two quarters. The highlighted quarter, which is the third quarter of 1991, corresponds to one of the quarters in which "C" is increasing. The marginal value of variable X is, therefore, shown on the lower part of the report as +10.00.

Variable "B" oscillates at twice the frequency of variable "C". It decreases in the highlighted quarter; its marginal value is −10.00. This combination, in which the X variable increases and the Y variable decreases, positions the limit cycle in the lower right quadrant, which is quadrant 4. Note that the quadrant position of 4 is indicated by the arrow at the top of the chart.

One can use the quadrant references to identify the orbit of the latest trajectory. Examine Figure 2.5 closely. The three quadrants visited before quarter 3, 1991, were 2, 3, and 1; hence the latest trajectory can be identified as quadrant series 2314. You may want to take a moment to mentally trace the limit cycle as it orbits repeatedly through the series 2314. Note the oscillations on the marginal history charts for "C" and "B" as you do this.

Velocity Measure

Velocity is the product of the two marginal values that form the limit cycle. One can view it as a measure of the combined "energy" in the system. If either variable is not oscillating, velocity is zero. Any oscillations that support each other will result in an increase in velocity, even if both variables are decreasing. When the oscillations of the two variables fail to support each other, the velocity will decrease. Think in terms of the quadrants visited. If both variables increase, the trajectory will visit quadrant 1 and velocity (the product of the two marginal values) will be positive. If both variables decrease, the trajectory will visit quadrant 3 and velocity will still be positive, since the product of two negatives is positive. Note that the farther the trajectory departs from the center of the phase plane, the greater will be the velocity. If one variable increases and the other decreases, either of the two off-axis quadrants (2 or 4) will be visited and velocity will be negative.

The velocity measure indicates the extent of supported and inverse oscillation in the system. If a limit cycle is supportive, as in a Period 2 trajectory, then the velocity measure will plot as a series of peaks on an otherwise flat baseline. There will be no negative velocity measures. The sample data used for Figure 2.5 produces a Period 4 trajectory that results from oscillations that are equally supportive and inverse (i.e., half the time the two variables are increasing simultaneously and half the time one is increasing while the other decreases). The marginal history chart of velocity is, therefore, equally distributed above and below the mean velocity value of zero. If a limit cycle results from two variables that are always oscillating inversely, then it will visit only quadrants 2 and 4 and the velocity measure will plot as a series of valleys dropping below a flat baseline. If the limit cycle is constant, then it has neither supportive nor inverse oscillations, and its velocity will plot as a flat line.

The velocity measure is useful for identifying changing intensity of a limit cycle, and it can indicate changes in the relation between the two oscillating variables. Increasing intensity of the limit cycle will be reflected as increasing range in the velocity; the peaks and valleys will grow. As the magnitude and severity of the oscillations decline toward a Period 1 condition, the velocity history will drop toward a flat line. One can compare the relative size of one wave with that of another to see changes in the relationships between two values. For example, if velocity becomes more negative during quarters 2 and 3 relative to positive velocity measures during quarters 1 and 4, it signals a bifurcation from Period 2 to Period 4. A similar practice of comparing relative size is regularly used by physicians to identify pathologies in electrocardiograms.

Determining Period

In Figure 2.5 a variable labeled P is shown as having the value 4. The reference is to the period of the limit cycle. Although the period of a limit cycle is obvious for the sample data provided, determining the period can get rather subjective when assessing actual corporate data. For this reason a method has been devised to objectively determine the period of a limit cycle. The procedure involves comparing the sequence of the four most recent quadrant visits with an established table of quadrant sequences. For example, if both variables maintain constant increases that position the limit cycle for four quarters in quadrant 1, then the quadrant sequence is 1111, which corresponds to one of the four possible series identified as a Period 1 limit cycle in Table 2.2.

Similarly, if the limit cycle trajectory sustains an oscillation in any manner between any two quadrants, its quadrant sequence will correspond to one of those identified as Period 2. The large number of Period 2 sequences results from the need to identify any of the four quadrants as the starting quadrant of the series. Table 2.2 also lists the series needed to identify all possible Period 4 trajectories.

The total number of possible combinations of four-quadrant trajectories is designated by 4 to the power of 4, since each quarter can visit any of

Table 2.2
Quadrant Series

===

                        Period 1 Series

1111 2222 3333 4444

                        Period 2 Series

1112 1113 1114 1121 1122 1131 1133 1141 1144 1211 1212 1221
1222 1311 1313 1331 1333 1411 1414 1441 1444 2111 2112 2121
2122 2211 2212 2221 2223 2224 2232 2233 2242 2244 2322 2323
2332 2333 2422 2424 2442 2444 3111 3113 3131 3133 3222 3223
3232 3233 3311 3313 3322 3323 3331 3332 3334 3343 3344 3433
3434 3443 3444 4111 4114 4141 4222 4224 4242 4244 4333 4334
4344 4411 4422 4424 4433 4434 4441 4442 4443

                        Period 4 Series

1423 1243 1342 1324 4123 4321 4231 4213 3241 3421 3142 3124
2134 2314 2413 2431

                        Period 8 Series

All 155 other quadrant sequences.

===

the four possible quadrants. This means that there are 256 possible sequences. Table 2.2 identifies 101 quadrant series, leaving 155 sequences unidentified. The remaining 155 series are defined, by default, as Period 8. This objective approach to determining the limit cycle period falls short of a mathematical proof of the limit cycle period, which is possible if a large number of observations is available. It does, however, provide a practical approach that allows us to classify a limit cycle with only a few observations.

Determining Axis

If a limit cycle returns to precisely the same position in an orbit, it will retrace that orbit indefinitely. Even if it fails to retrace the orbit, it will tend to adhere to its attractor so long as its trajectory is within the basin of attraction. A measure of the orbital consistency is given by the axis of the limit cycle.

If we use the center of the phase plane as our reference, we can compute the angle of each quarterly Poincaré position by simply taking the arc tangent of the difference between the coordinates of the Poincaré position and the origin and then converting the measure to degrees and minutes. The result is a measure that, when combined with the velocity measure, exactly

Figure 2.6
Axis Coordinates in Degrees

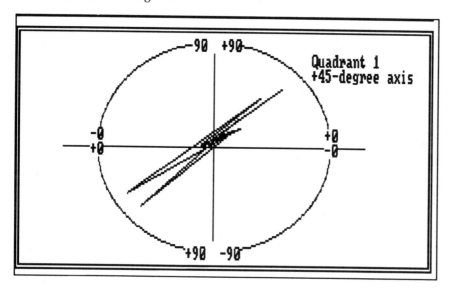

defines the orbital position. Velocity provides a measure of distance from the origin; axis provides the direction. One must look at both measures to determine the extent to which the limit cycle is retracing its orbit.[6]

Figure 2.6 indicates the coordinates of phase space in degrees if we compute the angle of the Poincaré point as described earlier. Note that quadrants 1 and 3, those that are associated with positive velocity measures, also have positive coordinates in terms of degrees. The off-axis quadrants, 2 and 4, have negative angular coordinates. Consider the axis of the Wal-Mart limit cycle shown in Figure 2.6 as it visits quadrants 1 and 3; it is clearly a Period 2 cycle. Take special note of the axis for quadrant 1. Recall that in quadrant 1 both variables (sales on the horizontal axis and profits on the vertical axis) are increasing and that oscillations between quadrants 1 and 3 are quite common in business; quadrant 1 serves as a reference for the beginning of the limit cycle trajectory. The axis of the trajectory in quadrant 1 is an important measure of the limit cycle's consistency.

Limit Cycles and Financial Ratios

Consider the information provided by a traditional financial ratio. When one computes net profit margin, for example, one reduces the information contained in both sales and profits to a single number that results from dividing profits by sales. Just as we lose information when we sum them to compute a total, we also lose information when we compute ratios. Ratios are just another way to simplify the data, and in so doing they discard much of the dynamic information that exists in the actual data. In business we commonly manage with totals and ratios, both of which mask information important to our decision-making. When we use ratios our simplification results in the loss of two types of information. We lose a measure of magnitude; 200 divided by 1,000 is 20 percent, just as 180 divided by 900 is 20 percent. Although we typically look at the total figures as well and would undoubtedly discover a change in magnitude, our use of ratios requires that we supplement our ratios with the original values.

We also lose a measure of proportionality. We know that when a ratio changes from 20 percent to 24 percent, the increase has not been proportional. We know the disproportionality is 4 percent, but 4 percent of what? Again we must refer to the original data for that answer. So what, precisely, do ratios tell us?

If we compare two ratios—for example, last year's profit margin and this year's profit margin—and they are identical, they indicate that the trajectory of the limit cycle is either Period 1 (the rates of change are precisely the same) or Period 2 (the rates of change of the two variables are proportional); we cannot tell which by looking at the ratio. If two ratios are not the same, then we know that the trajectory has deviated from perfect proportionality such as that given in a standard Period 2 limit cycle. It may still be visiting quadrants 1 and 3, or it may have ventured into an off-axis quadrant. We could not see whether or not it has established a Period 4 oscillation unless we examined the trajectory for several previous quarters, and we would never identify the oscillation by looking at the ratios. Business ratios are common, but they are of limited value. They do, however, show us where to look for new measures of corporate performance.

Here we have concerned ourselves only with sales and profits. Clearly, limit cycles for virtually any organizational performance measure can be computed to provide differing views of corporate activity. We can look at activity ratios such as asset turnover, days in inventory, or average collection period. We can look at any of the profitability or liquidity ratios. The traditional ratios are focused on the proper points to measure; they simply do an inadequate job of measurement.

In addition to the financial ratios, we would expect to find that structural characteristics of our firm have created attractors that affect safety, employee turnover, absenteeism, and a wide range of other operational concerns. We can expect to identify a corporate "ideal" in companies with multiple divisions or stores. With a limit cycle that represents the "corporate ideal," we can examine the limit cycles of individual stores to identify "unhealthy" conditions and behaviors; we can look for pathologies that call for intervention. Practices in cardiac medicine so closely parallel this approach that we can look there for concepts of diagnosis and methods of analysis that apply to industry.

NOTES

1. H. Richard Priesmeyer and K. Baik, "Discovering the Patterns of Chaos," *Planning Review* (December 1989): 14–21, 47.

2. Each pattern is presented as part of the Rabbit Survival/Market Share analogy plotted in Figure 1.1.

3. A regression technique will mistakenly refer to the difference as error.

4. Two other generic Period 4 limit cycles are also possible. The butterfly can rotate by 90 degrees, and the cycle can trace a trajectory through quadrants 1, 2, 4, and 3 or in the opposite direction through quadrants 3, 4, 2, and 1.

5. In many cases the organizational attractor is probably much more complex than Period 8, and in these cases Period 8 is a misnomer. It is, however, a convenient way to refer to an entire class of complex attractors.

6. Specifically, one can compute the angle in degrees and minutes using the following algorithm:

Theta   = ATN(((Y1(I) − MeanOfY)/RangeOfY)/((X1(I) − MeanOfX)/RangeOfX))

ANGLE = Theta * (180 / 3.141593)

MIN   = ANGLE − INT(ANGLE)

MIN   = CINT(MIN * 60)

ANGLE = INT(ANGLE)

IF MIN = 60 THEN ANGLE = ANGLE + 1:MIN = 0

Variables ANGLE and MIN will then contain angle in degrees and minutes.

Where   Y1(I) and X1(I) are arrays containing the marginal values of Y and X.

3

Organizational Heartbeats

Disorder emerges naturally from conditions of the system, and decisions create the system's condition. We decide what type of foods to eat and what type of exercise to get. We decide how to cope with stress. We decide whether or not to smoke. In making those decisions and others we establish physical characteristics that definitely will—or definitely will not—lead to heart disease. Heart disease is not random; it is the natural result of the system's condition.

Human and organizational heartbeats are not the same thing. One is an electrical signature of a biological activity; the other is a financial signature of business activity. But they share a common denominator, in that they are both nonlinear systems. They are like so many other biological and social processes; they are dynamic systems, and they adhere to an attractor that creates characteristic patterns of repeated performance. Organizations and human hearts can, therefore, be analyzed using the tools and terminology of chaos theory.

Physicians discovered a new view of heart activity when they learned how to record the electrical impulses that stimulate the heart. The discovery took a while. Kollicker and Mueller noted the heart's electrical activity in 1855. Ludwig and Waller subsequently showed that the heart's electrical stimuli could be monitored from the skin. Not until 1901 did Einthoven provide a way to record the rhythmic pattern of activity on photographic paper; he provided the first electrocardiograms (EKGs).[1] "We can record the heart's abnormal electrical activity and compare it with the normal," he said.[2]

The EKG does not show heart activity; it shows an electrical reflection of it. Similarly, financial statements do not show business activity; they are a reflection of business activities. To understand an EKG tracing one must understand the structure and process of the heart; one must know what is normal and what is abnormal. One must have experience identifying pathologies. To understand an organization's limit cycle and marginal history chart one must understand the characteristics of the firm and the conditions that create those patterns of performance.

When Einthoven first produced his EKG, the tracings defied description. There were no names for the peaks and valleys. When two EKGs were compared, the differences could be seen but not described. "This peak is higher here . . . this one is longer and flatter." The wavy line needed explanation and a system for interpretation. That is what we need here, so we'll look at what the cardiologists did and learn by analogy.

They labeled the waves. They recognized that the continuous tracing recorded a series of separately identifiable patterns that related to the *change in the electrical charge* of the heart. The unique structure and condition of the heart provide an equally unique electrical signature as it depolarizes during the contraction phase and repolarizes during the resting stage. During depolarization a positively charged wave flows through the negatively charged atrium, causing it to contract. As a result of this activity the EKG records a positive electrical impulse called a P wave. The electrical signal is delayed momentarily as it is conducted down the bundle branches to the ventricles. The delay is identifiable on the EKG; it starts at the end of the P wave and ends when the ventricles contract. The electrical signature resulting from the powerful ventricular contraction provides a pattern of activity that is recorded as a dramatically spiked QRS complex. The Q wave, if present, is downward (negative), the R wave is upward (positive), and the S wave is downward, back to the electrically neutral baseline. There is then another momentary delay before the heart begins to repolarize; when it does, a broad positive T wave appears, reflecting the electrical transition that prepares the heart for another contraction. The delay between the end of the S wave and the beginning of the T wave is called the S-T segment. After another pause of less than a second, the entire sequence begins again, when the sinus node up in the right atrium fires an electrical impulse that starts the next heartbeat. By labeling the waves, physicians could begin establishing standards for the shape and duration of the electrical signal. They can now identify pathologies because those pathologies have characteristic signals. They can identify changes by comparing a patient's recent EKG with one recorded earlier. They have built a science around EKG tracings and have turned it into a profession.

Cardiologists use multiple measures. They attach electrodes at different positions to obtain as many as twelve tracings that record the electrical phenomenon of the heart from different perspectives. The electrodes are oriented at regular angles circling the heart, and each of the several tracings has a standard notation so that any trained cardiologist can interpret the results. The human heart is typically oriented such that the electric wave associated with each contraction flows downward to the left (from the person's point of view). By comparing the EKG tracings one can determine the direction, or *axis,* of the electrical impulse. Because physicians know the standard axis, they can identify *axis deflections* and relate them to various pathologies. They document the axis in degrees and relate it to four quadrants that surround the heart.

Physicians look at the shape and size of the PQRS and T waves. They know, for example, that P waves should be regular in height and that an inverted T wave usually indicates ischemia—lack of blood flow. They know that Q waves are supposed to be small or absent, and that a Q wave more than one-third the amplitude of the QRS complex is considered pathological; it is an indication of infarction. They have terms we can use. *Diphasic* refers to an oscillation that extends equally above and below the baseline of the tracing. A standard Period 4 limit cycle like that given in Figure 2.5 produces a diphasic velocity history chart. *Retrograde* refers to an oscillation in the opposite direction of what is normal. A *sinus rhythm* is a normal rhythm. *Dysrhythmia* means an abnormal rhythm; *arrhythmia* means without rhythm.

ORGANIZATIONAL RHYTHMS

So what are the implications for our work here? To read the marginal history chart we can begin by labeling the waves. Using quarterly data, we can expect to get four waves, which we can call P, Q, R, and S. We can establish a rule that the P wave begins the cycle, and we can establish the beginning of the cycle as that moment when both the X and the Y variables go positive. This means that the P wave is designated as the wave that enters quadrant 1. The next three waves, regardless of which quadrant they visit, can be referred to as Q, R, and S. We can, therefore, establish a notation system to describe any trajectory. A Period 2 limit cycle that orbits only between quadrants 1 and 3 can be referenced as $1_p3_q1_r3_s$. A Period 4 limit cycle may have a trajectory of $1_p3_q2_r4_s$. Such is the case for Hechinger's marginal history charts. Examine the numerical sequence at the top of the graphs in Figure 3.1. Note the consistency of the quadrant visits from quarter 2 of 1981 through quarter 2 of 1987. The organization repeats the Period 4 series $1_p3_q2_r4_s$.

Like the cardiologist, we can look at the shape and size of the various waves. We know that P waves relate to quadrant 1 visits. In Figure 3.1 we can study the consistency of the P waves by examining the peaks of the waves in columns relating to quadrant 1 visits. Note that the P waves for the sales variable increase in amplitude over the length of the tracing; the only time it failed to increase in this trend was in quarter 2 of 1985. The P waves related to our Y variable, however, are regular. Note that they are of fairly consistent height starting in quarter 2 of 1983. Even though the tracing of the common share earnings variable appears more erratic, it

Figure 3.1
Hechinger's Marginal History Charts

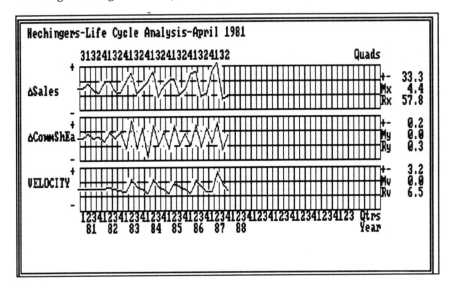

is actually quite consistently oscillating at twice the frequency of the sales variable. Look closely at the tracing of the earnings variable. Start at the top of the P wave in quarter 2, 1983. Now follow the tracing one quarter at a time and call out the letters PQRS as you go. The S wave in quarter 1, 1984, is exceptionally low, but other than that the tracing is surprisingly consistent.

The combined effect on the two variables becomes apparent when one looks at the velocity measure. The tracing shows a consistency in the peaks when both variables are either positive (quadrant 1) or negative (quadrant 3). It also shows consistency in the valleys when the trajectory visits either of the two off-axis quadrants 2 or 4.

Note that the tracing of the earnings variable is diphasic; its oscillations are about the same magnitude above the middle baseline as below it. This means that the rate of change of the earnings variable is fairly constant over the time analyzed. The sales variable, however, is not diphasic. Its magnitude above the line usually is greater than that below the line. This means that the rate of change of sales is growing. In other words, the rate of change in sales is expanding, whereas the rate of change in earnings per share is remaining fairly constant. This explains why Hechinger's limit cycle is increasing in width (the sales variable) but not expanding in height (the earnings variable).

The term *ideoorganizational* is useful. "Ideo" refers to one's own, so an ideoorganizational rhythm is an organization's own rhythm. In Figure 3.1

we are looking at Hechinger's ideoorganizational rhythm. It reflects the company's unique trajectory displayed in Figure 2.3. The limit cycle gives us a view of the company's heartbeat; the marginal history charts decompose that heartbeat activity into its components, which can be analyzed incrementally.

A manager has a major advantage over the cardiologist. There are far more direct and efficient ways to change the structural characteristics of an organization than there are ways to affect the functioning of a heart. The cardiologist often must work remotely with drugs to alter any dysrhythmia. One tries to avoid direct intervention by surgery or implantation of a pacemaker. A manager, however, guides the trajectory of organizational performance on a more regular basis—like driving a car. Management can monitor performance and change budget allocations, production quotas, and on-hand inventories to respond to changing conditions. Chaos theory, with its limit cycles and marginal history charts, offers managers a better view of the road and more control over the organization; it shows them the expected pattern of performance and reveals any deviations from that pattern. To the cardiologist all the information in an EKG is important. To the manager, all the information in a marginal history chart is important. Neither should throw away such an accurate history of performance by using some method such as traditional statistics that discards much of the information as error.

Normal and Abnormal Rhythms

Organizational limit cycles and marginal history charts vary considerably from one firm to the next. Some are rather constant, reflecting Period 1 patterns of performance. Some are oscillating, and correspond to Period 2 trajectories. Some, like Hechinger's, show stability at Period 4. Many organizations show limit cycles of such great complexity that we must classify them as Period 8, or chaotic.

Because industry conditions differ so greatly and operational characteristics vary considerably between firms, we can expect to see unique patterns of performance for each firm; we would expect the limit cycles of firms to be largely ideoorganizational. However, limit cycles and marginal history charts for similar firms in the same industry are comparable. What is normal, therefore, could be defined as what is common for firms in the same industry. Alternatively, normal could be defined as a sustained ideoorganizational rhythm or as a pattern of performance known to management. In any case, a firm's limit cycle and marginal history chart can be compared to patterns of performance that are considered at or near optimal.

Consider the retail store industry. Specifically, let's look at the majors in the discount department store business: K Mart Corporation, Woolworth

Figure 3.2
A Comparison of Limit Cycles in the Retail Store Industry

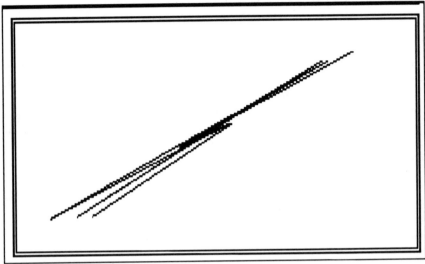

K Mart Corporation

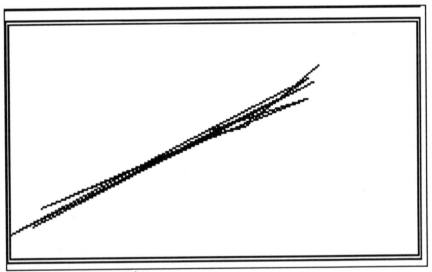

Woolworth Corporation

Figure 3.2 (Continued)

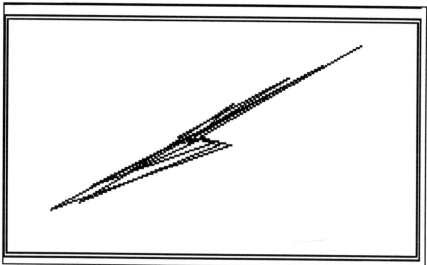

Wal-Mart Stores

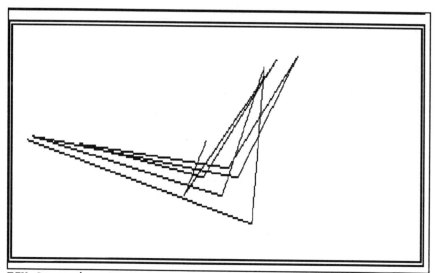

TJX Companies (Zayre)

Figure 3.3
A Comparison of Marginal History Charts

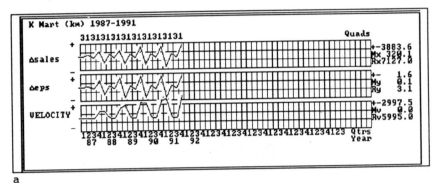

a

b

Corporation, Wal-Mart Stores, and TJX Companies (Zayre). Figure 3.2 provides the limit cycles of these four firms. As before, the horizontal axis of each phase plane is *changes in sales* and the vertical axis is *changes in earnings*.

Zayre's obviously different limit cycle is the result of major changes that occurred in 1989; at one time its limit cycle closely resembled those of its competition. Now it differs considerably from any of the other three. If we consider K Mart as having a normal rhythm for companies in this industry, then we can use it as a standard by which to examine TJX. Figure 3.3 shows the marginal history charts for K Mart and TJX.

Consider the differences between these two patterns of performance. Note the regularity of quadrant visits in Figure 3.3a, depicting K Mart; the $1_p3_q1_r3_s$ sequence is maintained throughout the period under evaluation, indicating a distinct Period 2 oscillation. In Figure 3.3b TJX, by comparison, shows several off-axis oscillations into quadrant 4, reflecting quarters when sales increases were associated with declining profitability. Compare the marginal history charts for sales of the two firms. Both firms suffer major decreases in sales in the first quarter of each year. K Mart, however, shows a diphasic pattern with increases in quarters 2 and 4 that offset the quarter 1 decline. TJX, however, shows pronounced decreases in quarter 1 sales and a flattening of the P wave associated with quadrant 1 visits.

The marginal history chart of K Mart's earnings reflects that of its sales; this proportionality is typical for a Period 2 performance. TJX, in contrast, shows a more irregular pattern of earnings performance. Although it has a pronounced increase in earnings during quarter 3 of each year, it often shows decreases in earnings during quarter 4 (particularly in quarter 4, 1989). A quarter 1 increase in earnings evident in the first two years dissipates and reemerges as a decrease in earnings in 1991.

The velocity history chart for TJX highlights two important events. Velocity decreases substantially in quarter 4 of 1989, reflecting an off-axis oscillation into quadrant 4; this was when sales were increasing but profitability declined. The unexpected increase in velocity during quarter 1 of 1991 occurred because both sales and earnings declined during this time. Previously, the company had been able to avoid major decreases in profitability during quarter 1.

We can describe K Mart as having a diphasic, sinus rhythm and a sustained PQRS complex. Its velocity shows mild hypotrophy, reflecting healthy growth in both sales and earnings. TJX, in contrast, shows a weakening P wave and an increasingly pronounced negative R wave in sales performance. Earnings are dysrhythmic, sustaining a $1_p4_q3_r4_s$ sequence during the last ten quarters. This sequence is of particular concern for those who expect profitability during the seasonal third and fourth quarters. The quadrant 1 visit of the P wave is followed by a decrease in profitability, which results in off-axis visits to quadrant 4 during the normally profitable fourth quarters. Decreases in both sales and profits during quarter 1 then take the R wave into quadrant 3. An improvement in sales during quarter 2 is not matched by improvements in profitability; the result is another visit to off-axis quadrant 4 during the S wave, resulting in continued decreases in profitability even while sales increase. The fact that the $1_p4_q3_r4_s$ sequence is maintained for more than two years indicates that this pattern of performance is not transitional, but is an established condition of the organization.

TJX provides an example of four pathologies: nondipolar P waves, Q4 deflection, dissociation, and paroxysmal escape. *Nondipolar P waves* result from the lack of diphasic oscillation in sales; changes in sales are more often negative and not offset by corresponding increases, like those at K Mart. *Q4 deflections* (quadrant 4 deflections) describe the visits to off-axis quadrant 4 in which sales are increasing while profits decline. This mismatch between the pattern of sales and profits performance suggests a *dissociation* between the two measures. A *paroxysmal escape* is the spontaneous emergence of an oscillation not associated with the normal sinus rhythm. In the case of TJX it occurs during quarter 1 of 1991, when the normally flat R wave on the velocity history chart appears as a sharp peak. The new R wave is the result of decreases in both sales and profits during that quarter. Apparently transitions from sinus rhythms to arrhythmia can occur as a slow, or chronic, transition. Alternatively, there can be a sudden shock to chaos as a result of slow internal or external forces that act on the pattern of performance. Examples of corporations that have experienced each of these episodes are available.

For an example of an organization shocked to chaos by sudden external factors, we can examine the Toro Company. For several years before 1979 Toro enjoyed the success of broadening its product line to include lightweight snowthrowers and chain saws; sales and earnings tripled through these years, reaching $358 million. An environmental shock presented itself in quarters 3 and 4 of 1979 when the first of two snowless winters arrived (see Figure 3.4a). The disruption pushed Toro away from its established pattern of performance (outside its basin of attraction), and the subsequent chaotic behavior was punctuated by the resignation of chairman McLaughlin, the firing of president John Cantu, and the dismissal of 125 other managers (see Figure 3.4b). A recovery engineered by the new president, Kendrick Melrose, involved cutting the work force by 50 percent, reducing administrative costs by 23 percent, and consolidating production from eight plants to five. The manufacture of snowthrowers was suspended for two years until existing inventories were depleted. These changes reestablished a new predictable pattern of performance. The results of these events are evident in Figure 3.4c.

Other Heartbeat Analogies

One can carry the analogy of organizations' heartbeats further to cite other concepts of cardiac medicine that may prove useful for organizational analysis. For example, the rate at which the periodic cycle is repeated is of primary importance to the cardiologist. When studying organizations we should recognize that organizational patterns will exhibit different rates. Specifically, activities within an organization show distinct cycle rates on much shorter intervals than the quarterly cycles shown earlier. For example, cycles associated with merchandise inventory and others associated with accounts receivable have been found at the monthly level. Project budget cycles have been found to cycle in phase with scheduled completion dates, which are not at regular time-oriented intervals. Various production processes have been found to cycle over two-day periods. The concept of rate is useful to us in that it specifies the appropriate level of analysis—quarterly, monthly, daily, hourly. It determines the frequency with which we gather data on an organization's continuously evolving processes.

Figure 3.4
The Toro Corporation

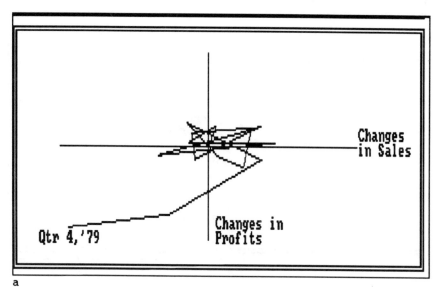

a

Changes
in Sales

Changes in
Profits

Qtr 4, '79

1980 through 1983

Changes
in Sales

Changes in
Profits

b

Figure 3.4 (Continued)

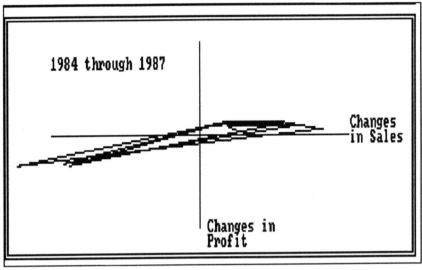

c

Rhythm is the second item a cardiologist checks. Rhythm describes the pattern of oscillation and creates a tracing like those given on the marginal history charts in Figure 3.3. To a trained cardiologist, rhythm describes the physical characteristics of the heart. The shape and relative size of each wave, viewed from the several vantage points of a standard EKG series, report dysrhythmias that can be identified and related to certain cardiac conditions. Rhythm is the richest source of information to the cardiologist because of all that has been learned about the function of the heart. Similarly, it will be the most valuable source of our understanding of organizations once we associate characteristic patterns with known organizational conditions. Perhaps one day we will have an "Encyclopedia of Organizational Disorders" in which we report normal and dysfunctional patterns of performance for various business activities in a variety of industries (see Figure 3.5).

The analysis of rate and rhythm has advanced to such an extent partly because EKGs are plotted on a standardized scale, thereby allowing comparison of one patient to another. Establishing a similar scale for the study and comparison of organizations is a logical and necessary step in the study of organizations as chaotic systems. Our current practice of using business ratios to standardize expenses or profits by dividing them by some other measure of business activity or scale (sales, assets, or equity) is a first step toward addressing this problem. Similarly, our normal reporting cycles are probably also appropriate measurement periods that can allow for comparisons over time and between firms. Put simply, we are probably

Figure 3.5
Normal and Abnormal Sales Rhythms in the Retail Industry

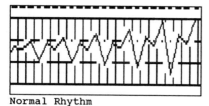

Normal Rhythm

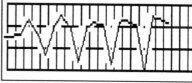

Sales Dysrhythmia

already collecting the right data frequently enough to study organizational rates and rhythms.

Blocking is a term used to describe restrictions or obstructions in the electrical pathways of the heart. The existence of a block typically results in a delay or complete absence in the heart's response to sinus contractions. One can imagine analogous blocks within organizations. Any activity that restricts or delays organizational response to signals from other parts of the organization constitutes a block, and lessens the organization's ability to respond to the external factors that affect it. Although the analogy seems somewhat strained, a comparison of organizational limit cycles clearly reveals that the structural characteristics of the organization clearly affect the ability of the organization to respond to cyclical changes.

Consider the two companies in Figure 3.6. As described earlier, the horizontal axis on each image is *changes in sales* and the vertical axis is *changes in profits*. Consider the challenge of managing inventory at the two firms. Atlanta Gas is easily able to vary their production capacity during the year. When demand increases, customers simply draw from the company's system of pipelines that provide natural gas to a large part of the South. When demand decreases, sales and profits decline. Management simply needs to maintain constant pressure in the lines to maintain a proper inventory. Although there are other significant challenges to managing this firm, such as purchase or construction of new distribution lines, the scaling ability of the firm is ideal. It is able to immediately respond to changes in demand. One should note that for Atlanta Gas, demand is fairly predictable; it serves a large number of users with an extended history, and although temperature has an effect on daily consumption, overall monthly demand is fairly predictable. The limit cycle of Atlanta Gas is typical of utility firms; Union Electric and Southwestern Energy reveal limit cycles that are almost identical to that of Atlanta Gas.

Tandy Corporation is faced with much greater challenges in predicting and meeting consumer demand. It operates in an industry where demand varies with personal disposable income and the strength of substitute products. Further, the company is vertically integrated, operating several large

Figure 3.6
The Effect of Blocking on Organizational Limit Cycles

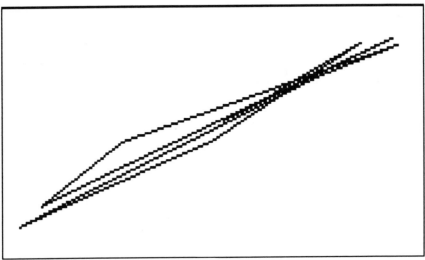

Atlanta Gas Company

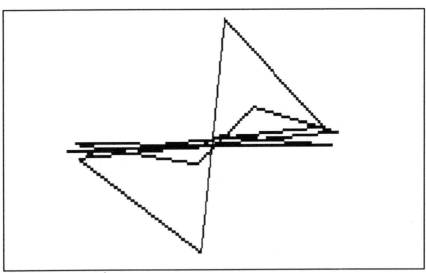

Tandy Corporation

Figure 3.7
The Demand-Response Matrix

		High	Low
	Low	1	2
Blocking	High	3	4

Predictability of Demand

manufacturing plants that must produce long before seasonal peaks in demand. Additionally, many of the company's products are purchased in international markets, extending the time between when orders are placed and products are received at the retail stores. Any requirements or activities that restrict the company's ability to immediately scale up or down in production capacity constitute blocks for the company. Blocks are represented by the need to place early orders, the need to warehouse inventory, the delay in distribution of products, the delay in accumulation of point-of-sale data, and the need to maintain raw materials at the manufacturing level.

The effect of blocking is less severe when demand is predictable, since management can allow for the anticipated delays and still meet the predictable demand. When demand cannot be predicted with precision, blocks in the production process inevitably result in decreased profitability. If demand is underestimated, the company suffers from stock outages, increased shipping costs, and overtime. If demand is overestimated, price decreases, inventory carrying costs, and inflated payrolls drive down profitability.

One can begin to see some of the managerial implications that flow from a study of organizations as nonlinear systems. The discussion above describes the differences in the limit cycles of these two firms as the result of two major factors, predictability of demand and blocking. Consider a matrix that combines these two characteristics and describes the ability of an organization to respond to changing demand.

In Figure 3.7 quadrant 1 describes Atlanta Gas' situation. Demand is quite predictable, and the company has few characteristics that block its ability to meet demand. We would expect the limit cycle of such a firm to be low order, and this is confirmed by Atlanta Gas and others in the utility industry, which exhibit a distinct Period 2 trajectory. Companies in quadrant 2 should also exhibit low-order limit cycles. Although demand is unpredictable, the absence of any major blockages should permit such firms to respond to changes in demand. Companies that are classified into quadrant 3 should also be able to maintain low-order limit cycles. Examples of such firms are Wal-Mart and Toys Я Us; both of these companies have shown the ability to trace Period 2 limit cycles despite the significant challenges of seasonable demand, lengthy order times, and major inventory handling requirements. Companies in quadrant 4 will typically exhibit limit cycles of higher order. Tandy and Hechinger's (shown in Figure 2.3) provide examples of distinct Period 4 limit cycles resulting from inherently unpredictable demand and significant restrictions in the ability to respond to changes in demand.

Figure 3.7 provides an interesting way to summarize organizations, and it points to the needed focus of the companies involved. For example, companies in quadrants 1 and 3 are "blessed" with predictable demand. Those in quadrants 2 and 4 are forced to deal with unpredictable demand. Companies in quadrants 1 and 2 have few obstructions to meeting demand, whereas those in 3 and 4 have many (or a few significant ones). Companies in quadrants 1, 2, and 3 should be able to maintain low-order limit cycles, whereas companies in quadrant 4 should not. The prescription for those companies in quadrant 4 is to either improve their ability to predict sales (perhaps by contracting with customers) or reduce the blockages that prevent the organization from responding to changes in demand. The matrix can provide a tool for researchers, managers, or investors who want a classification scheme for organizational limit cycles.

Industry Heartbeats

The discussion of the retail industry (i.e., Wal-Mart, K Mart, and TJX) and Atlanta Gas suggests that organizational limit cycles of companies in the same industry are similar. Undiversified companies that operate in the same industry do exhibit similar limit cycles, as suggested by those companies in the retail industry shown in Figure 3.2. This means that comparative studies are possible within an industry. Although there are many reasons why a company's limit cycle may differ significantly from others in the same industry, the information provided by examining a competitor can be combined with a knowledge of the differences between firms to reveal important strategies or tactics. For example, a comparative study of limit cycles may reveal a difference in axes between two firms. If one organization has an axis of less than 45 degrees and the other has an axis of greater than 45 degrees, it indicates that the profits of the first firm are less influenced by changes in volume (see *Determining Axis* in Chapter 2 and Figure 2.6).

Industry limit cycles also can be created. This can be done either by using total industry figures or by combining the sales and profit data of selected firms in the same industry. The resulting limit cycle and velocity history chart provide a "standard EKG" that can be used for analysis of companies in the industry or to compare one industry with another.

Figure 3.8
The Company Stability Matrix

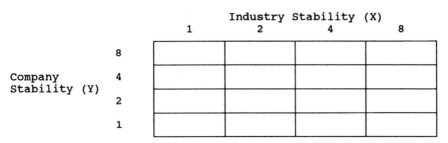

Alternatively, one can simply identify the period of the company under examination and compare it with the period of the industry limit cycle.

For example, consider the information provided by a matrix based on the profit margin stability of the industry and the profit margin stability of the company. We can use industry statistics for a measurement of the industry profit margin and company data for our company profit margin. The latest limit cycle period of each can be used as an objective measure of stability. Figure 3.8 provides a sample of such a matrix.

Any position in the matrix can be referenced by applying a traditional X,Y coordinate system, in which X represents industry stability and Y represents company stability. Consider the implications of various positions on the matrix. Position 1,1 describes the highest consistency of both the industry and the company; it also describes a relationship in which the company's stability matches that of the industry. Positions 2,2 and 4,4 represent positions in which the stability of the company and of the industry match with increasing disorder. Coordinate 8,8 describes instability in both the industry and the company profit margin and is also one of the matched coordinates that lie on the upward-sloping, *equal-stability* diagonal of the matrix. Because of common environmental and company structure characteristics, there is a tendency for industry stability to match company stability, resulting in matched coordinates; however, off-diagonal coordinates are surely possible and carry major implications. For example, coordinate 4,2 describes a situation in which the profit margin of the company (Y) is stabler than that of the industry (X); such is the case for any coordinate position below the equal-stability diagonal. Such a condition suggests a company that is more able to adapt to changes than other companies in the industry (i.e., fewer blockages). The company may be more able than others in the industry to maintain profits during the second quarter of the year, or it may have a more proportional increase in both sales and profits during the fourth quarter of the year. Whatever the difference, the limit cycles of both the industry and the company contain a wealth of data that will highlight their timing and nature. Similarly, coordinates above the equal-stability diagonal reflect situations in which the company is less stable than others in the industry.

The fact that industries have different and characteristic limit cycles has important strategic implications. It means that organizations collectively constitute an entity with unique structural characteristics that extend over time. It means that there is more to being an industry than simply a classification. Industries have common supply-and-demand conditions, and the businesses within them have common operating characteristics. Industries have "heartbeats" that are influenced by environmental events and that improve or degrade in performance. Industries have structural characteristics—physical plants, inventories, and technology—that define how they will respond to their changing environment. Their performance is driven only in part by current conditions; much of their performance is determined by historical decisions that have created the current state of the industry.

Strategic management theory provides a wide array of portfolio matrices that classify businesses or industries according to two (or more) criteria. For example, several position a business on a matrix that compares market share with industry growth rate (obviously one wants to be positioned with high market share in a rapidly growing industry). But such matrices fail to identify the chronology of an industry. They, like an annual financial report, are single-frame photographs snipped from an epic film. It is the evolution of the industry that is important in both the short and long run. Significant changes in the performance of the industry will result only from significant changes to the structural characteristics of that industry. A company's competitive advantage emerges when it fails to follow the pattern of operations that define and permeate the industry. Unfortunately, the attractor that defines an industry and the operations of businesses within that industry is extremely powerful; it is difficult to change the way business is done within an established industry. Fortunately, a minor change can make all the difference subsequently as it defines a new future for those companies innovative enough to try something fundamentally different. Success and failure come from being different.

Environmental Heartbeats

What drives the periodic oscillations that we know as business cycles? What is the source of exogenous shocks that disrupt operations, invalidate forecasts, and, occasionally, provide unexpected opportunities? Industries and the organizations within them are driven by a wide range of environmental events—factors exogenous to the firm. This is not a new concept; in the 1950s Kenneth Boulding identified organizations as open systems operating in a turbulent environment. What is new is the recognition that the environment is deterministic. The external threats and opportunities

identified in a strategic analysis of the external environment are there because of other underlying reasons. Traditional strategic analysis would
classify declining sales in a particular market segment as a threat, and
improving demand as an opportunity. But this level of analysis is much
like following a shadow; it allows you to follow the leader, but it fails to
recognize the true source or cause of the changes in direction. Sales decline
for a reason. They decline because of a change in consumer attitude or
because of the introduction of a new, substitute product. The threat is not
the sales decline or even the change in consumer opinion; the threat is the
failure of the organization to monitor the underlying determinant that is
causing the change.

Environmental factors, like changes in demand, changes in prices of raw
materials, and action by competitors, also adhere to an underlying attractor that can be mapped in phase space and analyzed on a marginal history
chart. A study of environmental limit cycles and a discovery of the patterns
of change in environmental phenomenon provide a new window on the
broad array of external threats and opportunities faced by a company.

A study of total rental property in a major metropolitan market revealed
an underlying attractor that bound rental rates to occupancy rates. A study
of gasoline prices revealed an underlying attractor that bound them to
crude oil prices. In another study the limit cycle that associates changes in
housing starts with changes in interest rates was displayed. Traditional
statistics have taught us to expect a correlation between these variables;
chaos theory teaches us that the association is much richer than a correlation statistic. There are distinct and constrained patterns of change that
associate one with the other.

Unlike many organizational limit cycles, environmental phenomenon
present higher-order attractors, patterns that are probably nonrepeating.
Such patterns appear random and may be entirely unpredictable even though
they are driven by entirely deterministic forces. Consider the limit cycle in
Figure 3.9 that binds the U.S. gross national product (GNP) to personal
expenditures. In the image, changes in GNP are on the horizontal axis and
changes in personnal consumption expenditures are on the vertical axis.

Does this limited data set provide any pattern? Is it bound in any way?
If it were not seasonally adjusted, it would probably oscillate with some
regularity. Even without seasonal adjustment it is clearly bound by some
limits as it progresses from quarter 1, 1990, to quarter 3, 1991.

It is not random, its trajectory traces the interaction of an *almost* endless
list of forces that collectively define the behavior of these macroeconomic
variables. This does not suggest that the future performance is any more
predictable. It does mean, however, that there are patterns of behavior—
some quite structured, others less so—for many of those exogenous, external events that we often accept as random. It also reminds us that there

Figure 3.9
The U.S. GNP–Personal Consumption Expenditure Attractor—
Seasonally Adjusted

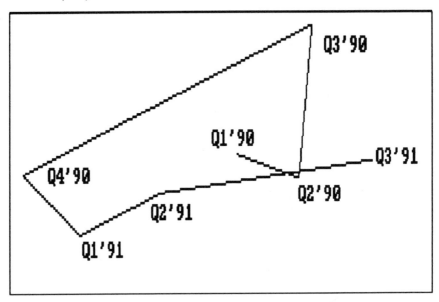

are causal determinants of these macroeconomic variables and that their future trajectories may be quite sensitive to minor structural changes.

Patterns at the Functional Level

From the micro to the macro level we find that the phenomenon of business and economics is addressable as a flow of transitions with intricate patterns of changes. Externally and internally to our organizations we can reexamine the many variables and ratios we typically monitor and see new patterns in them. Perhaps the most exciting realizations emerge when one considers traditional management functions in light of chaos theory. For the next several chapters we will look at the implications of chaos theory at the functional level. We will then examine specific decision-making activities such as forecasting and strategic planning. For this reassessment of management we need not apply mathematical procedures much beyond those already discussed, although occasional refinements will be introduced when describing particular applications or the results of certain studies.

The most important concept to keep in mind from these introductory chapters is that of determinism—that future performance of a nonlinear system emerges naturally from the current state of the system. At a functional level we will see that this greatly influences when and how we intervene in processes. We will see that this understanding directly affects our promotional planning and allows us to classify our products differently. We will see that financial analysis has another dimension and the complex production processes can be simplified using chaos theory. Even human resource management takes on a new view when examined from the chaos theory perspective.

Perhaps "view" is precisely the objective here. Chaos theory offers much more than a new mathematical procedure for manipulating numbers. It causes us to reconsider the very nature of those processes we measure and manage, and in doing that it offers us an opportunity for creative approaches and new perspectives on business.

NOTES

1. The acronym EKG is used instead of ECG to avoid confusion with EEGs, which are electroencephalograms.

2. For a readable, understandable, and educational text on EKGs see Dale Dubin, M.D., *Rapid Interpretation of EKG's,* 4th ed. (Tampa, Fla.: Cover Publishing Company) 1989.

PART II

APPLYING CHAOS THEORY TO BUSINESS

4

Marketing Applications

What impact, if any, does chaos theory have on common operations such as marketing? Does it offer only a new theoretical framework for researchers, or is it something for the sales representative and the ad manager? The answer is that it is both. Academicians will find chaos theory and the simple methods of analysis proposed here valuable for new research. Some of the implications eventually will make their way into the textbooks. Practitioners, however, will find that chaos theory, either as an analytic technique or by the new perspective it offers, influences virtually every marketing activity. It has profound implications regarding pricing, it can identify previously unseen opportunities for significant changes in market share, it causes us to rethink virtually every promotional tactic, and it compels us to review how we distribute our products. Beyond that, it enhances our understanding of competitive strategies and has strategic marketing implications. Chaos theory changes the theories and practices of marketing, not in some singular conceptual way, but in a myriad of practical ways.

This chapter examines some of the primary marketing functions of price, promotion, and distribution, and considers how a chaos theory perspective changes our view of those traditional activities. The results of several research studies are reported to illustrate major points. Also included are several "propositions" that summarize important points. Implications regarding competitive strategies and product portfolio issues are addressed after the discussion of functional activities.

PRICING ISSUES

Let's start with something practical and profound. Here's an opening proposition:

Proposition 1: Traditional supply-and-demand theory as we know it doesn't work. The sales of Coca-Cola sometimes go up when we raise the price.

In a recent graduate class titled Chaos Theory and Business Research one student, an information manager for a major grocery chain in the Southwest, collected data on Coca-Cola sales and price and demonstrated this fact with empirical clarity. Other students went on to show the effect with various other products. In all fairness to the economists, what chaos theory revealed to these students is in no way contradictory to basic economics. The key words in Proposition 1 are "as we know it," since most of us operate with a misunderstanding of what our economics professors were really saying.

Students in the graduate "Chaos" class were asked to identify some business activity and collect two variables that would measure the behavior of that activity. Some chose inventory management and used measures of sales and on-hand inventory; others chose budgeting and examined actual and budgeted expenditures. The revelation that provides Proposition 1 emerged when one student chose to examine the effect of pricing on unit sales.

Let's go back to our basic economics class. We all know that price affects quantity demanded. One of the first of many charts our economics professors put on the board resembled the one in Figure 4.1a.

We know the first chart *too* well. With a horizontal axis of "Quantity" and a vertical axis of "Price," Figure 4.1a tells us that increasing the price of any product (or service) will cause a decrease in quantity demanded. In other words, if we raise the price, we will sell less. "That's intuitive," we thought. "Economics won't be *that* bad," we muttered.

Then the complications set in. It was pointed out that even though the *quantity* demanded might be less, we will be selling that quantity at a higher price, so we might be better off with higher prices than with lower prices. It all depends on what our costs are, and that's when the supply curve got introduced (see Figure 4.1b).

The supply curve reflected the fact that the quantity supplied to the marketplace depends on the price that can be charged for the product. Put simply, if the market is willing to pay high prices for a product, more will be supplied. "So where the lines cross is important," said the professor. "That's the equilibrium point—that's the price and quantity that will exist in the marketplace."

We left economics class the first day knowing one thing for sure: If we raise the price, people will demand less of our product. But what we should have remembered was the concept of that equilibrium point. And when our instructors started shifting those lines around, we should have paid close attention because that's when the dynamics of the price–quantity relation emerged. We can criticize our economics professors for not shift-

Figure 4.1
Traditional Supply and Demand Curves

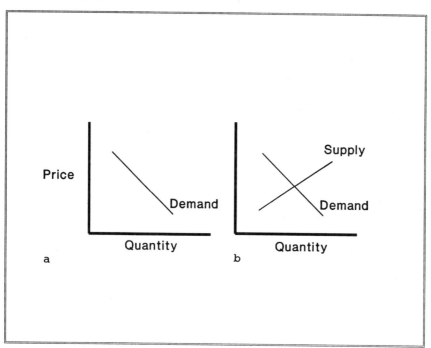

ing them often enough, fast enough. You see, there is another entire dimension that unfolds when you draw layer after layer of shifting supply-and-demand curves. Each chart is like a frame in a movie, and the equilibrium points on each chart are connected to one another. Imagine your professor drawing hundreds and then thousands of charts, each with shifting supply-and-demand curves. Imagine him drawing them with lightning speed—watch the behavior of the equilibrium point—see the movie? See the dynamic equilibrium point shifting upward for a while, then down to this position, and then oscillating periodically as it traces a trajectory from chart to chart, its future determined by its position on the previous chart and the changes that occur from chart to chart.

Your professor shifted the supply curve from D_1 to D_2 and said, "Of course, if demand increases, more will be sold at a higher price." At the time we didn't realize that shifting demand curves are more important than the static notion that demand decreases if we increase price. The relation between price and quantity demanded holds for a single chart, a single slice in time. But it does not describe the behavior of the equilibrium point over time, and *that* is what we experience, *that* is what is important.

So when our graduate student used chaos theory to analyze the relationship between the price of Coca-Cola six-packs and the quantity sold, he discovered an oscillating, orbiting equilibrium point with a fascinating trajectory. He put price on the horizontal axis and quantity sold on the vertical axis and then plotted changes in the two variables on a phase plane, using weekly data. The equilibrium point usually oscillated between quadrants 2 and 4. A visit to quadrant 2 reflected a decrease in quantity sold (the x axis) when the price was increased (the y axis). But sometimes, not too rarely, the equilibrium point visited quadrant 1 or 3, and that is when the discussion got interesting. "How did it do that? Why did it do that?" asked the class. Quadrant 1 means that quantity demanded *increased* when we raised the price ("Does that mean it's a Giffin Good, like potatoes in Germany after World War II? Does that mean it's a violation of some cherished principle of economics?") And what about quadrant 3? How can quantity demanded *decrease* when we lower the price?

Alas, the explanations were almost mundane. The equilibrium point visited quadrant 1 during Labor Day weekend and Super Bowl weekend. That is when prices were raised in anticipation of increased sales. And the visit to quadrant 3 occurred after Thanksgiving, when consumers had overstocked, overspent, and overstuffed to such an extent that no matter how low you lowered the price, sales would still decline. Although the explanations were mundane, they were still profound. They demonstrated that our experience with the relation between prices and quantities sold is better described as a trajectory over time rather than by a single—or several—supply-and-demand curve. They also reinforced the value of a single data point. Each data element was used in the analysis; nothing was discarded as an error, as traditional statistics would have us do. The outliers were most important as they reflected critical events with important managerial implications. Consider the fact that we were able to explain only some of the quadrant 1 visits. This means that there were other occasions when an increase in price was associated with an increase in quantity demanded. Our graduate student was eager to look into those other occasions. Although they may simply reflect other, uncontrollable increases in demand, like Super Bowl weekend, they might not; they might be associated with some promotional tactic that was particularly effective. They might be the result of some change in the display previously thought to be unimportant. They might identify an inexpensive means of escape from the price–quantity attractor and present one more way to influence the future with free will.

With Coca-Cola, it is generally true that price changes are inversely related to changes in quantity sold. But what of other products? What about the product or service you sell? And when are there exceptions to the rule that allow you to visit quadrant 1? The inverse relationship between price and quantity cannot be taken for granted. In the example above it's been demonstrated that it occasionally doesn't hold for Coca-Cola. There are other products for which it doesn't hold at all. The relationship depends on the nature of the product, availability of substitutes, and other attributes peripheral to the sale of the product. What one should begin to realize is that each product has a unique equilibrium point trajectory that we, as managers, should know and monitor. We should know the general shape and size of the equilibrium point's attractor, how tightly it is bound to its attractor, and when it is likely to escape that attractor. We need to know these things for practical reasons; not only do they affect every price change we plan to make, but they also show when we should make a price change.

PROMOTION ISSUES

Gasoline violates the rule. A study of the relationship between price per gallon and gallons sold at several retail locations revealed an attractor that stands almost vertically on the phase plane. With changes in price on the horizontal axis and changes in quantity on the vertical axis, the phase plane surprised the marketing manager of a major gasoline retailer. There was no evidence of an inverse association between changes in price and changes in quantity sold using many months of data. The economist would say that the price changes were not great enough to be significant. The statistician would find no correlation and then spend the rest of the afternoon analyzing the variance (the "error") in a desperate attempt to explain what his linear method could not describe. The chaotician would say that the equilibrium price and quantity are bound to an attractor that is defined by the structural characteristics of the system. Change the structure of the system—change the characteristics of the market or the way in which the product is presented to that market—and you can change the trajectory of the moving equilibrium point. Sure, the price of gasoline is important. But the relationship between price and sales is nonlinear. A price change of several cents per gallon won't make *any* difference in some markets. However, lower the price from anything over a dollar to 99 cents, and you're likely to be interviewed on the five o'clock news and have cars lined up around the block. The relation is nonlinear, and the company we studied now knows the limits of its price–quantity attractor for a few locations. To sell gasoline it can worry about other things besides price.

Proposition 2: High-order chaos offers opportunity and risk. Low-order chaos offers predictability and constraint.

Because each market has a unique set of characteristics and purchasing behaviors, each constitutes a separate system and, as any marketer knows, each should be analyzed separately. But what criteria do we have for determining if two markets are the same or different. We can test them for

Figure 4.2
Limit Cycles for Two Retail Gasoline Locations

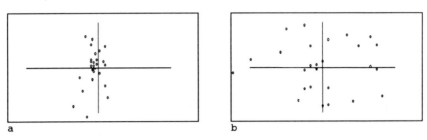

a   b

differences statistically: "Is the household income in this city significantly different from income in that city?" Or we can produce phase plane diagrams of the behavior in each market and compare them in much the same way we compare fingerprints.

The gasoline retailer cited above operates more than 800 locations that combine gasoline sales with a well-stocked convenience store. These stores are located throughout Texas with many locations in major cities. What is the market for these stores? How finely should the company define their promotional efforts. Is the entire Texas market homogeneous? Are the markets of the individual cities homogeneous enough to permit common promotional efforts within each city? Or are the markets even more unique than that, varying from each store to the next?

In our study of the price–quantity attractor we selected two locations just two miles from each other on the same major street. Although neither location showed an attractor sensitive to price, the two limit cycles were profoundly different. One was fairly bound to the vertical axis (Figure 4.2a), whereas the other appeared as an explosion of points reflecting larger price changes and much greater changes in quantity sold (Figure 4.2b). A quick check of the corporate records indicated that both locations were being supervised by the same area manager. The phase plane diagrams revealed new information that showed the locations to be fundamentally different, and those differences have a direct impact on any promotional efforts for the stores.

Further study revealed that one was considered to be a "destination location" and the other was not. A "destination location" is one that has considerable regular traffic. It might service a neighborhood, or be the obvious stop for regular commuters. The other store competed directly with several other retailers that were located within the same block. One should be able to deduce that the destination location was the one with the tightly bound limit cycle.

The company issues redemption stamps at all locations at a cost of more than $10 million per year. However, the analysis described above suggests that at some locations, the purchase patterns are tightly constrained to an identifiable attractor, whereas at others the characteristics of the market allow for much greater variability. If we were to decide that redemption stamps could be used at some stores and not at others, which stores should issue them? The characteristics of these two markets, just two miles apart, suggest a need for much more active promotions at the one with high-order chaos than at the one with greater equilibrium point stability.

What about the other 798 stores? How many of them have equilibrium point stability and how many require active promotional intervention? As Proposition 2 states, high-order chaos offers opportunity and risk. Low-order chaos offers consistency and constraint. It may take only minor promotional initiatives to make a substantial difference at the high-order location; its market is volatile and perhaps sensitive to adjustments. It presents both an opportunity and a risk. The low-order chaos location is bound by more powerful and restrictive forces. Price changes apparently have no appreciable effect, and discontinuing redemption stamps will probably make little, if any, difference. If it is profitable, it will probably remain so; if it is not profitable, it will probably remain unprofitable without some significant intervention that forces a change in the very structure that binds the market.

Consider the implications for this company on this single issue regarding redemption stamps and on the many other promotional issues. If an analysis of all 800 stores indicates that half have tightly patterned limit cycles, that presents a potential saving of $5 million. The effect of discontinuing redemption stamps at any location could be easily monitored by observing the behavior of the limit cycle trajectory. What about remodeling locations? Perhaps we should delay remodeling of those locations with low-order limit cycles and focus on remodeling those that offer a greater opportunity for significant changes in the market structure. Which ones should we expand? Which ones should we close? Because we are now able to identify profitable locations with reliable, low-order limit cycles, we can now identify the market characteristics that create this condition and use that information to select sites for new locations. Proposition 2 provides a new way to classify markets and a new criterion for selecting promotional activities. It will take time to discover the many implications of this classification scheme, but it seems that each market may be as unique as a fingerprint and that the limit cycle can provide that fingerprint.

A second example confirms the stability of market characteristics and contributes to the argument that high-order chaos provides opportunity. Remember ice cream drumsticks? You can still buy them in the freezer case at the grocery or convenience store. You can still find "Nutty Buddy" and others. Ice cream drumsticks are part of the ice cream novelty item category that includes ice cream sandwiches and ice pops. The product category is considered mature with many competitors, none of which command a significant market share. The seven largest competitors combined account for only 35 percent of total market share on a national level. However, within any single market there are only a limited number of products offered, and the market share of these products, as we will see, is quite stable. The category is obviously seasonal, and there is almost no mass marketing. Promotions in this category take the form of discounts to grocers.

When we isolated the market share of ice cream drumsticks as a percentage of total sales in the category and compared the change in market share with changes in price, we discovered a well-defined limit cycle that oscillated between quarters 2 and 4 (see Figure 4.3a). With changes in price on the horizontal axis and changes in market share on the vertical axis, this confirmed that promotional price decreases brought higher market share, but that market share was sacrificed when prices were returned to normal. It seemed that drumsticks were tightly bound by the characteristics of their industry to a catch-22—sacrifice profits for market share or market share for profits.

Then something major happened. A new chocolate ice cream bar was introduced by one of the major candy companies. The impact of that new entry did not simply draw down the market share of all other products in the category. Instead, it drew new attention to the category. It created new customers. Two consecutive price decreases for drumsticks were associated with substantial decreases in sales and then some price increases were associated with sales increases. The tight market share structure had been broken, the limit cycle escaped its attractor, and the future share of all products in the ice cream novelty business was unpredictable (see Figure 4.3b). High-order chaos had brought new opportunity.

The window of opportunity had opened temporarily. This was when new promotions and changes in product design might make a substantial and lasting impact on the future performance of the drumstick. The event was clearly not random; Snickers had planned at length the introduction of their ice cream bar. The turbulence of the market was defined by the nature of that system at the time and the decisions made by each competitor as it played out a defensive strategy.

Chaos theory forces us to recognize the relationship between the past, present, and future. The limit cycles that can be generated offer proof that there is a pattern in the behavior of economic variables as they create unique trajectories from yesterday into tomorrow. Promotional tactics allow us to intervene and attempt to influence the course of that trajectory, be it equilibrium price or market share. Sometimes those patterns of market equilibrium are more susceptible to influence than at other times. Generating the limit cycle provides a picture of the pattern we are managing and suggests the appropriate timing of our involvement. For ice cream drumsticks the new disorder represented opportunity for major changes in market share.

Figure 4.3
The Market Share-Price Attractor for Ice Cream Drumsticks

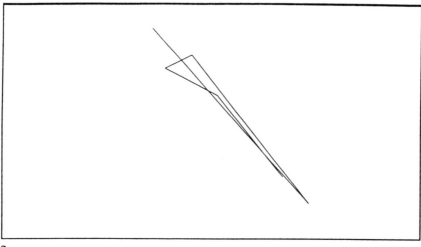

a

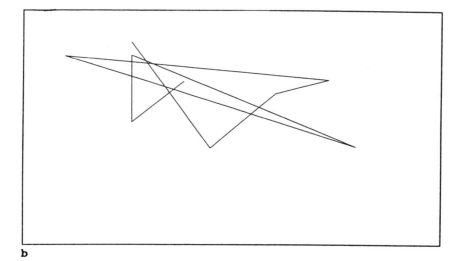

b

NONLINEARITY IN DISTRIBUTION SYSTEMS

The route by which products and services reach their markets constitutes a marketing channel. Traditionally, we view the participants in the
channel as suppliers, manufacturers, wholesalers, and retailers, although
sometimes there are jobbers, contractors, and other participants, depending on the product being distributed. Recently, there has been a trend to

eliminate the wholesaler as a separate channel member. The traditional role of the wholesaler who historically warehoused, sorted, or repackaged products is being assumed by others in the distribution system or by new technologies. For example, assortments of ready-to-wear garments are, in some cases, shipped directly from manufacturer to retailer, bypassing any intermediary. The manufacturer's ability to provide assortments and quantities according to demand stems from new information and manufacturing technologies.

Contrary to what some may believe, participants in a distribution channel are exceedingly cooperative with one another. They constitute a team with a mutual objective; their purpose is to get the right quantity of the right product to the market at a minimal cost. Although there is obviously negotiation between the participants as to who absorbs certain costs, ultimately the advantages of cooperation and the need for efficiency outweigh most disputes. The trend today is toward even greater cooperation than in the past. Instead of contracting multiple suppliers to ensure a reliable source of raw materials, manufacturers today are likely to get more heavily involved with a single supplier who commits to certain quality standards and delivery schedules.

Ultimately, the performance of a marketing channel is determined by the nature of the product and the market it serves, the structure and participants in the channel, and the policies and practices of the channel members. Collectively, these factors create a system with certain capacity, behavior, and efficiency.

Proposition 3: A distribution channel constitutes a nonlinear system with an overall behavior resulting from the behavior and interaction of the channel participants.

The flow of product from one channel participant to another creates a nonlinear relationship with a potential for chaotic behavior. The relationship involves more than simply the quantity of product in the channel; it includes prices, transportation costs and agreements, reimbursement policies, and a myriad of other policies and practices. Within certain bounds the channel structure is maintained; beyond those bounds the structure shifts, perhaps permanently, perhaps temporarily. Consider the ingredients of your favorite candy bar. Historically, it included a specified quantity of sugar made from sugar cane, and suppliers of sugar cane could count on relatively constant (or consistently changing) orders from the major manufacturers of candy in the United States. However, wide variations in the price of sugar created an intolerable condition for candy manufacturers, causing them to reformulate their candy bars in a way that allows varying levels of corn syrup to be substituted for sugar. That reformulation constituted a fundamental change in the distribution system, and it greatly affected all participants in the channel. Sugar plantations now faced changing demand for their product, changes that were related to the relative price of corn syrup. U.S. candy manufacturers realized much greater stability in their costs, as did all those channel participants who subsequently carry the product from manufacturer to the market. Even you were affected by the change in the channel structure. Your candy bar carries a more consistent price (or size), and its ingredients may change periodically (although you probably can't taste the difference).

Channel structures and their market conditions create channel performance that is constant, periodically oscillating, or chaotic. The entire channel has a nonlinear behavior, and each channel member contributes to the behavior of the overall channel by either increasing, dampening, or continuing the periodic oscillations it encounters from members further up the channel. The overall behavior can, therefore, be decomposed into its constituent parts to reveal sources of disorder and sources of dampening behavior. Consider the following proposition.

Proposition 4: The efficiency of a distribution channel is evident in the limit cycles that reflect the channel's behavior.

The phase plane diagrams in Figure 4.4 provide a different view of the common inventory turnover ratio. On these diagrams the horizontal axis represents changes in units sold to a customer and the vertical axis represents changes in the supplier's quantity of inventory on hand. Consider the implications of those positions labeled A, B, C, D, and E on the diagram in Figure 4.4a.

Position A at the origin reflects constancy. At A there would be no change in the rate of sales and no change in the quantity of inventory on hand. To maintain position A the company has to guard against sources of oscillation such as changes in demand, changes in supply, and changes in their own operations that would affect the on-hand inventory or the quantity of units sold. Such a situation may be rare, although a combination of long-term sales and supply contracts could create the condition. A bottler, contracted to deliver a specified quantity and supplied by a steady source of raw materials, provides a possible example. The bottling process of purchasing, producing, and distributing inventory is virtually continuous, resulting in no changes in sales and no change in inventory on hand.

For our example imagine that raw materials and finished inventory shipments are made each morning and that sales are recorded at time of shipment. What if it snowed at the bottling plant? If it snowed in the early morning before shipments were received and finished inventory was shipped, the disrupted shipments would cause the limit cycle to take a trajectory toward position B, reflecting a decrease in units sold and an increase in finished goods as the last of current raw materials are processed. By the

Figure 4.4
Limit Cycles of Channel Participants

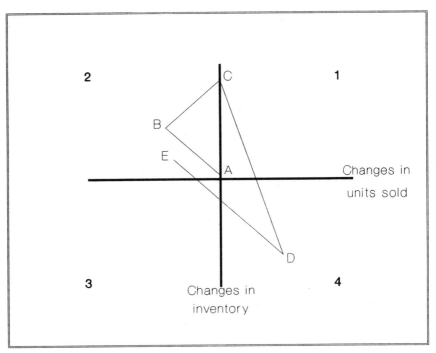

a

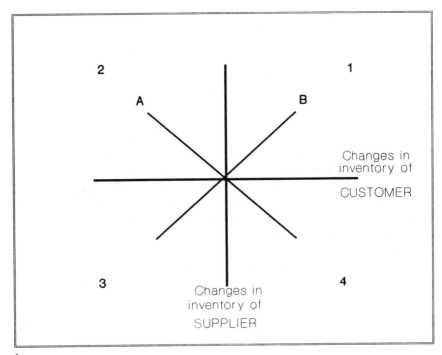

b

end of the next day our limit cycle would approach position C, reflecting a continued increase in finished inventory on hand and no change in units sold (relative to the previous day). The next morning, two days after the snow, we would ship our excessive quantity of finished inventory and receive another supply of raw materials. The limit cycle trajectory would visit position D, reflecting the increase in recorded sales and decrease in on-hand inventory. The next day, three days after the snow, the effect would still be identifiable in the trajectory as both sales and on-hand inventory decrease relative to the previous day. The snowfall, like the lack of snowfall in our Chapter 3 discussion of The Toro Company, shocked the continuous operations of this single channel member. The effect echoes through time as the company works to dampen the effect and draw back toward its Period 1 attractor. Events have signatures in the limit cycle trajectory.

One should note that if it had snowed just after the trucks left that first morning, it would have had no effect on the company operations. One should also note that the company might lose its sales contract because of this; the disruption in supply might be all that is necessary incrementally to cause its customer to take business elsewhere.

The disruptive effect of the snowfall ripples through the distribution channel. Admittedly, the effect in this example would probably be minor, since buffers of inventory hedge against such minor disruptions in distribution. The effect of the inventory buffers dampens the effect but usually increases inventory carrying costs for one or more channel participants.

Most companies are not so insulated as the bottler described here; they are exposed to changes in demand. Cyclical changes in demand will cause periodic oscillations in the inventory turnover limit cycle, and if production processes can't be scaled to match that changing demand, there is going to be a cost associated with the resulting inefficiency.

Let's consider the implications of positions in quadrants 1, 2, 3, and 4 in Figure 4.4a and relate them to the traditional concept of inventory turnover.

Inventory turnover rates commonly are computed to assist in the control of inventory levels by relating them to sales. The ratio computed essentially measures "what has been sold" relative to "what is on hand." Specifically, the computation divides cost of goods sold by average inventory at cost. It usually is reported on an annual basis. For example, if the value of inventory sold in a year is four times the value of inventory normally in stock, the turnover rate will be four times. Inventory turnover rates can be computed for any product or product line and can be computed over intervals shorter than one year. The measure is essential to determining how much replacement inventory to buy or manufacture.

An attractor that holds the limit cycle in quadrant 1 or a temporary visit to quadrant 1 suggests increases in on-hand inventory and increases in unit sales. The result may be no change in the inventory turnover rate, although average inventory increases (there may be a minor change in the turnover rate if the two increases are not proportional). A visit to quadrant 3 reflects the inverse of this; both on-hand inventory and units sold decrease, and again there may be no change in the inventory turnover rate. A trajectory visiting quadrant 2, however, suggests a decrease in sales while on-hand inventory increases; the result would be a decrease in the turnover rate. A visit to quadrant 4 implies a decrease in on-hand inventory while sales increase, resulting in an increase in the inventory turnover rate. Cyclical changes in demand invite instability in the trajectory and the inventory turnover rate. However, as long as any oscillation can be contained to quadrants 1 and 3, the turnover rate will be reasonably stable. Any trajectory into quadrant 2 or 4 will cause major changes in the turnover rate.

Although the discussion above suggests that cyclical oscillations increase costs and invite higher-order chaos into the distribution channel, a much more positive view can be taken toward channel management. Because most companies are faced with changes in demand, they typically have opportunities to decrease costs by improving coordination between participants in the distribution channel. Because phase plane diagrams so effectively reveal any turbulence, disruption, or systematic patterns in the distribution process, they provide a valuable way to describe and communicate channel behavior. Retailers can use phase plane diagrams to image the disruptive patterns caused by inconsistent shipments by suppliers. Suppliers can illustrate the pattern of supply and work with retailers to smooth shipments into regularly oscillating or consistent behavior. Only by knowing the *precise* behavior of the distribution process can the channel member hope to improve it beyond any conventional, statistically controlled process.

Figure 4.4b suggests a way to understand the behavior of the relation *between* two channel members. In Figure 4.4b the horizontal axis has been changed to measure changes in the on-hand inventory of the *customer* and the vertical axis has been changed to measure changes in the on-hand inventory of the *supplier* (the customer has been placed on the horizontal axis, since the customer's inventory level is more likely to drive the inventory supply of the supplier). The diagram effectively displays the behavior of inventory levels in the relationship between two channel members.

Both supplier and customer would benefit if the relationship was characterized by a Period 1 attractor, allowing constancy in inventory levels to both. Although such stability may be possible, changes in demand will probably cause some form of oscillation to emerge. Consider which line, A or B in Figure 4.4b, is preferred.

If we measure the inventory levels of both channel members at the same time (i.e., no time lag to allow for distribution of inventory), we can expect to see a limit cycle tracing line A. The supplier's on-hand inventory would oscillate into quadrant 4, which reflects the decreasing inventory level of the customer while the supplier's inventory level is increasing. Similarly, after inventory is shipped by the supplier, the decrease in on-hand inventory should be matched by an increase in inventory at the customer level. This takes the limit cycle to quadrant 2.

If we consider the inventory levels each would maintain over longer periods of time such as quarterly, we are likely to see a limit cycle tracing line B. Consider the implications of a visit to quadrant 1. An oscillation into quadrant 1 suggests that the supplier is increasing on-hand inventory at the same time the customer does, and there may be many good reasons for doing this. For example, manufacturers and retailers need to accumulate inventories together to meet demand during the Christmas sales season. Deviations off of line B might suggest an inefficiency in the distribution function, with disproportional changes for the two channel members.

One can readily see the merit of "just-in-time" or "on-demand" distribution strategies. Cooperation between market channel members results in efficiencies for all. Even when the relation is complicated by having many customers and many suppliers, the dynamic behavior can be described by a limit cycle relating the channel members.

Proposition 5: The source and type of information in a distribution channel greatly determine the ability of that information to stabilize the channel.

Information is the resource necessary to gain control over the dynamics of a distribution channel. The difference between a channel that collects its sales data in the traditional manner and one that uses down-channel information is depicted in Figure 4.5. The phase planes in this figure represent the inventory turnover limit cycles of the individual channel participants. Specifically, they relate change in units sold (on the horizontal axis) to changes in inventory on hand (on the vertical axis). In figures 4.5a and 4.5b changes in final market demand create an oscillation between quadrants 1 and 3 at the retail level. Recall that the inventory turnover rate can be stable even with this oscillation, since on-hand inventory can be scaled proportionately to changes in units sold.

But what price is paid for this stability? In Figure 4.5a the wholesaler collects data in the traditional manner—sales are recorded as they are shipped to the retailer. However, because there is a stock of inventory at the retail level, sales by the wholesaler do not precisely match sales at the retail level. The result is some occasional excessive on-hand inventory and some occasional shortage in inventory at the wholesale level. To avoid stock-outs the wholesaler probably carries sufficient safety stock and incurs the costs associated with doing so. Similarly, the manufacturer in Figure 4.5a records sales as orders are received from the wholesaler. Sometimes those

Figure 4.5
Sources and Effect of Channel Information

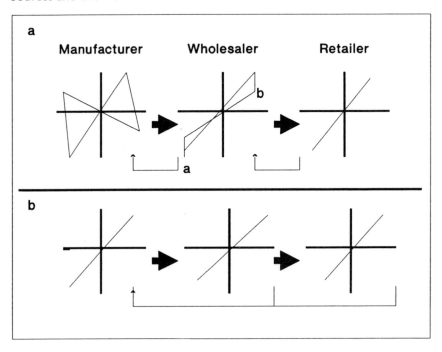

orders are relatively large, particularly when the wholesaler finds the inventory condition at position A with demand expected to increase and stock *unexpectedly* low. Sometimes those orders are substantially less, which they would be when the wholesaler finds inventory conditions at position B. At these times the expected decrease in demand (which will occur when the system oscillates back to quadrant 3) is further decreased by *unexpectedly* high inventories. In both cases the unexpected adjustments to inventory purchases are due to the inappropriateness of the sales information being used by the wholesaler.

The manufacturer, who is probably the channel member least able to scale inventories up or down, is faced with oscillations in demand that are even greater than those of the wholesaler. The fact that a single manufacturer might supply many wholesalers does not guarantee that changing demand will smooth out. In fact, those errors might be compounded, as all wholesalers are likely to find themselves unexpectedly overstocked or understocked at the same time. The phenomenon we are seeing here is much like the game one plays that involves passing a secret down a line of several people. The secret, as announced by the person at the end of the line, bears little resemblance to the one that was started at the front of the line. In that game everyone laughs when they compare the original message with the last one received. In business no one laughs when they compare actual sales with the production schedule that was used. There is a high price for the inaccuracy.

By analogy, Figure 4.5b is much like the person at the front of the line directly reporting the secret to the person at the back of the line. Information on sales is recorded not *as received* from the retailer, but *as sold* by the retailer. And this information is delivered to the manufacturer at the start of the channel. Conceivably it could even be provided to suppliers of the manufacturer to stabilize the supply of raw materials. The manufacturer allows for the level of inventory in the distribution system (including that held by the wholesaler) and plans sufficient production to replace inventories. Sales forecasts at the retail level are used to drive changes in production when changes in demand are expected.

The discussion above describes a method of channel management well known to major manufacturers. However, recognizing that each channel member's inventory system is a nonlinear system gives one an appreciation for the precarious balance necessary to achieve efficiency. Further, this view highlights the way in which errors are compounded as traditional information is transferred down the channel. It further demonstrates how real savings can be obtained by allowing lower safety stocks and avoiding excessively high inventories. One should note that the sales information reported in Figure 4.5a is not *wrong;* it simply is the wrong information to use to manage the channel. Supplying retail sales data creates a synchronous effect throughout the channel. It provides a sort of metronome that keeps all the channel members in time, even if that time is something more complex than a simple oscillation.

Two companies, Dillard's Department Stores and Johnson & Johnson, provide concrete examples of how a distribution system can be stabilized by collecting data down the channel and feeding it back to manufacturing. We all know Dillard's for its wide array of ready-to-wear items and housewares. Consider the challenge of stocking those ready-to-wear garments. They include fashion products with limited seasonal life expectancies and unpredictable demand—and Dillard's has to carry them in a wide range of sizes. If a product fails to sell, you're faced with excessive inventory and you "take a bath" in markdowns. If a product gets "hot," you probably have nowhere near sufficient quantity and you suffer the heartbreak of stock-outs. To complicate matters many of the products are made in Taiwan and, therefore, have excessive lead times. The distribution channel from Taiwan to the sales floor of Dillard's is simply too inefficient to economically support the sales of a wide variety of fashion goods.

A solution was proposed by domestic garment manufacturers. Although these producers are faced with substantially higher labor costs, they have the strategic advantage of being closer to their market geographically. They proposed a system by which they would monitor sales of their products by "reading" the point-of-sale data collected by each store. They would then respond by immediately manufacturing and shipping replacement inventories to those stores that required them. If a particular shirt or blouse becomes popular, the manufacturer responds to those sales increases by delivering new inventory within days. The advantages of this approach are substantial. Dillard's can afford to carry a wider selection of styles because it does not have to carry it in as much depth as before. Dillard's warehouses don't have to carry the finished goods inventory, and even the manufacturers don't have to carry finished goods inventory. If a certain style doesn't sell, it simply is never manufactured in quantity. The cost savings are so substantial that domestic garment manufacturers are able to effectively compete with importers, despite the relatively high labor costs. We as consumers also receive the benefits of wider product selection and more reliable availability when we shop Dillard's or any of the other major retailers who participate in the same way with domestic suppliers.

Johnson & Johnson (J&J) provides an example even more like that depicted in Figure 4.5b. J&J obviously sells many of their products through major discount retailers such as K Mart. In a relentless search for greater efficiency J&J focused on the excessive costs of stock-outs and holding costs caused by inaccurately forecasting sales of their many products. These inaccuracies were caused by using data on sales *to* K Mart (among others) to establish subsequent production requirements. Like the garment manufactures, J&J went all the way to the source and began collecting sales data at the point of sales. They then assumed control over distribution of the products all the way through the K Mart warehouses. In fact, the ownership of some products doesn't change from J&J to K Mart until the point of sale. The new information has reduced the disorder in the distribution channel and improved the efficiency with which it operates.

Nonlinearity in a marketing distribution channel can be observed by use of a simple computer model (see Appendix 4.1 at the end of this chapter). We can simulate demand by using a simple logistic equation like that given in Chapter 1. In our simulation the logistic equation provides a demand function that drives actual demand. In other words, demand is described as a multiple of the underlying demand function (see Equation Set 1 in the Notes). This means that the behavior of demand can be controlled as a nonlinear system. If we set the demand constant at some low level (i.e., 2 to 2.75), we will find constant demand and, hence, constant inventory levels and purchases at all levels in the channel. At somewhat higher levels (i.e., demand constant of 3.00) demand will oscillate with a period of two. For example, when the demand constant is 3.25, demand oscillates continuously between 81 and 51. At still higher levels the demand function adopts a Period 4 behavior. At a demand constant of 3.5, for example, demand cycles repeatedly in the following series; 50, 87, 38, and 83. At 3.75 de-

mand becomes truly chaotic, and with a demand constant of 4.0 the behavior of the demand function escapes and approaches infinity. We can
see the effect these varying levels of disorder have on a distribution channel by creating simple models of inventory control at the retail, wholesale,
and manufacturing levels.

For the retailer we define the level of inventory as current inventory less
demand plus any purchases by the retailer. We define purchases as the
difference between demand and current inventory (see Equation Set 2).
Similarly, our simulated wholesaler maintains an inventory that is defined
as current inventory less any sales to the retailer plus any purchases from
the manufacturer. The size of those purchases is determined by the difference between sales to the retailer and the wholesaler's on-hand inventory
(see Equation Set 3). Finally, our manufacturer maintains an inventory
that is reduced by sales to the wholesaler and increased by production (see
Equation Set 4). Throughout the simulated channel, sales are limited to
the level of inventory on hand, and inventory cannot be returned to the
previous channel member (i.e., no negative purchases).

We can observe the behavior of this system using phase plane diagrams
like those described in Figure 4.4b. Recall that in these diagrams the horizontal axis represents changes in the customer's inventory and the vertical
axis represents changes in the supplier's inventory. A proportional oscillation between quadrants 1 and 3 suggests efficient and coordinated changes
in the level of inventory in the distribution channel.

The images in Figure 4.6a, 4.6b, and 4.6c illustrate the disorder that
emerges even in this entirely deterministic model. The simulation program
produces inventory and purchasing data for the retailer, wholesaler, and
manufacturer. As mentioned above, demand becomes truly chaotic when
the demand constant is set to 3.75. The top three figures in Figure 4.6
show the limit cycle trajectories for this simulated data when plotted using
the procedure described in Chapter 2. Specifically, Figure 4.6a relates changes
in the manufacturer's inventory (on the vertical axis) to changes in the
wholesaler's inventory (on the horizontal axis). Figure 4.6b relates changes
in the wholesaler's inventory (on the vertical axis) to changes in the retailer's inventory (on the horizontal axis). Finally, Figure 4.6c illustrates the
behavior of the entire channel by relating changes in inventory at the manufacturer's level (on the vertical axis) to changes in inventory at the retailer's level (on the horizontal axis).

The bottom three images in Figure 4.6 illustrate the effect of feeding
final demand information back to the wholesaler and manufacturer. The
simulation program at the end of this chapter was modified to create this
effect by substituting the variable for final demand (i.e., DEMAND) for
the variable representing sales to the retailer in Equation Set 3 (i.e., RET-
purch). Similarly, final demand was substituted into Equation Set 4 to replace the variable that represented sales to the wholesaler (i.e., WHOLE-

Figure 4.6
Comparative Market Channel Stability

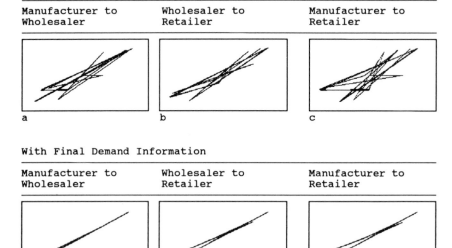

Without Final Demand Information

Manufacturer to Wholesaler	Wholesaler to Retailer	Manufacturer to Retailer

a
b
c

With Final Demand Information

Manufacturer to Wholesaler	Wholesaler to Retailer	Manufacturer to Retailer

d
e
f

purch). These changes meant that all channel members were controlling inventory by using final demand rather than the sales to a subsequent channel member. Figure 4.6d, 4.6e, and 4.6f indicate the resulting consistency that emerges as a result of the new information.

One should note that the level of disorder in this dependent system increases from retailer to wholesaler to manufacturer. Figure 4.6c reflects a level of disorder greater than either of the two other linkages individually. The manufacturer, therefore, endures the greatest instability and, hence, has to make the greatest changes in production to accommodate demand in the channel. It follows that the manufacturer has the greatest to gain by improving channel communications.

Although this demonstration focuses on nonlinearity in a channel of distribution, it is entirely transferable to any interdependent system. The simulation program could be considered a model for distributing inventory between stores at a retail level or between multiple warehouses. We would expect to see similar behavior in any other interdependent system, such as accounts receivable collections, human resource training, and quality control.

STRATEGIC MARKETING AND NONLINEARITY

Beyond the operational functions of marketing we can find important applications and examples of nonlinearity at the strategic marketing level. Here, although the concepts are a bit more abstract, we discover new perspectives that cause us to reconsider the validity of common strategic marketing tools. In marketing, a life cycle for a product or industry has become cliche, so much so that most marketing strategists shy from the concept, if not for valid professional reasons, then simply because the concept is overused. The product life cycle is, however, an excellent place to start in our discussion. It provides a common reference with which most of us are already familiar and it illustrates how an understanding of chaos theory concepts can radically change one's perspective of something so well known.

First, let's review the product life cycle concept. Products are commonly viewed as being positioned at some stage on an evolving cycle that is measured by time. The earliest stage of this cycle is the introduction stage, which is characterized by a new product meeting an undeveloped market. In the introduction stage marketers must work to educate the public on the value and potential utility of the product. As the product is accepted by the market we begin to see the market size grow and the sales of the product increase with this market growth. Appropriately, this stage is called the growth stage, and it is characterized by new entrants into the market. Other companies, seeing the market potential, enter into the same market with those already there. Further development of the market over time transitions the cycle into a stage where the competition between products and a waning of the market growth rate cause consolidation and the exit of some competitors. During this shakeout phase the product becomes more generic and standardized. As the market continues to evolve and surviving competitors stabilize and defend their market share, the product enters the maturity stage of the life cycle. During maturity, prices are bid down to such an extent that only major economies of scale or some other form of significant competitive advantage allow profitable operations. Finally, some time later, life cycle theory depicts a decrease in market size for the product. This stage, called the decline stage, is characterized by declining profits and the exit of major competitors.

Each stage of the life cycle is associated with a broad spectrum of marketing strategies ranging from the importance of product development to how to distribute and price the product. For example, product development is important at the introduction phase to create a single viable product model; it is important in the growth stage to differentiate your product from that of competitors. Similarly, pricing at the introduction stage can take the form of penetrating pricing, such as when Texas Instruments priced electronic calculators below actual production costs. In the growth and maturity stage prices are supposed to reflect the differentiation of the product; those with premium features and quality command higher prices than those that are more generic. IBM's premium pricing of their personal computers for many years provides one simple example of pricing according to product differentiation.

A product life cycle is, therefore, traced by sales for that product over time. It is a gradually upward sloping curve that peaks at the maturity stage and then declines to approach the horizontal axis in the decline stage. The horizontal axis for the cycle is "time," although the theory recognizes that there is no specified amount of time for each of the stages. In other words, the theory proposes what will happen, but not when it will happen. Associated with the sales curve is a curve depicting the behavior of profits for products on the life cycle. The profit curve is negative during the introduction stage, struggles into profitability during the growth stage, peaks late in the growth stage or early in the maturity stage, and drops back into unprofitability sometime during the decline stage. The product life cycle provides, therefore, a plot of the trajectory of two related variables over time, and this suggests that the relationships it describes can be viewed as an interaction of forces within a nonlinear system.

The notion that products evolve through a life cycle has invited the idea that industries follow a similar cycle. If a single product exhibits such behavior, why shouldn't the sum of all products of competitors in an industry create an industry life cycle? In fact, product life cycles and industry life cycles can be observed in the historical financial data of companies. Video games, like those at the local bowling alley or neighborhood bar, exploded on the scene in the early eighties and entered the growth stage with the game named "Pacman." Amusement operators subsequently endured increasing competition as other operators entered the market. Continued product development by manufacturers could only fuel the growth rate for so long; the maturity stage occurred sometime around 1987. Ever since, operators have returned to the more traditional games such as pinball and pool that have been the mainstay of that industry. Similar cycles are evident when one considers the market behavior for personal computers, facsimile machines, and cellular telephones. Although these may or may not have hit a decline stage, their faithful tracing of the introduction, growth, and shakeout stages provides confidence that the notion of product or industry life cycles is a valid one. It also suggests that the cycle applies equally to services, such as cellular telephone service.

So what new perspective does chaos theory provide? Start by considering that the market is deterministically defined. Although it evolves in complex ways, guided by the free will decisions of suppliers and consumers who participate in that market, it apparently often traces a common pattern of evolution. There are apparently forces in the industry and its market that cause the trajectory of total sales and the trajectory of total profits to follow a common path. Chaos theory causes us to consider not only the nature of these different forces, but also that there is an industry attractor that binds the behavior for the entire length of the life cycle. Further, it allows us to view the evolving relationship of sales and profits within the industry as an interaction that changes over time.

Proposition 6: Product and market evolution traces a trajectory defined by an interaction of forces. The trajectory's behavior over time is bound to and defined by an industry attractor.

What does the commonly known life cycle look like when described as a nonlinear system? What are the forces that create the characteristic life cycle pattern? To view the limit cycle of a market's evolution over many years, we must change the focus on our phase plane. Rather than plotting the behavior of a product on a quarterly basis, which provides a view of seasonal and annual transitions, we must look for longer-term patterns of change. Perhaps annual data would trace the evolving trajectory and eliminate the seasonal "noise" for the relatively quick life cycle of the video amusement products. Perhaps a limit cycle of five-year data would be more appropriate for those products with long-term cycles.

To create a limit cycle that will reflect the evolving trajectory of a product life cycle we include the same two variables that define the life cycle. However, we focus on the rates of change in these two variables to discover the characteristic pattern of their interaction on the phase plane. Following the conventions applied in Chapter 2, we place the variable considered most independent on the horizontal axis and the dependent variable on the vertical axis. In this case, "changes in profitability" is most likely defined by "changes in total sales," so it is placed on the vertical axis with changes in sales on the horizontal axis.

Figure 4.7 depicts the limit cycle and velocity history of a product following the classic life cycle. The dynamic interaction of sales and profit measures are shown to visit different quadrants of the phase plane as the product traces a trajectory from introduction to decline. (The quantitative data that support the images in Figure 4.7 are given on the Chaos Software Report in the Notes at the end of this chapter.)

At the time of introduction both sales and profit increase, pushing the limit cycle into quadrant 1. Note that significant increases in profitability will probably occur even though overall profitability may still be negative. This is because any newly generated revenues will typically begin to cover at least some costs.

As the product is more accepted into the market, its performance in both sales and profits improves. This growth stage is reflected by the fact that the trajectory pushes further into quadrant 1. At the upper right of the phase plane both sales and profits are increasing at their most rapid

Figure 4.7
Limit Cycle and Velocity History of a Simulated Product

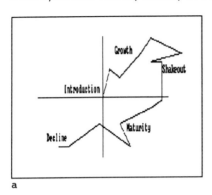
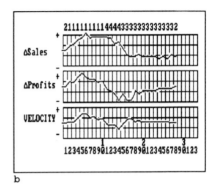

a   b

rates. Note that throughout this evolution the specific position of the trajectory on the phase plane is defined by individual points that reflect the current stable positions of the system; in this case the system can be defined as the product and its market. Also note that the growth phase is characterized by a trajectory with a 45-degree axis.

The transition from growth phase to shakeout is characterized by a reversal in the trajectory that reflects decreases in the rate of growth in profits while the growth rate in sales remains relatively constant. Recall that as long as the trajectory remains in quadrant 1, both sales and profits are increasing. As the trajectory drops toward the horizontal axis it reflects a decrease in the rate of growth of profits. The fact that it remains in roughly the same position on the horizontal axis relates to the constancy in sales increases. We can define entry into the maturity stage as the time when the change in rate of sales drops below the horizontal axis and enters quadrant 4. In quadrant 4 profits are truly declining while sales continue to increase. Note, however, that the trajectory is moving back toward the vertical axis during this time; it does so because the rate of sales increases is also declining. When the trajectory crosses the vertical axis and enters quadrant 3, the product can be defined as being in the decline stage. In quadrant 3 both sales and profits are decreasing.

The related marginal history charts also depict these changes but describe the contributing behavior of each variable. Although they may resemble the life cycles commonly known, they are not the same thing. These marginal history charts reflect the rate of change in each variable over time. The velocity history chart at the bottom of Figure 4.7b combines the behavior of the two by plotting the product of the two marginal values.

This new view of traditional product evolution causes us to ask what forces are at work to define the trajectory of the product's limit cycle. Further, it offers a new tool for empirically observing the behavior of a product's trajectory. Its focus on rates of change makes it more sensitive than traditional methods and will probably reveal patterns of behavior that would otherwise go unnoticed. But what forces are at work? The trajectory's meandering and our understanding that such meandering can emerge from entirely deterministic systems suggest that there are specific reasons—albeit many of them—why the trajectory is drawn to follow this path.

The process of designing, producing, and marketing a product and the very characteristics of a product's marketplace provide a complex pattern of structural characteristics that define the trajectory. There are production capacities, limits to the size of the initial promotional budget, and limits to the rate at which customers will adopt new products. These factors, along with a myriad of others—like the reaction by competitors, the availability of substitute products, and the efficiency of the product's distribution channel—constrain the moving point of stability—the trajectory—to a specific path. Some of these factors contribute to the success of the product during its growth stage, pushing it upward and outward. Some forces restrain it. The resulting path can be viewed as the course of least resistance between these two sets of competing forces.

Viewing the behavior of a product's evolution on a phase plane will provide no new or revolutionary factors that can help create a product's success. However, it does cause us to focus on the incremental. *Constant* growth in Figure 4.7 is represented by a stationary point. What we see is the moving trajectory with a path that is traced incrementally. It shows that the incremental *changes* are the things of importance. Our question should not be how to *increase* sales, but how to increase the *rate of increase* in sales. It shows us that the critical relationship is that interaction between a product and its market and that changes in the product or the market can result in changes in the path of the trajectory. The moving point of stability also causes us to recognize that the relation is *constantly* moving and suggests that product design should also be constantly changing (within the limits of economic feasibility) to fit the evolving market. Finally, we should reflect on the other attributes of nonlinear, chaotic systems. Their future performance can be highly dependent on initial conditions; the future position of the limit cycle may be highly dependent on minor changes that affect the position of the trajectory early in its development. Also, there is a basin of attraction about the limit cycle; although we do not see the actual attractor that guides the path of the limit cycle in Figure 4.7a, we can infer that the trajectory displayed is following some sort of underlying attractor. Over the long run that attractor may be a single point in the center of the phase plane, since ultimately any product will probably decline in utility to the market and both sales and profits will decrease until the product is discontinued. From this perspective, the trajectory in Figure 4.7a is simply a clockwise orbit about the center point of the phase plane, an orbit that began when the product was launched into quadrant 1 and that will end in an eventual collapse to the center when the product is removed from the market after having remained in quadrant 4 for some length of time.

Given the way in which a product satisfies fundamental needs of the marketplace, it may be more helpful to consider the trajectory as an approximate trace of the underlying attractor. It may be that the boundary of that attraction about the limit cycle is quite broad, meaning that the future course of the trajectory cannot be easily influenced even if substantial *temporary* changes are made in the limit cycle's position. Alternatively, it may be that the basin of attraction that binds this product to its specified pattern of performance is quite tightly bound to the attractor. In such a case, the relationship being traced could be quite brittle, and a substantial shift in the current position—caused by product design, changes to the market, or changes in the marketing effort—could allow an exit from the attractor and permit repositioning of the trajectory onto a more favorable path with a more favorable future.

Marketing professionals know that in some cases it is entirely possible to prolong the length of the maturity stage for a product. This is done by prudent intervention in a way that fundamentally changes the relationship between a product and its market. Arm & Hammer Baking Soda provides an appropriate example. The basic product has been held in a late growth or maturity stage by expanding its uses from a cooking ingredient to an air freshener to toothpaste to a carpet cleaner. The tactic is not unfamiliar, but it takes on new meaning when we observe how it can be used to define an entirely new future trajectory for a product. Besides simply finding new uses for a product, it may be possible to manage a product's trajectory by changing its target market, how it is distributed, and how it is promoted, or by attaching it to other complimentary products or to emerging social issues (such as making it "ecologically safe").

Traditional product cycles or industry cycles have been criticized for a variety of reasons. Generally, they are considered simply descriptive and overly simplistic to provide meaningful strategic information. However, the discussion above provides some measure of the new insight available by analyzing even such a simple model from a nonlinear perspective.

There are, however, other strategic management tools that have been developed to describe the relative position of a product in its market. For many of these there are associated strategies or tactics that have been recommended and relate to the specific position of the product in the market. A number of such matrices relate some measure of competitiveness to the growth rate of the industry and provide some measure of the relative position of one product to another; often *competitiveness* is measured by market share.

Figure 4.8
A Strategic Portfolio Matrix and Its Nonlinear Counterpart

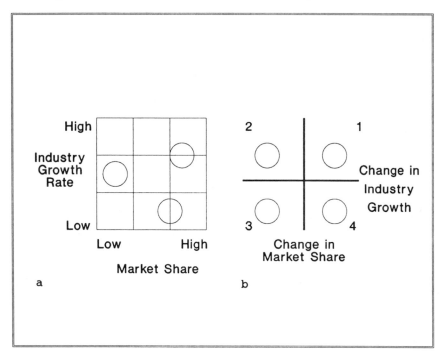

a   b

Proposition 7: There are strategies for managing products when analyzed using conventional marketing matrices. However, when products and their markets are analyzed as nonlinear relations, the products get reclassified and these new classifications suggest strategies that can be completely contradictory to the conventional ones.

A generic matrix of this type is provided in Figure 4.8. The circles in Figure 4.8a define the general domain of various products in a company's portfolio. In some matrices the size of the circle is made to reflect the size of the market for that product, and in some cases the total market share pie is sliced to indicate the percentage of market share commanded by the product being analyzed. These additional items of information are simple enhancements to a concept of relating a product's strategic marketing position to the growth rate of the industry and the percentage of market share it commands. Fundamentally, those are the variables of perceived importance. Clearly, industry growth rate has to be important, and ample research is available to justify the contention that market share is important (it provides economies of scale, provides visibility, allows control over distribution systems, and provides greater control over price).

The conventional product matrix in Figure 4.8a provides a static picture of product positions with regard to the two criteria of industry growth rate and market share. That is informative, but it causes one to manage on the "totals" rather than on the transitional edge. It shows where you are but not which way you are going. It is entirely possible that the product in the upper right portion of Figure 4.8a is rapidly losing market share. It may be that the industry for the product in the lower right portion of Figure 4.8a has just recently experienced explosive growth. Although the current positions are interesting, information about recent changes in industry growth rate or changes in market share is important to the marketing decisions that are to be made.

One could argue that the conventional matrix in Figure 4.8a can be enhanced by showing the historical and current positions of the product to provide a sense of evolving direction, and in some cases this modification to the matrix has been proposed by some as an approach to product portfolio planning. Such an approach is helpful but requires that transitions be identifiable at the aggregate level rather than at the marginal level. As a result, such an approach if far less sensitive to recent transitions. The interesting patterns are in the *rates* of change. Consider the interpretation of Figure 4.8b. In that image the horizontal axis represents changes in industry growth and the vertical axis represents changes in market share. (The question of which variable is dependent and which is independent has become more difficult to answer; on this phase plane we will simply consider them fundamentally related in some way.) Four positions, depicted by circles, indicate the domain of a product's position on the phase plane. Here the circles indicate the general vicinity of the product's attractor.

A product in quadrant 1 experiences increases in both industry growth and market share. A move toward this quadrant, *regardless of where the trajectory is on the entire phase plane,* is a movement in the "right" direction. Here, our concept of axis can be usefully applied. Any movement with an axis between 0 and 90 degrees is good. We can consider such a product a *"well-managed winner"*—*well managed* because its market share is increasing and a *winner* because it is in a growing industry. It may suffer from currently low market share and a small market; it may even be quite unprofitable, but on the margin it is moving in the right direction.

A product that visits quadrant 3 or moves toward quadrant 3 from any place on the phase plane suffers from decreases in both industry growth rate and market share. Consider such a product a *"poorly managed loser."* Again, its current market share and industry growth rate may be substantial, but its future is directed toward a decrease in both of these measures.

The off-axis quadrants of 2 and 4 define positions of marked failure and success. Quadrant 2 is the home of our *"well-managed losers."* Although the industry growth rate is declining, the product is gaining market share.

Such a product might be found in the lower left corner of the conventional matrix and might, therefore, be classified simply as a source of cash flow. Using conventional approaches, management would follow conventional wisdom and withhold any substantial investment or product development funds, thereby failing to realize the potential gains in market share that might be possible. Here is a product that demonstrates emerging success even in a declining market; it is being selected more frequently than others by a market that is becoming more and more selective. "Well-managed losers" have important potential that should not be ignored, particularly if a substantial residual market is expected to remain after a long period of market decline.

In quadrant 4 the industry growth rate continues to increase while market share erodes. Consider this product a *"poorly managed winner."* It represents a product in an industry with excellent potential, but one that is being marketed or managed so poorly that it fails to keep up with others in the market share *on the margin*. Note that it may have the highest actual market share on the conventional matrix in Figure 4.8a, and if it did, it would be viewed as a winner somewhere in the upper right portion of that diagram. A manager using the conventional matrix would be satisfied with its current position and direct efforts elsewhere. A manager using the phase plane diagram would immediately intervene to identify and attempt to correct the relationship between the product and its market right there on the edge, where the future direction of the trajectory for that product is being determined.

Any of the products identified on the phase plane can exist anywhere on the conventional matrix in Figure 4.8a. *"Poorly managed winners"* can be positioned at the lower left of the conventional matrix, but as described above, they can also be classified as winners in the upper right of the conventional matrix. This is because the two approaches measure fundamentally two different things: one measures the current state of the system and the other measures the direction of transition in the system.

So which products get the increased promotional budget? Which ones get redesigned? Which product manager gets rewarded? Which manager gets retrained? If we want to manage on the leading edge of that wandering trajectory, we need to develop strategies for *"well-managed winners," "poorly managed winners," "well-managed losers,"* and *"poorly managed losers."* We have the free will to intervene and change the course of a product's path on the phase plane; we can change the relation between a product and its market. But out there on the edge we find ourselves wondering what to do. What is the appropriate strategy for a "well-managed loser" when it has high market share? Do we redesign it, reposition it, or siphon cash flow from it? Although it is difficult to propose any reliable intervention strategies, we can at least make the questions clear and propose some initial prescriptions.

Table 4.1
Classifications on the Industry Growth–Market Share Phase Plane

Quadrant	Abr.	Classification	Description/Intervention
1	WMW	"Well-Managed Winner"	Both market share and industry growth rate are increasing. Maintain current strategies or do more of most recent changes in strategy.
2	WML	"Well-Managed Loser"	Market share is increasing but industry growth rate is declining. Product may survive a shakeout. Refocus on market niche and develop as needed to continue increases in market share.
3	PML	"Poorly-Managed Loser"	Both market share and industry growth rate are decreasing. This may be your source of available cash flow. If product has high market share consider selling it.
4	PMW	"Poorly-Managed Winner"	Market share is decreasing while industry growth rate increases. Reassess. Substantially change how it is designed, marketed, and managed. Invest and differentiate product to reposition it in the expanding marketplace.

The Industry Growth–Market Share Phase Plane (i.e., Figure 4.8b) provides us with a new tool that classifies products according to the descriptions in Table 4.1.

The many possible marketing applications of chaos theory are derived from the fundamentally different perspective chaos theory offers. It causes us to reexamine our conventional tools and strategies; it offers new questions and forces us to consider new answers. Ultimately, it will raise the level of competition as the new tools and perspectives are picked up by some and used as competitive tools in marketing.

APPENDIX

A simple program for simulating demand, inventory levels, and purchases in a distribution channel:

```
'SIMULATION OF A DISTRIBUTION CHANNEL
DemandConstant = 1.75
CLS
FOR X = 1 TO 20

'Parameters
        DemandConstant = DemandConstant + .25
        DemandFunction = .5
        RETinv = 100
        WHOLEinv = 100
        MFGinv = 100

PRINT "On hand Inventories    Purchases and
Production"
PRINT "Demand  Retail Wholesale Manufacturer   Retail Wholesale
Production"
FOR N = 1 TO 20
'Equation Set 1: Demand Function
        DemandFunction = DemandConstant * DemandFunction * (1 -
DemandFunction)
        Demand = DemandFunction * 100

'Equation Set 2: Retail Level

        RETinv = RETinv - Demand + RETpurch
        IF RETinv < 0 THEN RETinv = 0
        RETpurch = Demand - RETinv
        IF RETpurch < 0 THEN RETpurch = 0

'Equation Set 3: Wholesaler Level

        WHOLEinv = WHOLEinv - RETpurch + WHOLEpurch
        IF WHOLEinv < 0 THEN WHOLEinv = 0
        WHOLEpurch = RETpurch - WHOLEinv
        IF WHOLEpurch < 0 THEN WHOLEpurch = 0

'Equation Set 4: Manufacturer Level

        MFGinv = MFGinv - WHOLEpurch + Production
        IF MFGinv < 0 THEN MFGinv = 0
        Production = WHOLEpurch - MFGinv
        IF Production < 0 THEN Production = 0

PRINT USING " ##### #####  #####   ######  #####
#####   ######"; Demand; RETinv; WHOLEinv; MFGinv; RETpurch;
WHOLEpurch; Production
NEXT N
PRINT
PRINT USING "Demand Constant = ###.##  Demand Function = ###.##  ";
DemandConstant; DemandFunction;
Z$ = ""
LINE INPUT Z$
NEXT X
```

CHAOS SYSTEM SOFTWARE REPORT
Limit Cycle Data

| DATA FILE: | PLC.WKS |
| TITLE: | Limit Cycle of a Traditional Product Cycle |

VARIABLE X (INDEPENDENT): Sales
VARIABLE Y (DEPENDENT):   Profits

SEQUENCE #	ACTUAL X	ACTUAL Y	MARGINAL X	MARGINAL Y	VELOCITY	P	Q	DEG	MN
1	100.00	−15.00	+0.00	+0.00	0.00	0	2	0	0
2	102.00	−12.00	+2.00	+3.00	6.00	0	1	77	58
3	105.00	−10.00	+3.00	+2.00	6.00	0	1	54	19
4	110.00	−5.00	+5.00	+5.00	25.00	2	1	54	19
5	116.00	2.00	+6.00	+7.00	42.00	1	1	56	10
6	125.00	7.00	+9.00	+5.00	45.00	1	1	33	48
7	131.00	11.00	+6.00	+4.00	24.00	1	1	41	58
8	138.00	15.00	+7.00	+4.00	28.00	1	1	36	34
9	145.00	17.00	+7.00	+2.00	14.00	1	1	22	35
10	152.00	20.00	+7.00	+3.00	21.00	1	1	30	4
11	159.00	19.00	+7.00	−1.00	−7.00	2	4	−5	52
12	165.00	17.00	+6.00	−2.00	−12.00	2	4	−16	5
13	168.00	13.00	+3.00	−4.00	−12.00	2	4	−62	3
14	172.00	6.00	+4.00	−7.00	−28.00	1	4	−66	19
15	173.00	2.00	+1.00	−4.00	−4.00	2	3	84	42
16	171.00	−5.00	−2.00	−7.00	14.00	2	3	61	9
17	168.00	−12.00	−3.00	−7.00	21.00	2	3	54	19
18	165.00	−14.00	−3.00	−2.00	6.00	1	3	17	20
19	163.00	−18.00	−2.00	−4.00	8.00	1	3	44	8
20	160.00	−20.00	−3.00	−2.00	6.00	1	3	17	20
21	157.00	−22.00	−3.00	−2.00	6.00	1	3	17	20
22	154.00	−24.00	−3.00	−2.00	6.00	1	3	17	20
23	151.00	−26.00	−3.00	−2.00	6.00	1	3	17	20
24	147.00	−27.00	−4.00	−1.00	4.00	1	3	4	27
25	144.00	−28.00	−3.00	−1.00	3.00	1	3	5	29
26	140.00	−29.00	−4.00	−1.00	4.00	1	3	4	27
27	138.00	−30.00	−2.00	−1.00	2.00	1	3	7	8
28	135.00	−30.00	−3.00	+0.00	0.00	2	2	−7	9

QT=Quarter I=Period Index (1/2/4/8) Q=Quadrant

Velocity History Chart (VHC) Scale, Means, and Ranges
Variable VHC Scale   Mean   Range

Variable	VHC Scale	Mean	Range
X	+− 7.8	1.3	13.0
Y	+− 6.4	−0.6	14.0
V	+− 36.5	0.0	73.0

5

Applications in Managerial Finance

Financial analysis is not a simple thing. The more we learn about it, the more we realize that there are other patterns, other trends, and other interactions to be considered. At each level of analysis one feels satisfied that the analysis is correct, but there is always that feeling that we should dig a little deeper, that there's something we're missing.

In this chapter we examine the contribution chaos theory can make toward improving managerial finance. We will not concern ourselves here with the entire spectrum of financial management, but only with those issues practicing managers typically need to know. We'll look at leverage positions, income statement analysis, ratio analysis, and cash flow. The discussion does not address forecasting, which is the topic of Chapter 8.

At the most rudimentary level financial analysis involves an examination of the values reported on the income statement, the balance sheet, and the cash flow statement. Anyone who has ever examined these statements knows, however, that some computations are essential to put the raw values into perspective. It is simply not enough to know that net profit before tax was $126,328. That value, by itself, means almost nothing. (It does, however, indicate that the value is positive, not negative.) The value only takes on some importance when it is viewed relative to some other measure. For example, we often compute a net profit margin that divides profit by total sales. If sales were $1,579,100, then the net profit margin is 8 percent; at least we now have some feel for how much of sales ultimately emerged as net profit. Alternatively, we could assess our level of profit relative to the total value of assets at the firm. Dividing net profit by total assets computes return on assets (ROA); if our total assets were $1,052,733, ROA would be 12 percent. Again, we now have some relative measure of profitability.

So this is how we begin the plunge into managerial finance. First comes an understanding of what the values represent. Then comes an attempt to understand those values relative to each other—but it doesn't stop there. Is 12 percent better than last year or the year before? Thus enters the *time* dimension. Now we are looking at the movements and behavior of relative measures. And then we begin to ask whether our profitability ratio is going up while our debt ratio increases. We wonder if general improvement in the gross profit margin has been translating into a general improvement in net profit margin. As we examine the historical data we see that sometimes they seem related and sometimes they do not. And these are only matters of profitability and debt. What about cash flow, asset utilization, and the quality of all those accounts receivable? Financial analysis is not a simple thing.

All the numbers in a business simply reflect some measure of activity or value. Total sales is not simply $126,328. Sales are driven by the nature of the relation between the products or services we sell, how we attempt to sell them, and the characteristics of the marketplace at the time. The total sales value is nothing but an accumulated sum of a dynamic activity that has occurred over time. Similarly, profits are not simply a number; instead, they reflect the combined effect of the selling activity and the cost of operational activities within the firm. The ratio of these two values, the net profit margin, is an expression of that dynamic relationship that changes daily, monthly, and yearly and traces some evolving pattern. We all know that the numbers simply represent business activity, but our focus on their analysis sometimes causes us to forget that fact. What we are interested in is the interaction of those activities, not simply the interaction of the num-bers—and there *is* a difference. The numbers are periodically reported; the activities are continuous.

Failure to consider the patterns in business activity as they emerge in-vites failure at controlling the future of the business. Without a perspective of past patterns we are like the sugar ant that meanders left, then right, then left, and then right again. The sugar ant apparently has no knowledge of where it has been and it seems to have no plan for its future, since it often circles and crosses its own path and continues to wander until you get tired of watching. We would never buy a business without reviewing its history, and we wouldn't want to run one without a historical perspec-tive. For these reasons we keep the records, print the "year-to-date" col-umn on our reports, and compute percentage changes compared with last year. But this information does little to reveal emerging patterns in the dynamic activities of business. A single column of "percentage change" is like that single note from a symphony—there are intricate patterns of change that are simply being ignored.

One foggy night out on Lake Ponchatrain, just north of New Orleans, a massive barge was making its way across the lake toward the Gulf of Mexico. The Ponchatrain Bridge, one of the longest bridges in the United

States, slices across that lake. For most of its many miles it skims the surface; it only rises up above the lake for a short distance near the center of the lake to permit the passage of ships. That night, the barge wandered from its designated course and struck the bridge. It took out a number of supporting pillars and caused a large section of the bridge to collapse; several motorists suffered the obvious consequences.

Consider the activities of the barge pilot just before this accident. He probably saw the potential danger before the accident and reacted by reversing the engines, steering full port (or starboard), and sounding an alarm. He probably intervened in every way he possibly could to change the course of the multiton behemoth in his charge. But the future was set, determined by the actions he took or did not take before realizing the danger. Unquestionably, the ship had deviated from its designated course. Unfortunately, the deviation had not been realized early enough to sufficiently alter the course; had the deviation been discovered a few minutes before, the required adjustment would have been minor. History *is* important because patterns in the future emerge from those in the past. We manage on the leading edge where "what has been" meets "what will be," and we manage by injecting *changes* in events as they occur.

We can consider the Lake Ponchatrain incident a "maritime bankruptcy." It represents a disastrous event that resulted from failure to identify deviations that accrued over time. The incident was probably not simply a case of "pilot error." More likely it was the result of a failure to effectively deliver information about the course deviation to the pilot. Similarly, any financial analysis must report any changes between the course being traveled and the course preferred.

Proposition 8: Financial analysis requires more than simply a study of the current relationships between various financial measures. Understanding and prudent intervention require an awareness of the chronological patterns in the activities those measures represent.

The raw financial measures are not enough. Ratios of one measure to another are not enough. Even the historical record of financial ratios is not enough. To intervene in the course of events we need to know the patterns of change in emerging financial relationships. The phase plane offers the necessary added dimension, and like the previous chapter it causes us to reconsider our understanding of a major functional activity in business.

NONLINEAR INCOME STATEMENT

We can examine changes in income statement relations by simply plotting those relationships on a phase plane. It is useful, however, to divide the analysis and consider separately measures of profitability and measures of cost.

Figure 5.1 provides two phase planes: one representing the behavior of a profitability measure and the other representing the behavior of a selected expense item. By combining net profit and sales on a single plane we can examine the pattern of behavior for the common net profit margin. Quadrants 1 and 2 will be visited any time the rate of change in net profits increases. Quadrants 3 and 4 will be visited any time there is a decrease in net profits. Similarly, quadrants 1 and 4 reflect increasing sales and quadrants 2 and 3 will be visited whenever sales decline. The extent to which each variable contributes to the behavior of the net profit margin is then revealed by the location of the trajectory on the phase plane.

An oscillation between quadrants 1 and 3 should be expected. As sales increase and decline with market demand, we can expect some reaction by the net profit margin. That reaction, however, may be buffered or accentuated. If the business is able to accommodate sales decreases by contracting certain expenses, this buffering effect will be revealed by a trajectory like that traced by line A. Line A describes a company that is able to avoid a proportional decrease in net income when sales decline. Similarly, when sales are available, the company is able to accommodate them and generate proportional or greater than proportional profits. Whether the oscillation being examined is seasonal or occurs over a period of several years, interpretation of the trajectory is the same. A company following a trajectory like line A can be considered "adaptive."

Line B represents the trajectory of a firm that suffers disproportional losses when sales decline. Such a company might have considerable fixed costs that cannot be scaled down when sales decline. A firm represented by line B is "rigid" in that its characteristics or the way it is managed causes it to be less able to respond to changes in demand.

Note that the net profit margin for a firm represented by line C is constant over time. If profits decline in perfect proportion with sales, the computation of profits divided by sales will provide the same ratio. Hence a phase plane like that in Figure 5.1a reports not only changes in the ratio, but also changes in the aggregate measures that make up that ratio.

It is entirely possible for quadrants 2 and 4 to be visited as the moving stability point makes its way through time from one financial statement to the next. A visit to quadrant 2 implies improvements in profitability accompanied by decreasing sales. Although the possibility of this occurrence seems remote, it is more common than one might expect. Marginal sales carry marginal costs, and often a company pays a premium price for sales increases. For example, the cost of supporting sales and service staffs in a particular state may be proportionally higher than in other market areas. Leaving the costly market will improve net profit margin performance even though sales decline. (Whether it actually improves will depend on the

Figure 5.1
Phase Plane Diagrams of Income Statement Accounts

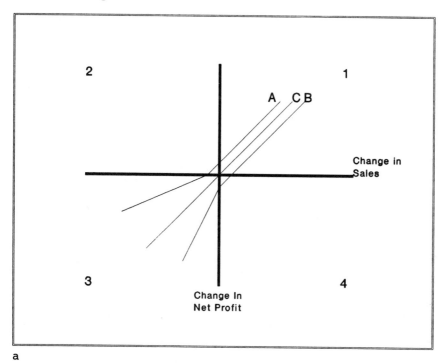

a

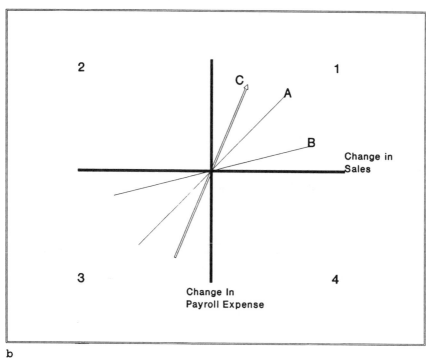

b

extent to which general overhead costs increase for the remaining sales districts.) Quadrant 2, therefore, reflects a good, but unsustainable position. It is good because profits are improving while sales decline. It is unsustainable because it also represents declining sales.

Quadrant 4 is precisely the opposite. Here sales are increasing while profits decline. A high price is being paid for whatever marginal sales are being attained. The additional cost may be an increase in unit cost (i.e., an increase in the cost of goods relative to sales) or an increase in operating expenses as a percentage of sales (that can easily be determined by subsequent analysis).

One cannot expect all companies to trace systematic oscillations between quadrants 1 and 3. Some businesses are faced with conditions that cause profits to move in an opposite direction of sales. These conditions are important to identify because quadrant 4 is inherently bad and quadrant 2 is the inherently good correction to the inefficiencies of quadrant 4.

Phase planes of the net profit margin are essentially identical to those presented in Chapter 3. There, quarterly measures of sales revenue and earnings per share provided the basis of our discussion of methodology. This is worth noting because in that discussion we viewed numerous examples of companies able to sustain Period 2 oscillations between quadrants 1 and 3 (Atlanta Gas, Wal-Mart, and Toys Я Us are good examples). Those companies with limit cycles that visit quadrants 2 and 4 often exhibit sustained Period 4 limit cycles (the classic example was Hechinger's). The primary reason for this higher-order cycle was identified as a scaling problem. Here, at the income statement level, we can begin to identify the specific source of that problem.

Quarterly data usually provide an hourglass pattern that begins to resemble a Period 4 oscillation. Retail firms, for example, typically have a strong increase in sales and profits during the third quarter. This combined increase causes the trajectory to move sharply upward into quadrant 1. During the next quarter sales continue to increase, often at an increasing rate, pushing the stability point further to the right on the "change in sales" axis. The improvement in profits is maintained or may increase at a decreasing rate so that the point visits a position in quadrant 1 somewhat lower and to the right of its previous one. Quarter 1, the first quarter of a new year, is reflected by a major decrease in both sales and profitability, resulting in the trajectory entering quadrant 3. The following quarter 2 may show some marginal improvement over the previous one, pushing the limit cycle upward and to the right somewhat but still remaining in quadrant 3, where both sales and profits are decreasing relative to their overall annual rate. When quarter 3 arrives again, the improvement in sales and profits closes the limit cycle into its hourglass shape.

The direction in which the limit cycle orbits reflects the degree of "rigidity" or "adaptability" of the firm. If the limit cycle orbits clockwise through quadrant 1 and counterclockwise in quadrant 3, as described above, then it can be considered relatively adaptive, since it is able to capitalize on rapid increases (i.e., the entry into quadrant 1) and adjust to rapid decreases as it enters quadrant 3. Alternatively, an orbit that is counterclockwise in quadrant 1 and clockwise in quadrant 3 suggests a degree of rigidity that prevents the firm from adjusting quickly enough to the quarterly changes to maximize available profits.

One of the first questions asked by those who reviewed the initial research papers applying chaos theory to organizational performance measures related to this issue of seasonality. "What if we adjusted for seasonality?" they asked. "Isn't the trajectory on the phase plane simply the result of seasonality?" Some additional research revealed what one would expect. The limit cycle resulting from quarterly data is the result of seasonality and everything else. When an appropriate seasonal index is applied to the data, the resulting limit cycle changes—it does lose much of its regular, systematic behavior, but not all. Seasonally adjusting the data simply strips away one layer of the forces that control the pattern. Here is an avenue for the entry of traditional statistics. One could use some traditional explanatory model such as regression analysis to extract from the limit cycle known patterns of behavior. Specifically, what one could do is independently regress on each of the two limit cycle variables using various independent variables and then use the resulting regression model to compute expected values of the dependent variable. The new limit cycle would be generated by using the error terms between the expected and the actual values of each variable. Viewed this way, chaos theory can be used as a sort of analysis of variance showing longitudinal patterns of behavior in error terms. However, one must be cautious here. The methods, applications, and results so far demonstrated here have all avoided any form of estimation. They have all applied all of the available data and not made any attempt to simplify the relation by making an approximate fit of an equation to the data. It may be that we know no more by seasonally adjusting or applying any other variables to adjust the data. In fact, we see more of the actual behavior of the nonlinear system by including all those seasonal forces.

Figure 5.1b provides the phase plane for a typical expense item. The interpretation of trajectories of this cost are fundamentally different from that of a performance measure such as profit. Line A in Figure 5.1b depicts proportionality. However, a position in quadrant 1 on line A indicates proportional increases in the payroll expense as sales increase. A position in quadrant 3 on line A indicates proportional decreases in the expense as sales decline. We typically expect expenses to be less variable than direct proportionality would suggest. In other words, we would not expect payroll to increase as rapidly as sales, and we typically don't expect it to decrease in direct proportion to decreases in sales. Hence we would expect the trajectory of an expense item like payroll to behave more like the trajectory depicted by line B. It is a flatter trajectory oscillating more in alignment with the "change in sales" axis.

It is possible for an expense item to take a trajectory like that depicted by line C. The primary concern here would be when the movement of the limit cycle is from quadrant 3 to quadrant 1 along line C. Such a behavior indicates an expense that increases at a rate greater than proportionality. It reflects a cost that increases greatly as sales increase. The reason for this type of costly behavior should be identified.

The implications for quadrants 2 and 4 with regard to the behavior of costs should also be considered. A limit cycle that visits quadrant 2 indicates poor expense control; payroll costs are increasing even while sales decline. Quadrant 4, however, suggests excellent expense control (or possibly economies of scale), since expenses decline while sales increase.

Limit cycles representing profitability and expense measures can provide insight into the timing of cost behavior. If quarterly data is used, one can readily determine when extra expense control initiatives are needed. If longer-term data is used—annual, for example—one can identify long-term transitions in cost behavior that may require intervention. These longer-term patterns of behavior will probably be currently unknown because of the traditional tendency to examine aggregate rather than marginal data.

The approach described above provides a way to study the behavior of individual profit or expense measures on the income statement. A more comprehensive picture of the income statement can be obtained by examining the interactive behavior of two key percentage-of-sales ratios: the gross margin percentage and the operating margin percentage. Gross profit is sales less the cost of goods sold. The gross profit *margin* is computed by dividing the dollar value of gross profit by total sales. The gross profit margin is, therefore, a measure of profitability after covering the cost of goods but before consideration of all operating expenses. A gross margin percentage of 40 percent indicates that 40 percent of sales is recognized as profit after the cost of goods is subtracted; it also means that 60 percent of sales goes toward cost of goods. Because management controls the amount by which products (or services) will be marked up over their cost, the measure reflects two important operational activities in business. It shows the behavior of unit costs (i.e., the cost of goods sold) and reflects pricing practices. Put simply, gross profit is that which we have left after paying to produce or paying to buy from a vendor the products or services we sell. Gross profit margin is gross profit as a percentage of sales.

The other critical income statement percentage is the operating margin, which reports total expenses as a percentage of sales. If expenses increase without a corresponding increase in sales, operating margin goes up. If sales decline and expenses are maintained at their previous level, operating margin goes up.

As most managers know, it is the difference between these two measures that is important; the difference between gross margin and operating margin is the net profit margin. Hence anything management can do to increase the gross margin or decrease the operating margin will improve overall profitability. Although the two ratios are computed similarly, they are influenced by two quite different things. For example, if sales volume goes up, there is little or no effect on the gross margin, since the cost of goods sold to capture those sales will go up proportionally. Operating margin will typically decline rapidly as sales go up, since many expenses, such as rent and utilities, are likely to remain constant. The result will be an increase in the company's net profit margin. The opposite reactions relate to a sales decrease. Operating margin will rapidly increase because some expenses cannot be proportionally decreased, resulting in a decreased net profit margin. The behavior of these two measures, therefore, accounts for the behavior of the net profit margin and points to the type of management action necessary to control the income statement.

Figure 5.2 provides phase planes for the limit cycle that traces a trajectory describing the interaction of the gross margin and operating margin percentages; it allows us to plot a limit cycle of the net profit margin.

Unlike some of the other limit cycle trajectories we have examined, the phase plane for this relationship is quite prescriptive; it suggests specific types of management intervention that can be used to control the limit cycle trajectory. Unlike the challenge of managing a market share trajectory, for example, here we begin to feel some degree of control over what happens. This phase plane is a window through which we can watch our course and take corrective action. This fact should not be taken lightly. In many of the previously mentioned applications of chaos theory the number and variety of forces at work cause us to wonder whether information about the behavior of a nonlinear relationship is of any value—control over such complex relationships appears so difficult. Here, however, we know many ways to change the course of events. Observing a limit cycle of the net profit margin provides us with a better understanding of its behavior and allows greater control over its future.

A visit to quadrant 1 on the 45-degree line A represents an improvement in gross profit margin associated with an increase in operating margin. Along line A in Figure 5.2a the net profit margin will remain constant. If the limit cycle is on line A in quadrant 1, total profits (in dollar terms) will increase. Any deviation off line A suggests that operating margin is changing disproportionally to increases in gross margin. Point 1, for example, will be associated with a mild decrease in the net profit margin as an increase in operating margin erodes some of the increase in gross profit margin. At point 2, however, net profit margin will improve despite an increase in operating margin because of the even greater increase in gross margin. Now consider point 3. Here, although the gross margin percent-

Figure 5.2
Interpretation of the Net Profit Margin Phase Plane

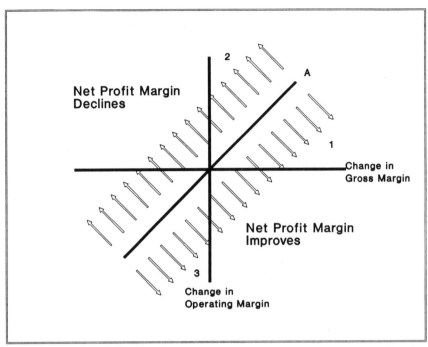

a

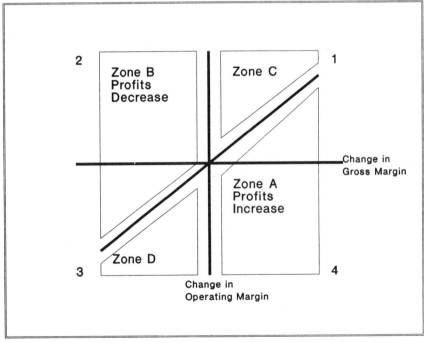

b

age is decreasing, operating margin is declining even more rapidly. The result would be an improvement in the net profit margin despite the fact that profits, in terms of dollars, would likely be decreasing. We can begin to see that when a trajectory visits any position *northwest* of the 45-degree line, net profit margin will decline, and any visit *southeast* of the 45-degree line will cause an increase in the net profit margin.

Figure 5.2b provides a map of the behavior of total profits, which differs from the behavior of the net profit margin. In Zone A, profits will improve, since nowhere in its domain does operating margin increase sufficiently to erode increases in the gross margin percentage. Conversely, anywhere in Zone B total profits will decline because operating margin never decreases sufficiently to offset the decreases in gross margin. In Zone C there are increases in both gross margin and operating margin. Although the net profit margin will decline, total profits can still improve if there is a sufficient increase in sales. Likewise, total profits can also decline in Zone C if the marginal increase in gross profit (resulting from the increase in gross margin) is insufficient to cover the increase in operating expenses. Similarly, total profits in Zone D may be either high or lower. The actual result depends on the specific location of the limit cycle when it visits these zones (D and C) and the amount of increase or decrease in sales.

Now that we have some feel for the behavior of net profit margin and total profits at various positions on the phase plane we can consider the appropriate intervention strategies for controlling the trajectory of the limit cycle.

Although the behavior of the net profit margin and total profits differ at different places on the phase plane, the intervention strategies are directly related to the four quadrants. In quadrant 1, for example, we should try to maintain whatever activities are causing an improvement to our gross margin and do whatever we can to hold down the operating margin. The improvement in gross margin will inevitably be traced to either some practice relating to the pricing of goods or to some success at holding down the cost of goods that are sold. The increasing operating margin can be traced to some specific expense or group of expenses that are increasing or to a decrease in sales that will cause the operating margin to increase. (Recall that operating margin is computed as total operating expenses divided by sales.)

In quadrant 2 profitability will decline because of the combined effect of increases in operating margin and decreases in gross margin. Tactics that hold down unit cost and simultaneously reduce expenses are necessary. If sales can be increased, operating margin will drop, and the limit cycle can be redirected to quadrant 3.

Quadrant 3 calls for efforts to improve the gross margin percentage. In quadrant 3 operating margin is declining, offering good potential profits;

any improvements in the gross margin will translate into substantial improvements in the net profit margin.

Finally, quadrant 4 is the desired locale for the net profit margin limit cycle. Here, gross margin is increasing while operating margin declines. Although it may be difficult to sustain a position in quadrant 4 because of limitations that prevent continuous reductions in unit cost, growth in sales can help sustain continuous decreases in operating margin, holding the limit cycle in either quadrant 3 or 4. In quadrant 4 one needs only to continue, at an increasing rate, those activities that are improving gross margin and lowering operating margin.

Figure 5.3 provides both an actual net profit margin limit cycle and the general prescriptions that apply to each quadrant. These phase planes are consistent with those given in Figure 5.2; the horizontal axis represents changes in the gross margin percentage and the vertical axis represents changes in operating margin. The limit cycle in Figure 5.3a is that of Engelhard Corporation, a leading provider of specialty chemical products and specialty materials. The four positions that are numbered relate to different years in the company's recent history. Specifically, they relate to the change that occurred from one year to the next. For example, position 1 could be labeled 1987–1988, since it reflects the difference between the values at 1988 and those values in 1987. In other words, it reflects the changes that occurred during 1988 (after the close of the 1987 statement but before the close of 1988).

Interpreting the net profit margin limit cycle is easy when one considers the prescriptions associated with each quadrant. At 1 the company should simply try to maintain the increasing gross margin and declining operation margin. When the trajectory moved to 2 it did so because it was unable to maintain gross margin while continuing to decrease the operating margin. A movement to position 3 in quadrant 1 reflected an improvement in pricing or unit cost control concurrent with increased expenses that drove up operating margin. The fact that position 4 is so near position 3 indicates that the company sustained these rates of change for two years. Although the current increases in gross margin are desirable, the company should look for ways to cut expenses and lower the operating margin.

Proposition 9: Phase plane diagrams provide a way to express the current state of an income statement's relationships. Because certain zones on the phase plane can be related to specific conditions, appropriate intervention strategies are prescribed directly by observing the current position of the limit cycle on the phase plane.

One should begin to see how limit cycle trajectories reveal the dynamic behavior of the income statement relationships. Because specific positions on the phase plane can be related to various intervention strategies, one can easily determine the type of intervention needed. Further, because the

Figure 5.3
A Net Profit Margin Limit Cycle and Prescriptions

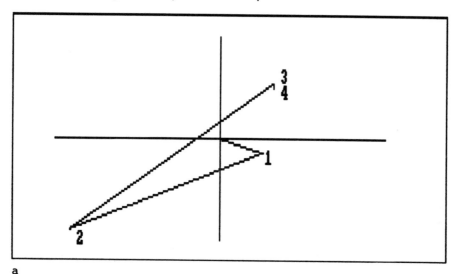

a

2	1
Lower unit costs to raise gross margin. Cut expenses to lower operating margin.	Maintain prices and unit cost control. Cut expenses to lower operating margin.
Focus on pricing and unit cost control. Maintain control over expenses.	Continue pricing, cost control and expense control activties. Do more of same.
3	4

b

trajectory can be viewed as an emerging pattern from the past, one can quickly see the result of previous decisions and relate those to plans for the future. (Consider the potential this implies for forecasting and budgeting issues that are addressed in later chapters.) And so far, we have only considered the income statement; other new views of a firm's financial status appear when we apply this same approach to the balance sheet.

NONLINEAR BALANCE SHEETS

Assets = Liabilities + Stockholder's Equity. Although the equation never changes, the values in the equation change continuously. They may only be reported quarterly or annually, but they, like the values of the income statement, are in transition over time. The numbers on the balance sheet reflect the values of various assets and liabilities. However, the changes in those values from period to period reflect specific *activities* that collectively guide the balance sheet accounts from one period to the next. We manage on the edge, making changes to the various accounts by the things we do. If the balance sheet is a "snapshot picture" of the firm's current capital position, then the trajectories of change in each balance sheet account are the "movie." Studying only the balance sheet is much like seeing the final scene of that movie: We would understand the final frame much better if we saw all the action that preceded it.

Like our discussion of the income statement, we need not address all the possible accounts and ratios that could be analyzed. Instead, we will consider some of the primary ones and use them as representative examples of the type of additional information possible with this approach.

Consider leverage. The assets listed on the balance sheets are either financed with debt (creating liabilities) or not financed with debt, in which case their value to shareholders is recorded as shareholder's equity. If additional funds are borrowed to purchase new assets, the amount of total assets increases relative to shareholder's equity. The increased debt is said to increase the leverage of the firm in that it allows shareholders to obtain higher returns on their equity. Higher leverage, however, usually is associated with higher risk; so although the return may be greater, so is the risk. Leverage is typically measured by either one of two ratios, *debt to total assets* or *debt to equity*. The two ratios measure fundamentally the same thing: the amount of debt relative to other values on the balance sheet.

We can see the changing relationships on the balance sheet by plotting a limit cycle of the leveraging effect. Although several alternate balance sheet measures could be selected, it seems logical to consider changes in liabilities and changes in total assets.

Figure 5.4 maps the phase plane for the leverage relationship. On it, changes in liabilities have been placed on the vertical axis with changes in

Figure 5.4
A Map of Conditions on the Leverage Phase Plane

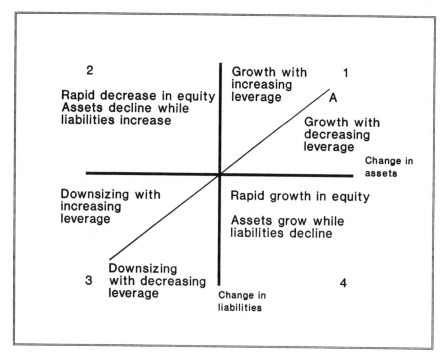

assets on the horizontal axis. Like the phase planes we have previously examined, different positions can be related to specific changes in the financial condition of the firm.

In this case, changes in assets can be related to changes in the leverage position. In quadrant 1 we find both assets and liabilities increasing. Below the 45-degree axis in this quadrant the company will experience growth (in terms of assets) while the leverage ratio declines (despite the fact that liabilities are increasing). This is because line A on the 45-degree axis represents proportionality, and any position below it in quadrant 1 represents increases in assets greater than increases in liabilities. This zone, which lies above the horizontal axis but below the 45-degree line, is a desirable position for many companies because it allows them to reduce their leverage through growth.

Above line A in quadrant 1 we still experience growth but with increasing leverage. This is not necessarily an undesirable condition, particularly if the firm is seeking additional leverage. Acquisitions that involve additional debt will send the trajectory into this zone because of substantial increases in both assets and liabilities.

Quadrant 2 causes rapid decreases in equity, since total assets are decreasing while liabilities increase. To visit quadrant 2 a company has to be incurring more debt while somehow divesting (or restating the value of) assets.

Quadrant 3 mirrors the conditions in quadrant 1. In quadrant 3 assets are decreasing, reflecting a downsizing of the organization. At the same time, liabilities are also decreasing, suggesting that the sale of assets is being used to pay off debts. The relative rates of these two activities determine whether leverage will increase or decline. If the trajectory is above line A in quadrant 3, then the rate at which assets are being divested is greater than the rate at which debts are retired, resulting in downsizing with increasing leverage.

A company that is having to liquidate assets to retire debt is likely to find itself in this position. Below line A in quadrant 3 debts are being retired at a rate proportionally greater than the rate of decrease in total asset value. A profitable firm that divests of assets to reduce debt will probably fall in this zone. (One can assume that the company is profitable or has healthy cash flow because it is retiring debts of greater value than the assets that are sold; the difference has to come from operations.)

One has to consider the type of data traditionally reported on the balance sheet to appreciate the clarity of the description provided by the phase plane. Balance sheet data evolves deterministically over time, just like the other business variables we have considered. Like the phase plane describing the net profit margin, changes in the relationships of balance sheet data can be related to specific changes in the firm's financial position.

NONLINEAR MEASURES OF PERFORMANCE

Managerial finance becomes really interesting when we combine income statement and balance sheet data to examine the behavior of their interaction. ROA is a common such measure that ties the two statements together. ROA, computed as net profit divided by total assets, reflects profits relative to the value of all assets required to produce those profits. Hence ROA captures a variety of other financial measures. Because profits are affected by sales, gross margin, and operating margin, all these measures are embodied in ROA, in addition to the measure of total assets. Similarly, *changes* in ROA will reflect activities that changed any of the elements contributing to ROA.

Figure 5.5 provides a phase plane for the ROA trajectory. Changes in total assets have been placed on the horizontal axis and changes in net profit have been plotted on the vertical axis. Our quadrant interpretations provide a fresh perspective of the forces that drive changes in ROA.

We are able to separate the contributions of the income statement and the balance sheet management in the behavior of the ROA measure. Horizontal movements result from changes to the total asset account. Vertical

Figure 5.5
The ROA Phase Plane

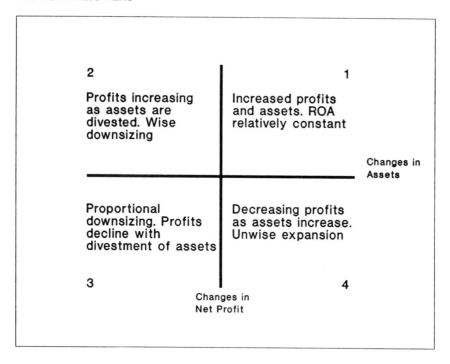

movements relate to change in profitability as reported by the income statements. Because profits are posted to the balance sheet, we expect to find the ROA trajectory in quadrant 1 with both profits and total assets increasing. One might say that profitable companies are able to find or create some kind of a Period 1 attractor that will hold them in quadrant 1. Similarly, companies with poor performance that is sustained are bound to an attractor in quadrant 3, where both profits and assets continuously decline. Oscillations between these two quadrants would not be unusual; however, sustained positions in quadrant 3 should be of concern.

The off-axis quadrants of 2 and 4 reflect conditions in which one statement is increasing while the other statement is decreasing. Whether that is good or bad depends on the specific actions being taken. For example, in quadrant 2 profits are improving while assets are declining. For these conditions to exist the company most likely is deliberately divesting assets. Divesting of unprofitable assets would create the conditions necessary to visit quadrant 2. We can consider quadrant 2 an indication of prudent downsizing. Quadrant 4, however, is just the opposite of this. Here the company is expanding, and as it does, net profits decline. Although initial startup costs of new ventures might be one explanation for this effect, a

Figure 5.6
Selected ROA Limit Cycle Trajectories

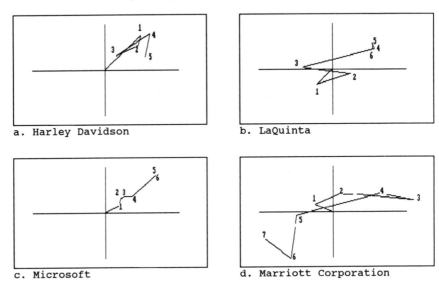

a. Harley Davidson

b. LaQuinta

c. Microsoft

d. Marriott Corporation

visit to this quadrant might also signal excessive investment in unproductive assets. Avoiding this quadrant may be considered a management objective.

The value of the phase space definitions becomes clearer if we examine the trajectory of an actual ROA limit cycle. We can then relate the conditions of the firm to the interpretations in Figure 5.5.

Figure 5.6 provides some ROA limit cycles for this purpose. Examine the limit cycles and relate them to Figure 5.5. Consider which companies are in the most preferred position. What changes are probably occurring in each firm to cause the specific shape of each trajectory?

The companies in Figure 5.6 were arbitrarily chosen, yet their phase plane diagrams provide a diverse set of limit cycles to interpret. Recall that on these phase planes the horizontal axis represents changes in assets and the vertical axis measures changes in profit. The numbers on each chart identify incremental years so you can follow the chronology of the limit cycle.

Harley Davidson in Figure 5.6a shows increases in both profits and assets. Its limit cycle traces the years after its emergence as a division of AMF. Many are familiar with Harley's dramatic success as a manufacturer of high-quality motorcycles in the heavyweight class. Management at Harley Davidson implemented modern quality-control approaches to manufacturing that required extensive employee involvement. The overall effect of Harley's new management system (actually more of a way of doing business rather than simply a management style) resulted in its adherence to an attractor in quadrant 1. The changes have caused its ROA trajectory to orbit a position in that quadrant (follow the trajectory through its chronology). The result is that Harley's ROA has increased almost continuously over the five yearly intervals displayed. One should stop and consider the implications of this adherence to a reasonably finite domain in quadrant 1 and the fact that management created the conditions that have resulted in the limit cycle's behavior.

Management created the attractor and maintains it by the actions it takes. The limit cycle is following a natural course, one that results from the attractor and the forces that work on it. This means that management can actively intervene to create conditions that control the limit cycle. Had management been aware of the limit cycle's behavior, it might have been able to constrain its orbit in quadrant 1 even more closely to an almost constant point of stability. The additional changes necessary to maintain a constant level of performance may be minor; in fact, it is possible that additional information about the performance pattern might have made managing the firm easier. There may have been some difficult decision that Harley's management made that would have been much easier, given this new perspective about the performance of their firm.

LaQuinta, a national chain of value-priced hotels, provides an opportunity to consider the implications of each quadrant. In year 1 both net profit and total assets declined into quadrant 3, suggesting a proportional reduction in each. The next year an increase in assets was not matched with proportional increases in profits, resulting in a visit to quadrant 4. Recall that sustained positions in quadrant 4 are undesirable because they reflect continued investment in nonprofitable assets. However, LaQuinta's increase in assets was only a temporary one, and in year 3 there was an offsetting decrease in assets while profitability increased. The trajectory, therefore, visits quadrant 3, which reflects improved profitability with a reduction in total assets. The subsequent years of 4, 5, and 6 show a sustained expansion in both profits and total assets. Note how tightly the trajectory is bound to an almost single point in quadrant 1. LaQuinta should be encouraged to maintain these constant improvements.

Microsoft in Figure 5.6c provides an example of a company with a sustained increase in its rate of increase in both profits and assets. The stability point for Microsoft is following a trajectory that advances progressively further out into quadrant 1; it is increasing at an increasing rate. Note, however, how the minor disproportional changes during years labeled 2 and 3 (reflecting proportionally greater increases in profits) are clearly evident. Also note how the last two positions (5 and 6) are in precisely the same place on the phase plane, indicating that the advancement of the trajectory seems to have recently slowed to constant increases rather than accelerating increases.

Table 5.1
Alternate Asset Turnover Ratios

Equation	Sales		Assets		Asset Turnover	Change
5.1	100	/	50	=	2.0	
5.2	110	/	55	=	2.0	0
5.3	90	/	45	=	2.0	0
5.4	100	/	40	=	2.5	+.5
5.5	125	/	50	=	2.5	+.5
5.6	100	/	66.66	=	1.5	-.5
5.7	90	/	60	=	1.5	-.5

Marriott Corporation provides evidence of a different type of trajectory pattern, one that traces a more long-term behavior. Note how the limit cycle progresses rightward from year 1 through year 3, reflecting increases in total assets (at increasing rates). Years 4 and 5 show a reversal in the rate of increase followed by a drop in profitability (year 6) and somewhat less of a drop in profitability in year 7 associated with continued decreases in total assets. Unlike more rapidly changing patterns such as that of LaQuinta, Marriott and Microsoft demonstrate the long-term behavior of limit cycles.

There are other ratios that relate income statement performance to the balance sheet. A common ratio that does this is asset turnover, computed as total sales divided by total assets. Unlike ROA, which provides a measure of the efficiency with which assets generate profits, asset turnover provides a measure of the asset's efficiency at generating sales. It is a particularly appropriate ratio to monitor when a company is more sales-oriented rather than manufacturing-oriented and when the firm carries a considerable finished goods inventory. This ratio, like all other business ratios that combine two variables into one, suffers from the loss of information that occurs when the ratio is computed. The effect can be clearly seen by examining the computations in Table 5.1.

Consider that Equation 5.1 is the asset turnover rate for the company during the *previous* reporting period and that Equations 5.2 through 5.5 are different possible asset turnover ratios for the current reporting period.

The table demonstrates quantitatively the effect we have been seeing in the various phase plane diagrams. That is, a ratio, because it combines two values into one, necessarily loses some information about the two original values. When one is comparing a ratio with its previous value, therefore, one is unable to see certain changes that may have occurred. For example, if Equation 5.1 is last period's asset turnover rate, Equations 5.2 and 5.3 can represent subsequent periods in which the turnover rate remained precisely the same, although there were changes in the actual values. Equation 5.4 reports an improvement in the turnover rate resulting from decreases in assets (perhaps inventory), whereas Equation 5.5 also reports the same increase in turnover rate resulting from improvements in sales volume rather than inventory reductions. Similarly, a reduction in asset turnover rate may be the result of increases in inventory (Equation 5.6) or decreases in sales (Equation 5.7).

This is a rather simple notion but one that invites serious interpretation of issues when studying financial data. Instead of simplifying the analysis by computing the ratio, one ends up examining six values to understand the changes that have occurred. Specifically, these values are (1) the latest ratio, (2) the previous period's ratio, (3) the latest sales figure, (4) the previous period's sales figure, (5) the latest total asset figure, and (6) the previous period's total asset figure. Did you really simplify things by computing the ratio?

In fact, even if there is no change in the ratio, one still has to examine the various underlying values to make sure that one of the changes that can be hidden by ratio analysis didn't occur. It makes one wonder why one would want to compute a ratio that discards so much valuable information and requires so much further inquiry.

Proposition 10: Phase plane diagrams report financial information that is often used for ratio analysis in a way that much more effectively displays the behavior of the contributing measures.

On a phase plane we would place changes in assets on the horizontal axis and changes in sales on the vertical axis. If there was no change to the relationship between sales and assets, our trajectory would remain at the origin, reflecting no change in either value. If there was a proportional change, the trajectory would move either into quadrant 1 at 45 degrees (if conditions were like that in Equation 5.2) or downward proportionally into quadrant 3 (if conditions were like that in Equation 5.3). Improvements in the asset turnover ratio would always be to the northwest of the 45-degree diagonal because of increases in sales associated with decreases (or less than proportional increases) in total assets. Reduction in asset turnover would occur when the trajectory ventured southeast, since total assets would be increasing at a rate proportionally greater than the changes in sales. If the trajectory entered quadrant 4, assets would be increasing while sales decline, signaling a condition of major concern for management. The trajectory itself, in its movement from one position to another, provides information regarding the current position relative to the previous period's position. Both the previous state of the system (the system being the sales and asset management process) and the current state are clearly evident. Although the phase plane may seem somewhat alien as a means of displaying traditional financial ratios, its benefits, precision, and sensitivity are apparent.

NONLINEAR CASH FLOW ANALYSIS

Cash flow statements are the only common financial reports that focus on changes—in this case changes in receipts and disbursements from the main sources and uses of funds. The overall result reported on the statement is simply the amount of increase or decrease in cash flow experienced by the business during the latest accounting period. It is like a single point on a phase plane; it reports the current state of the system, but in the case of the cash flow statement it fails to show any pattern to the changes in the system. To view changes in cash flow as a nonlinear pattern of behavior we can place sources of cash on the horizontal axis and uses of cash on the vertical axis. One can then interpret the four quadrants as follows.

Quadrant 1 would report increases in both sources and uses of funds. A movement up the 45-degree axis would reflect proportional increases in both, resulting in no change to the net cash flow. Similarly, a movement along the 45-degree axis into quadrant 3 would also result in no change to net cash flow, since both sources and uses would decline proportionally. However, like those phase planes described above, any movement toward quadrant 2 will result in increases in the variable on the vertical axis relative to that which is plotted on the horizontal axis. In this case that would mean a proportional increase in uses, resulting in a decrease in cash flow. Similarly, movement to the lower right toward quadrant 4 would result in increased cash flow, since movements rightward result in increases in sources of funds and movements downward result in decreases in uses of funds. The movement of a cash flow limit cycle would provide a detailed picture of any pattern of behavior. The current position of the trajectory at any moment would reflect changes in both sources and uses simultaneously and the net of those values would be the actual increase or decrease in cash flow for the latest period. The trajectory's position relative to its previous position indicates how the cash flow position has changed and whether those changes are more a result of changes in sources or changes in uses (any horizontal movements are due to changes in sources; vertical movements are due to changes in uses). So the trajectory presents the past and the present.

Analyzing this relationship on a phase plane becomes particularly interesting when one considers forecasting cash flow or the prescriptions that can be related directly to the phase plane diagram. The limit cycle of a company may show a fairly systematic pattern of seasonal behavior. Although the financial officer will probably be aware of this pattern in the cash flow, it is likely that there are subtle transitions that would be evident in the trajectory but otherwise unnoticed. Although both the traditional cash flow statement and the cash flow limit cycle are each based on the same raw data (changes in the sources and uses), the limit cycle offers the advantage of providing a pattern of the emerging relationship over time.

Such patterns are typically not evident by looking at the latest or even the last few cash flow statements.

Besides revealing long-term patterns of cash flow behavior, the cash flow limit cycle can also be used to better control cash flow by offering a way to set objectives that are consistent with those previous patterns of performance. Knowing that the future performance of a system will emerge from its previous patterns of behavior reminds us that any new objectives we set must be consistent with those previous patterns or at least not so different as to require a substantial break from the attractor that binds the system's performance. Viewing the previous patterns of behavior will allow us to better identify a future position that is attainable and consistent with the past. We can target a single point on the phase plane that specifies a desired level of cash flow—and specifically the amount of sources and uses consistent with that level of cash flow. We could even monitor the movement of the trajectory over the accounting period as it moves from its current position to the target position.

The phase plane offers an opportunity to identify generic prescriptions that are associated with each quadrant. These prescriptions are as follows. Because quadrant 1 reflects near proportional increases in both sources and uses, the actions that take a trajectory there can be considered the result of normal growth. The only prescriptions might focus on attempts to decrease the uses of cash flow. Quadrant 2, because it represents the combined effect of a decrease in sources and an increase in uses, calls for substantial intervention. Efforts might be directed at selling off assets to increase the sources of funds, while at the same time attempting to cut the use of funds. This can be done by allowing liabilities to increase, or one can inject cash into the firm by increasing its net worth with new stock issues. (One should, however, carefully consider the wisdom of using equity funds to finance operations with a poor cash flow.)

Quadrant 3, as mentioned before, represents reductions in both sources and uses. The prescription for any trajectory that visits this quadrant is related to actions that will increase the sources of funds.

Quadrant 4, representing the best possible position on the phase plane, offers rapid increases in cash flow. A company able to sustain a position in this quadrant should probably increase its investment in earning assets (thereby reducing its accumulating liquidity) or should decrease liabilities by paying off any such debts with rates higher than the cost of capital.

OTHER FINANCIAL APPLICATIONS OF CHAOS THEORY

The discussion here is meant to provide some hint of the potentially new insights that are available if one considers activities that drive financial measures to be nonlinear, chaotic systems. It has been demonstrated that the data does not have to reflect quarterly, seasonal patterns of performance. In fact, patterns of transitions are typically found in annual data, and the interpretation of that data takes on new meaning when viewed as an evolving trajectory on a phase plane. Other ratios can be analyzed. Any expense item can be viewed relative to sales, and any measure of profit (gross profit, profit before tax, profit after tax, or even earnings per share) can be combined with a measure of investment (assets or equity) to provide a better understanding of company performance. Various liquidity ratios can be examined; one could easily plot a trajectory of the quick and current ratios. Like the ratios discussed above, these will reveal intervention strategies associated with each quadrant. Any of the activity ratios could likewise be examined. One could study changes in accounts receivable or inventory turnover. Clearly, the ratios to consider are those of interest to the firm, whether they be traditional or not.

Beyond simple ratio analysis, chaos theory offers a way to discover the underlying instabilities in a business. Because performance measures such as return on equity reflect such a great number of management actions, it is common to decompose the measures so as to consider the contributing activities. For example, a leverage ratio such as debt-to-total assets or debt-to-equity can be used to better understand changes in return on equity. Likewise, behavior of the return on asset ratio can be better understood by examining the overall performance of the income statement as reported by the net profit margin (sometimes called return on sales).

The important point here is that the sources of instability can be discovered by examining the limit cycles of the contributing ratios. For example, if the return on equity limit cycle is unsteady, the source of that instability will be evident in either the behavior of the limit cycle reflecting leverage or in the limit cycle tracing profitability. Alternatively, some ratios may be deliberately altered by management to stabilize an otherwise unstable measure of performance, such as return on equity. For example, in the analysis of one major corporation it was found that the effect of major, erratic capital purchases was offset by appropriate adjustments to the leverage ratio, thereby stabilizing return on equity. It was interesting to note that in that case, the company worked to offset the capital purchases but didn't adjust leverage to offset changes in earnings, preferring instead to allow those instabilities through to the return on equity measure.

Finally, one can't avoid some comment regarding the use of chaos theory in the capital markets. Some authors have addressed chaos theory in the stock market and proposed methodologies for analysis. Unquestionably, market activity is nonlinear, and chaos theory is an appropriate tool for those who are looking to gain some temporary advantage. But focusing on the stock or commodity markets can cause us to avoid the practical applications that the theory holds at the functional, operational level in business. That has been our concern here, and that is the approach we will take as we examine chaotic behavior in processes of production.

6

Production as a Chaotic System

Chaos theory was born in the physical sciences, where things vibrate, oscillate, stabilize, and sometimes break. Their behavior is typically predictable but occasionally surprising—sometimes with disastrous consequences. So it is in the processes of production. The machines we employ, combined with the human resources we employ, constitute a dynamic system that either remains within an acceptable range of performance or escapes to cause costly rework. Machines are usually predictable because powerful physical laws govern their behavior. Unfortunately, machines are also unpredictable because those same laws allow for an occasional escape to bad behavior.

In this chapter we examine how chaos theory can greatly simplify some production processes. We also take a close look at the new approaches to statistical quality control and consider new perspectives that chaos theory can provide there. We will see that there is room for substantial improvement in statistical control approaches that recognize randomness and allow for errors within tolerance. Chaos theory, having gained popularity since the emergence of modern quality-control techniques, fits nicely into the classic statistical approach and can simplify data analysis. It also allows for earlier detection of errors and permits easy measurement of more complex relationships.

In Chapter 4 we discussed and modeled distribution processes as nonlinear systems. Here, we see that the interdependency of the production process creates an even more dynamic system to be monitored and controlled. We also see that current trends in manufacturing such as just-in-time delivery extend the distribution process off the manufacturing floor to the shop floors of suppliers and customers. As we look for additional ways to drive out inefficiency in the production process we will discover the value of sensitively monitoring changes in these increasingly complex, interacting systems.

Efficient timing is important to maintaining quality and reducing costs, and there are ways to use phase plane diagrams to improve the timing of our production processes. As we begin to understand the need for continuous improvement in production processes we will realize the need for information systems that are continuous rather than discrete. Continuous improvement requires frequent intervention and frequent changes that can substantially alter the processes and their relationships to one another. Chaos theory, which describes these processes with limit cycle trajectories, basins of attraction, and velocity history charts, offers that new continuous-monitoring technique.

Regardless of what we are producing or how it is produced, we are asked to control specific activities that are related to one another. Because these activities are typically periodic, cycling repeatedly, the limit cycles of these processes will reveal their behavior in detail. Similarly, because each activity inevitably has relationships with other functions, we will find our phase plane an appropriate domain in which to study the behavior of the interrelations.

Proposition 11: Chaos theory is particularly appropriate as a monitoring system for production processes, since production typically involves periodic process and processes with many interrelationships. The process of production inevitably requires the management of a chaotic system.

The interaction of production activities need not be very complex to produce quite complex patterns of behavior. Our simple computerized model of a distribution channel demonstrated this fact by showing that disorder can easily emerge from the interaction of simple, interrelated processes (see Chapter 4). That distribution model also demonstrated how the behavior of the system at one level can propagate through the system and drive the behavior of other processes in that system. Recall how an erratic demand function caused increasingly higher-order patterns of behavior within a distribution channel. Remember how the way in which information was exchanged in that simulated distribution channel greatly affected the behavior of the system.

Unlike our simulated distribution channel, actual production processes involve far more activities and relationships; there can easily be hundreds or thousands of individual processes that combine in some systematic way to produce the final product. These relationships—and therefore the entire process—are clearly nonlinear; a minor breakdown in one part of the system can require that the entire production process be instantly stopped. Accordingly, it is possible that a very minor change in a procedure can result in a substantial improvement in production quantity and quality or a substantial cost savings. In our distribution model we drove manufacturing with a final demand function. Although that may be an appropriate view with regard to the demand for a particular product, it fails to recognize the many forces on the supply side that affect production. Everything from the quality of production equipment, the way it is maintained, and the cost and quality of raw materials influences the behavior of the production process. Let's look at the production process generally—from materials supply through distribution—as a nonlinear system and consider what new perspectives chaos theory can offer.

Modern manufacturing has advanced to a highly sophisticated and technical level. Highly efficient quantitative models are marketed by major software houses and management consulting firms. Researchers in universities and business produce a continuous flow of newly proposed models that address virtually every conceivable issue regarding the production process. There are models for reorder, models for timing the delivery of supply, models for controlling the balance of supply between vendors, and an entire class of models to optimize the use of production equipment. Here, we do not intend to address those models directly; instead we will attempt to view the production process generally from the perspective of a "chaotician."

Consider the notion of sensitive dependence on initial conditions—that the future performance of a system can be highly dependent on very minor changes made early in the development of the system's behavior. Also consider that we manage a nonlinear system at the moment events actually occur by controlling how those events occur. The actual production process is only part of a much larger system; it is distinguishable from the rest of the system by the fact that it typically is the most complex part of the process. It is where everything really has to be right.

IMPLICATIONS OF CHAOTIC CHARACTERISTICS

Sensitive dependence on initial condition suggests that any change early in the system's development can greatly affect the system's subsequent behavior. We have demonstrated, however, that early alterations do not necessarily change future performance. The effect depends on the nature of the system; minor changes are either sustained, compounded, or dampened. The issue has considerable importance because production processes that are highly resilient to change are far less likely to be disturbed as a result of changes in input. That is, it is valuable to know how stable a production process is. Further, whether a process is inherently stable or on the threshold of a transition to high-order chaos has implications regarding costs, asset utilization, quality, and production capacity.

Systems that are stable are stable only at limited volume levels; any system—an oscillating pendulum, an individual piece of production equipment, or an entire production process—will become unstable at some higher-volume level. This fact is clearly described as the process of bifurcation, and it was demonstrated in Chapter 1. A system that is operating well below the level at which it becomes unstable is sure to contain excess resources that assist in maintaining its stability. These resources inevitably represent excess capacity. Consider how a production process responds to changes at either the input or the output end. If excess raw materials are received, they are typically stored in a warehouse until the production process needs them. The warehouse allows the system to absorb occasional, temporary increases without disrupting production, and it constitutes a buffer that helps dampen the effect of the increase in input and helps ensure stability of the system. Alternatively, if the raw material input is in the form of a perishable commodity—milk or produce, for example—then the production process may be designed to enable rapid increases in production capacity, allowing the additional input to be processed. In each case control over the production process is maintained by the presence of some additional resources. In these examples, however, the behavior of the production process on a phase plane will be quite different. If we were to examine the relation between the actual input of raw materials into the production process and the output of finished goods, we would discover that warehousing the goods provides Period 1–like stability, whereas scaling production volume up to process perishable supplies will provide an oscillating, Period 2–type trajectory.

PRICE OF STABILITY

The warehouse is a very inefficient resource. Its value exists only in the benefits it provides due to the nature of other characteristics of the supply-and-demand system. It may, for example, permit purchasing in economic lot sizes, or it may permit more rapid response to increases in demand. Its value may be simply that it prevents the need for excess production capacity, and by doing that it saves money. The warehouse is only valuable to the extent that there are other inefficiencies in the process. As these inefficiencies are driven out, so is the need for maintaining inventory buffers and the costs associated with them. These are the reasons behind just-in-time delivery systems.

If inventories are inefficient, so is excess production capacity. The costs associated with maintaining inventory buffers cannot be avoided by simply increasing the capacity of the system to process those occasional increases in supply. The cost of such increases in capacity can easily offset any savings in warehouse costs.

The dynamics of the production process are compounded by changes in the demand for finished goods. It is one thing to manage changes in raw materials inventory; it is quite another to manage the dynamics of the production floor when there are changes in both supply and demand; the interaction of supply-and-demand changes creates a condition not unlike that of a train that jolts sequentially from car to car as momentum hits inertia coming out of the station.

Consider the characteristics of a production process when it is operating at low volume, well below its capacity level, compared with when it operates near capacity. At low volume it has considerable excess capacity at all stages. This capacity permits it to rapidly adapt to changes in supply and demand, resulting in a stabilized, Period 1–type behavior. Any temporary changes are processed by the system, which subsequently returns to a constant-production level. The excess capacity, however, represents considerable inefficiency. At near-capacity levels of production assets are much more fully utilized, but the ability to maintain stability in the production process is reduced. Additional increases in supply can actually disrupt production as labor or equipment is redirected from the production process to manage the incoming supply. Similarly, a temporary decrease in demand can also disrupt production as resources are redirected to manage accumulating finished goods inventories. Consider the implications of both of these events occurring at the same time. When a system operates near capacity it is subject to much greater risk because excess capacities do not exist to help stabilize the system. The behavior of a production process, viewed at this level, is clearly nonlinear.

We can begin to better understand the behavior of a production process by examining the relation between supply, work in process, and output of finished goods. Production inevitably involves many stages of separate processes—some parallel, some sequential—that interact in some determined way to produce the finished goods. We know some of these processes to be continuous and others to be periodic, or batch. We can gain real insight by relating changes in one stage of the process to changes in another. At the simplest level we can relate supply to work in process and work in process to finished goods inventory.

Consider the diagram in Figure 6.1a, which relates changes in raw materials supply to changes in work in process. Two separate trajectories are given that describe possible responses to a temporary increase in demand for finished goods; in both cases we have made the assumption that the manufacturer has sufficient excess capacity to adequately scale up production volume.

Trajectory A reflects a theoretical ideal demonstrating a proportional increase in supply as work in process increases. As demand declines, so does the raw materials supply until it returns to a constant level at the origin of the phase plane. Such a trajectory would only be possible with close coordination between customers, the manufacturer, and suppliers. Information regarding demand would have to be communicated to raw materials suppliers in a timely enough manner to exactly match materials

Figure 6.1
Interaction of Generic Production Activities

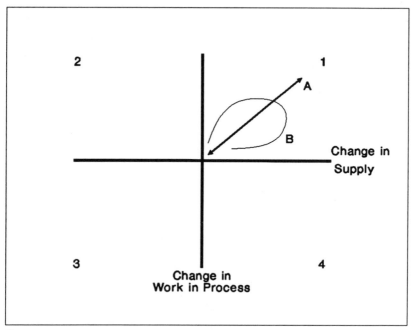

a

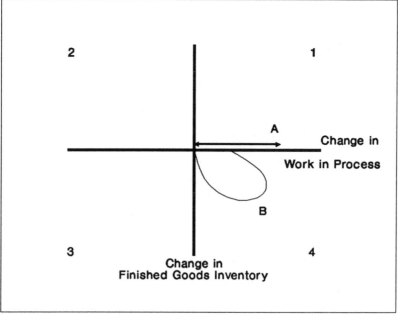

b

Figure 6.1 (Continued)

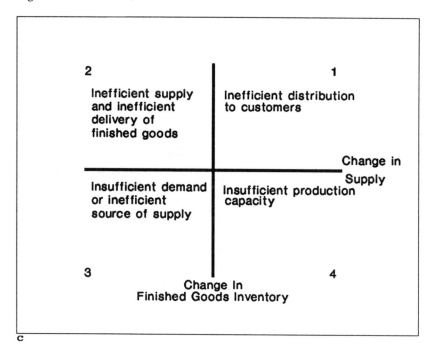

c

supply to increasing levels of production. Similarly, decreases in demand would also have to be efficiently communicated to suppliers and the manufacturer.

A pattern of performance like that in Trajectory B in Figure 6.1a is far more likely to be found. As demand increases, the manufacturer responds by increasing work in process, initially consuming some of the raw materials inventory that acts as a buffer in the system. During this stage the trajectory moves upward, reflecting the disproportional increase in work in process relative to changes in the raw materials supply. When the rate of increase in work in process begins to slow (halfway through the clockwise orbit of the trajectory), changes in raw material supply continue to increase, thereby replenishing the materials inventory buffer. Although Trajectory B is common and orderly, it does represent inefficiency in the ability of the system to respond to changes. In fact, any movement away from the 45-degree axis suggests some form of inefficiency.

Similar trajectories can be used to describe the relation between changes in work in process and changes in finished goods inventory. Trajectory A in Figure 6.1b provides a theoretical ideal. The trajectory moves directly to the right, reflecting the fact that increases in work in process should have no corresponding increase in finished goods inventory, since finished goods should be absorbed proportionally by the customer. Trajectory A would be possible only if there is no finished goods buffer and all finished goods are distributed as they are finished. Such a case is only possible with excellent coordination between manufacturer and customer, and again, the manufacturer must have the ability to adequately scale up production volume. It also requires the ability to deliver goods at any required volume level.

Proposition 12: Study of production and distribution as a nonlinear process can reveal inefficiencies in the system.

Trajectory B in Figure 6.1b provides the more realistic pattern of behavior between work in process and finished goods. Here we see the counterclockwise orbit begin as finished goods inventory rapidly depletes because of an increase in customer demand. The manufacturer subsequently responds by increasing the level of work in process in an attempt to meet the accelerating demand. As demand subsides, work in process continues to increase until the decrease in demand is communicated. When the finished goods inventory buffer is refilled, production volume returns to a constant level, indicated by the return of the trajectory to the origin.

PRODUCTION AS AN INPUT/OUTPUT SYSTEM

We can examine the behavior of the entire system by looking at the interaction of the supply input and the finished goods inventory. Figure 6.1c provides interpretations of each quadrant that describe the state of the system while visiting each of the domains on the phase plane. In quadrant 1 the supply of raw materials increases while finished goods inventory also increases. The implication is that although production has increased, inefficiencies in the distribution channel to customers have caused an accumulation of inventory in the production process. Quadrant 2 describes conditions that reflect both an inefficiency in delivery to customers (due to the increase in finished goods inventory) and a problem with supply (suggested by a decrease in supply while finished goods inventory increases). Accordingly, quadrant 3 is visited when both supply and finished goods inventory decrease. This could occur as a result of decreased production owing to declining demand or a shortage of raw materials supply. Finally, if raw material supply increases while finished goods inventory decreases, as in quadrant 4, one would expect inefficiencies in the production process.

Measuring the behavior of complex production processes at only three stages is clearly insufficient to provide real insight into the complex interaction of processes on the production floor. This simple example is useful, however, for describing how the relationships between different production processes can be decomposed to identify sources of instability. Although the interpretation of the various quadrants will differ, depending on the application and the variables used, it is quite conceivable that the interaction between all the assembly processes could be examined. Doing so would provide a description of the dynamics in the process and would clearly illustrate which processes are continuous (Period 1), which are oscillating (Period 2), and which have higher-order levels of behavior (Period 4 and greater). No doubt some processes will be related to others in a way that causes truly chaotic behavior. For these, an intervention strategy that synchronizes or paces the two processes might be a worthwhile intervention tactic.

Proposition 13: Sometimes highly complex production processes can be adequately controlled as a "black box" with nonlinear behavior.

Modern data-collection and data-processing techniques have allowed us to monitor complex and high-speed production processes. Our information systems have, in most cases, been able to record and report production levels as products make their way from one stage of production to the next. As the complexity and speed of the production process grow, numbers alone are often not enough to allow an intervention.

One application at a major electronics manufacturing plant involved nine major stages of production with four related product designs. Some of the designs required considerably more time at certain stages than others, yet several of the processes on the front and back ends of the assembly process were shared. To add to the dynamics of the process, the first stage of production involved a stamping activity performed by an expensive, high-speed device that, because of its economics, was required to operate continuously with only limited downtime for preventive maintenance. The stamping machine could be quickly programmed to change the type of board it produced, thereby controlling the quantity of units in production for each model. Because of the complex substitution effects between the models in the eight subsequent stages, management was unable to determine the actual quantity of products of each model that would reach finished goods at any particular time. This unpredictable output was of major concern, since the manufacturer was a just-in-time supplier to a major automobile manufacturing plant. It also increased costs, since sometimes overtime was necessary to finish adequate quantities of some products and idle time was spent when production levels unexpectedly exceeded requirements. Labor was the buffer most often used to dampen output and match it to demand. In some cases the form of transportation for finished goods was changed to expedite materials to the auto manufacturer. These substitutions from trucking to air freight carried a high price.

Information regarding demand was not a problem. The parts manufacturer was "on line" with the auto assembly plant and knew demand requirements with precision three days before required delivery. The assembly process, however, required one day and shipping required one additional day, leaving only twenty-four hours slack time.

The manufacturer had available, in real time, the quantity of products in process at each stage of production, and this information was broken down by model number. However, because of the speed and complex interactions in the production process and the great quantity of data supplied by the production management system, the data were virtually useless. The information could not be interpreted fast enough and often enough to allow for timely intervention.

The behavior of the production process became more understandable when all the interim production data was ignored and the system was analyzed as a nonlinear "black box." The phase plane diagram for this application used the horizontal axis to measure *change in work in process* for a particular model, and the vertical axis to measure change in quantity at final assembly *one day later*. The limit cycle on this phase plane traces the relation across time. Consider the value of the information such a trajectory can provide.

The black box phase plane could exhibit a Period 1 limit cycle only if there was a constant input and final assembly quantities remained constant even after the complex interactions of the various processes. This was never observed, since the input quantity was continuously adjusted in attempts to meet final demand requirements. If the limit cycle adhered to an attractor with a Period 2 oscillation, then one could expect work in process one day later to respond proportionately to the change in input. This was, in fact, identified as the goal. If management would alter inputs carefully enough, the relationship could be stabilized to prevent the nonlinear responses that caused unpredictable overtime or idle time.

Without intervention, the production system was adhering to a pattern of performance that was quite complex. For example, an increase in input quantity of 4,000 units per hour might result in increased final assembly of 3,000 units the next day, whereas an incremental input of 6,000 units might result in an increase of only 4,000 units in final assembly. The system was bound by certain internal constraints that determined how it was going to respond to adjustments. Although those constraints were reported in all the numbers generated by the production management system, the true behavior of the system wasn't apparent until the black box phase plane was generated.

One of the most exciting characteristics of this concept is the ease with which it provides for intervention. By observing the normal trajectory of the limit cycle that relates input to output across time, one sees its behavior and domain on the phase plane. One knows with considerable reliability that a certain level of input on the horizontal axis is typically associated with a certain level of output on the vertical axis one day later. Hence one begins to know the levels at which the production process behaves predictably and when it will probably provide a nonlinear response. Further, one can observe previous mistakes and learn by them. Any oscillation off of a 45-degree axis is associated with some specific event. Identifying the source of the constraint that caused the nonlinear response can allow one to improve the performance of the system.

MEASURING INTERVENTION

We have seen that the relationship between production processes can be studied as a nonlinear pattern of performance. We have also seen that sometimes complex processes can be better understood when they are monitored as a black box that delivers certain output as the result of changes in input. Now consider a third application of chaos theory that allows one to immediately identify the effect of changes in the production process or changes made as intervention strategies.

Proposition 14: Chaos theory can be used to identify specific sources of instability or stabilizing effects by relating changes in input or changes in the production process to measures of subsequent output.

Consider a phase plane that relates production volume to some measure of quality at any stage of the production process or after final assembly. If we place production volume on the horizontal axis and quality on the vertical axis, we would expect to find a trajectory that traces a line from quadrant 2, through the origin, to quadrant 4. Increasing production may cause a decrease in quality, but does it? What is the nature of this relationship? A traditional statistical correlation relates a change in one variable to a corresponding change in another variable, but it does this by matching an individual period and, therefore, fails to describe the rebounding trajectory that emerges when the independent variable is changed. (Even if the data is lagged, correlation only describes the association of one variable to another when taken as independent observations; it fails to provide any description of the chronological trajectory that describes the relationship.)

Is it true that quality goes down when volume goes up? Might it be that the inverse is true, and that when production volume is decreased quality suffers? More likely the association adheres to an attractor that lies horizontally along the production axis on our phase plane. A great number of structural characteristics, such as material specifications, inspections, and product design, bind quality to constancy. Alternatively, production volume may be allowed to vary considerably to meet changes in demand. Hence we have here a variable regarding the production process (i.e., volume) that relates in some way to a measure of production performance (i.e., quality). The behavior of that relationship and the limits of the basin of attraction that binds that relationships are important to management. Recall that the phase plane is scaled on the *changes in production* and the *changes in quality*. A trajectory that maintains a position in quadrant 1 reflects continuous improvement in both volume and quality (a desirable place to be). Quadrant 2 provides improvement in quality at the cost of production volume. Quadrant 3 is a degradation of quality associated with decreasing volume, and quadrant 4 reflects improving volume at the cost of quality. Constancy, as before, lies at the origin.

If one redefines quality as a measure relative to competitive products, the phase plane takes on new meaning regarding competitiveness. Changes in volume result from greater acceptance in the marketplace, whereas changes in relative quality result from continuous redesign and improvement.

One should begin to see the implications of this type of analysis. Because the production process is deterministic, we know that every production characteristic has some association with any final measure of production quality. It may be that most changes in production processes have little effect on the final product because of buffers that dampen or compensate for their effect; however, it is also true that some patterns of relationship can be recognized. Put simply, if a low-order limit cycle is discovered between changes in a production process and a subsequent measure of production quality, then that relation can be exploited to improve quality.

Similarly, the effects of any intervention in the production process will be immediately revealed by the phase plane. Consider a phase plane that relates changes in finished product production rates to changes in time spent at work station 1 inspecting raw materials. Imagine we intervened and invested six additional minutes to ensure proper quality and grade of the raw materials. There is no need to collect a statistical sample size to determine if the intervention has had an effect. If the production process is considered deterministic, then the phase plane describes the behavior not generally, but specifically. A sample size of *one* may be all that is needed to signal a change in production volume. A second observation confirms the new orbit of the limit cycle that relates the increased inspection time to changes in production rate. A third orbit provides additional confirmation; by the fourth or fifth oscillation the reliable trace on the phase plane will confirm that a newly established trajectory has resulted from any intervention. The statistician will still be waiting for an adequate sample size to correlate *average volume* to *average inspection time*. By the time the relation emerges as a statistical association (and it is questionable whether it ever would), the employee at work station 1 will have already perfected the new inspection procedure.

Admittedly, this example is based on many simplifying assumptions, but it emphasizes that every process and any intervention in the production process are deterministically related to final production measures. To the extent that we can discover association between our activities and the finished products we gain a better control over the process.

BEYOND QUANTITY

As implied by the discussion above, the nonlinear behaviors in a production process include more than just production quantities. Quality measures will behave nonlinearly; costs will behave nonlinearly. We can expect customer satisfaction to respond in a nonlinear manner to the interventions on the production line.

Proposition 15: Nonlinear behavior in production is not limited to simple quantities of production. The behavior includes attributes such as the quality and cost of the goods that are produced.

The phase planes that so sensitively report changes in the behavior of a system are a new tool that can be used on the production floor. Black box associations between any stage of production and any subsequent production activity can provide feedback through the system, allowing workers to view the effect of any changes in process. The effect of any incremental improvement in method will be immediately evident. The effect of any disruptive activity—even if it occurs only once—can be made evident to those who have the ability to control the process.

Cost Control

But what of production costs? Production activities are inevitably measured financially, providing a consistent series of data reflecting the performance of the production process. Like financial measures on the traditional income statement, balance sheet, or cash flow report, data regarding production activities are typically reported as aggregate values, reflecting total costs over some specified period. We often use this data to compute a measure of unit cost that is subsequently used for pricing and budgeting. However, like the financial reports, information on production costs fails to address the incremental. Although we compare this period with the last, we fail to plot the trajectory of change over time, which can reveal so much about the underlying forces at work. We see instability in the cost per unit—sometimes seeing it go up and sometimes seeing it go down—but are never quite sure which collection of production costs accounts for the random-appearing behavior. Although we can study the changes in cost figures from one period to the next and know with confidence the accounts that caused a cost increase, in the next period the behavior will be different, and a similar analysis will reveal another set of changing costs that account for the difference.

The question is not "Which costs change?" It is "Where is the source of instability?" If we know which costs are unstable, we can direct our efforts at controlling the sources of those costs. If we can't control their instability, we may be able to better anticipate their behavior by looking at the patterns in their rates of change. This new information about the changes in costs may enable us to offset some current instability and better control actual costs.

Proposition 16: The effectiveness of various costs and expenses can be determined by examining their association with total costs on a phase plane. Further, sources of instability in production costs can be identified by decomposing total production costs into a series of limit cycles that reflect the various cost components.

Production costs are typically divided into operating and maintenance. Operating costs usually are defined as labor, raw materials, machining, tool, work-in-process inventory, setup costs, and quality-control costs, although much more specific accounts may constitute these general categories. Instabilities in any of these costs are readily revealed by examining their relation to the total operating cost.

Consider a phase plane on which changes in an account such as direct labor are plotted on the horizontal axis and changes in total operating costs are plotted on the vertical axis. The association could be based on any time frame, such as weekly, monthly, or quarterly. What would be the preferred trajectory on such a plane? As usual, if there were no incremental changes in either measure, the trajectory would remain in the center of the phase plane at coordinate 0,0. Two very different possibilities emerge when one considers the nature of this relationship. If the trajectory ventures into quadrant 1, we know that an increase in labor costs relates to an increase in operating costs. That would be normally expected. Similarly, if the trajectory visits quadrant 3, then operating costs decline with decrease in labor costs. An oscillation between quadrants 1 and 3 is quite normal, therefore, representing attempts to hold down labor costs to minimize unit cost. But what about an oscillation into quadrant 4? Such a visit means that an increase in labor cost was associated with a decrease in operating costs. Although that seems illogical, it could be the result of the activities performed with that incremental labor. In fact, any time labor is effectively used to decrease other costs, the trajectory will move into quadrant 4.

The implications of this analysis are considerable. One can afford to experiment by investing labor into activities with potential cost savings. Any action that substantially lowers and maintains operating expenses into quadrant 4 can be considered effective. Although there are many other costs that affect the changes in the operating expenses, these forces will combine to create a limit cycle pattern on the phase plane. The effectiveness of the intervention will be visible as a change in the shape, location, and behavior of the limit cycle. A visit to quadrant 2 tends to confirm this relationship. In quadrant 2 operating costs increase when labor costs decline. Hence an oscillation between quadrants 2 and 4 emerges when the relationship between labor costs and total operating costs is inverse. Conversely, an oscillation between quadrants 1 and 3 reveals a direct relationship between labor costs and total operating costs.

It would be possible to monitor the effectiveness of labor's efforts at controlling costs by studying the trajectory on such a phase plane. The most undesirable relation would be reflected in an oscillation between quadrants 1 and 3 that is near vertical. In this case changes in labor costs almost directly affect total operating costs. Improvements in the effectiveness of labor at cost control would emerge as a rotation in the oscillation to one that still oscillates between quadrants 1 and 3 but lies almost flat approaching the horizontal axis. Increased expenditures in labor become an investment when the limit cycle continues to rotate and oscillates between quadrants 2 and 4.

In much the same way changes in other costs, such as raw materials, machining, and tooling, will be revealed either as contributors to total operating costs or as investments that can help decrease operating costs. We all know that raw materials are a major part of total operating costs; our traditional accounting systems adequately report that to us. But what about *changes* in raw materials costs? The relationships between these variables *on the margin* may be a fundamentally different thing. It is quite possible that purchasing higher-quality raw materials can result in marginally lower operating costs. It simply is not enough to know what the costs are; one must know how they change relative to each other.

Instability in the operating cost can easily be traced to those costs that contribute to its total. Some of the phase plane diagrams relating these costs to operating costs will show high-order chaotic patterns. One or more will probably show a low-order, Period 2–type limit cycle. In this analysis a low-order limit cycle identifies two costs that are closely associated with each other; hence one can recognize those most responsible for changes in the total operating cost.

Production Budget Control

Often production activities are managed by project budgets that attempt to control costs over the length of the project. This form of production control often is used in both service industries and construction to control costs relating to long-term projects. In these settings the budget takes the form of an "attractor," to which actual expenditures are bound. The cumulative nature of both the budget and the expenditures creates a condition in which subsequent adherence to the budget is greatly dependent on previous expenditures. It also is true that exceeding the budget at one moment often results in the ability to save relative to the budget at a later time. One application of this concept at a major research laboratory demonstrated that some projects were closely bound to their budgets, whereas others quickly departed from the planned budget and accumulated increased variances over time. In that application *changes in the budget* were plotted on the horizontal axis and *changes in actual expenditures* were plotted on the vertical axis. Because one would expect increases in expenditures to be coordinated with increases in the budget, one can expect the trajectory on the phase plane to oscillate along the 45-degree axis. Any variation from the 45-degree axis represents a variance from the budget. A movement toward quadrant 2 reflects increasing expenditures when the budget calls for reductions in expenditures; a movement toward quadrant 4 reflects a situation in which increases in the budget are not matched with increases in actual expenditures.

Proposition 17: Chaos theory offers a new level of control over production budgets. By relating changes in actual expenditures to changes in the budget, one can identify departures from budget sooner than with traditional approaches.

This approach to project control offers immediate reporting of any deviation between actual and planned expenditures. Because it focuses on *changes,* it is more able to identify deviations from budgets, than traditional means. Further, it offers a new way to control budgets, demonstrating how overexpenditures, which appear as oscillations into quadrant 2, for example, can be offset with a counter-oscillation into quadrant 4. Budget control becomes a process of managing the trajectory as it evolves. One makes many minor adjustments in the rate of change to guide overall expenditures of the project to completion.

This approach to budget control also readily reveals that deviations from budget are as likely to result from inaccurate budgeting as from uncontrolled expenditures. When viewing the trajectory that describes deviations between budgeted and actual expenditures, one begins to realize that many of the variances are simply the result of failing to adequately detail the budget. Changes in actual expenditures often reflect activities that were actually needed to accomplish the project. It is likely that patterns of actual expenditures for various types of projects eventually may emerge by reviewing the course of the trajectory after each project's completion.

Quality and Process Control

Statistical *process* control is an approach to improving quality by focusing on controlling the *way* products are produced rather than simply inspecting finished goods. By continuously improving the processes used in production, one continuously reduces the opportunities for error and thereby improves the quality of the final product. An integral part of the technique is the use of quality-control charts by those employees who are involved in producing the goods. In these applications chaos theory offers an improved quality-control chart that more readily identifies significant variations and significantly raises the quality of information in quality-control analysis.

Proposition 18: Chaos theory offers a simple way to increase the precision and sophistication of quality control beyond those levels possible with statistical quality control. Because intervention always takes the form of a change to the system, changes in the system's behavior should be measured.

Consider the quality-control charts shown in Figure 6.2. The two traditional charts report two production measures (A and B) as they commonly would be reported. Confidence bands are typically established that suggest that variation within the bands is acceptable, whereas any measurement outside the bands requires intervention. But the aggregate measures reported on the traditional chart mask the evolving behavior patterns. This fact may not be immediately apparent but becomes clear when one compares the information on the traditional and the nonlinear control charts.

Locate the peak in Measure A at observation 12; it is the highest point on the "Traditional QC Plot" of Measure A. Also locate it on the top marginal history chart on the "Nonlinear QC Report"; its position corresponds to the sequence value of 12 labeled on the bottom of the charts. Now compare the two charts with respect to the next value after observation 12. On the traditional chart the value has moved back to a midpoint between the bands labeled 30 and 40. The nonlinear chart, however, reflects that the latest adjustment is actually an overadjustment. Although it returned the quality-control measurement to the center of the confidence bands, it should not be sustained. At observation 14 the actual value of Measure A continues to decline and nears the value of 30 on the traditional chart. The error that caused this is obvious on the marginal history chart by the fact that observation 14 is still below the center of the chart, which represents no change in the measure.

Note that when Measure A on the traditional chart drops below 30 at observation 17, this is reflected as a *sustained* condition below the center line on the marginal history chart. The fault that resulted in a drop below 30 actually began with observation 16. Left uncorrected, the condition continued until acted on at observation 18. The subsequent stability of the system is evident on the marginal history chart as a relatively flat line with occasional upward movements.

Measure B demonstrates how an emerging oscillation in performance would appear on a traditional chart and on a nonlinear one. Begin by

Figure 6.2
A Comparison of Traditional and Nonlinear QC Reports

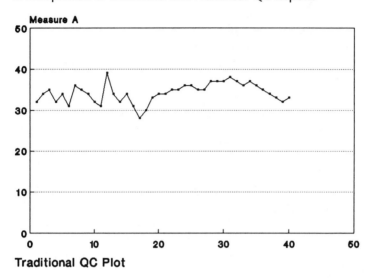

Traditional QC Plot

Traditional QC Plot

Figure 6.2 (Continued)

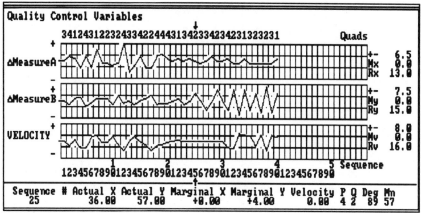

Nonlinear QC Report

comparing the two charts, starting with observation 20. On the Nonlinear QC Report above one can see an oscillation between observations 20 and 23 that continues through to observation 40. On the traditional plot the first oscillation is not evident until observation 25.

Note that the focus of the nonlinear chart is on that incremental difference, which translates into incremental quality. Although the traditional charts suggest this process is sufficiently controlled the focus should be on the incremental changes where the process is not adequately controlled. Traditional quality-control charts identify error relative to the total measurement, whereas the nonlinear control chart shows error relative to zero, which is the desired error rate. Incremental quality is gained by intervening into the system to control that which is not already controlled.

Velocity measures the systematic changes in the two measures. Note that the velocity measure is unstable through observation 20, reflecting instability in both A and B. The velocity measure becomes stable, however, for observations 20 through 30, even though Measure B is oscillating. This is because the fluctuations in B are independent of any changes in A. The velocity measure responds noticeably after observation 30 when changes in A begin to be associated with those in B. Recall that the velocity measure here is simply the product of the two measures. Therefore, both marginal measures must be non-zero for velocity to be non-zero.

If A and B respond directly (both positive or both negative), then the velocity measure will be positive and rise above the center line. Likewise, inverse associations will be revealed as drops below the center line of the velocity measure.

There are underlying philosophical merits to using the nonlinear approach. Traditional statistics suggest that there will always be some level of random error that cannot be controlled. Hence zero-error quality control becomes a relentless pursuit with no hope of success; one can only hope to *approach* perfection. Chaos theory suggests that no error is truly random and that by identifying the contributing forces, one can control the final product deterministically. It suggests that a zero error rate is attainable.

Proposition 19: Phase planes can be used to sensitively examine the behavior of a single measure over time, thereby offering a simple, more efficient substitute for traditional statistical quality-control charts.

It is not essential that one combine two measures of a process to generate a phase plane of the measure's behavior. Because one dimension on all the phase planes presented is *time* (represented by the evolving trajectory), one can examine the changes in a variable over time by comparing the changes in a value at time *t* with changes in the variable at time *t-1*, where *t-1* represents the changes in the variable during the previous observation. If one places *t-1* on the horizontal axis and *t* on the vertical axis, a phase plane diagram can be developed demonstrating evolving patterns of behavior for a single measure. The interpretation of such a phase plane is particularly interesting. For example, if the trajectory visits quadrant 2, it suggests that when the variable decreases (a movement left on the X axis), it tends to be followed by an increase during the next observation (a movement upward on the Y axis). Hence a trajectory that alternately visits quadrants 2 and 4 reflects an oscillation in the measures, with each measure being followed by a subsequent increase or decrease. A visit to quadrant 1 suggests that increases tend to be followed by another increase. Hence if a trajectory remains in quadrant 1, the variable is continuously increasing. Accordingly, if the trajectory remains in quadrant 3, decreases follow decreases, so the variable is constantly declining in value.

If one expects to maintain a constant measure, one tries to maintain the value near the center of the phase plane. Figure 6.3 describes the behavior of Measure A, which was presented above. Three phase plane diagrams illustrate the changing behavior of the variable at subsequent stages over time. Note that in Figure 6.3a the trajectory oscillates between quadrants 2 and 4. In Figure 6.3b the trajectory assumes a clockwise orbit, suggesting some underlying mechanism driving the variable's behavior. Note that this *pattern in the rates of change* is completely unnoticed on any traditional quality-control chart. It represents the following complex behavior: (1) a decrease after a decrease, (2) an increase after a decrease, (3) a decrease after an increase, (4) a decrease after a decrease, (5) another increase after a decrease, and (6,7) increases after increases. The complex pattern is readily apparent by the consistent orbital behavior of the limit cycle.

Figure 6.3c shows the limit cycle of Measure A at a later stage. Here you can see that the changes are greatly reduced and the trajectory tends

Figure 6.3
Phase Planes and Velocity of a Single Measure

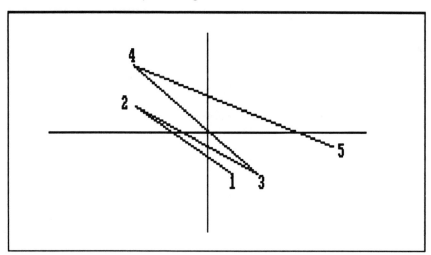

a

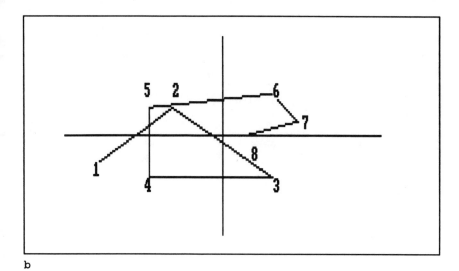

b

Figure 6.3 (Continued)

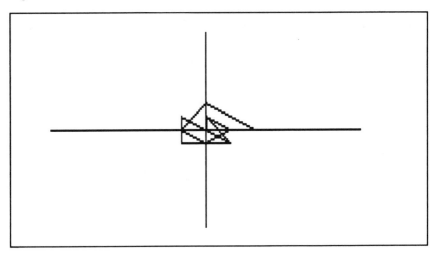

c

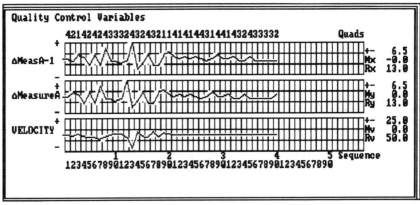

d

to adhere to the origin on the phase plane. The velocity history chart in Figure 6.3d provides another way of viewing the single measure's behavior. Note the disorder evident in the early stages and the stability apparent during the later stages. The velocity measure in this case represents the products of the changes in the measure at times t and $t-1$. When these changes decline toward zero, the velocity measure stabilizes to a constant flat line.

Consider the value of this information in a production setting. Every measure of dimension, every reading of electrical resistance or voltage, every measure of weight, every measure of quality is subject to this type of analysis, which can reveal systematic, emerging patterns of behavior in the production process. One need not simply wait until the incremental changes finally push performance outside the tolerance levels; instead, one can make the central coordinate (0,0) the objective and strive for stability in the production process. This approach offers a new plateau for quality control. Just as it is deemed insufficient to control quality by observing the quality of the final product, so it is insufficient to control production by measuring current performance levels; one must focus on changes in current performance and control processes on the margin as undesirable patterns of performance emerge.

Proposition 20: Phase plane diagrams can be used to reveal additional information about data beyond that provided by many common quality-control charts. They also suggest certain weaknesses of some conventional statistical charts.

Charts other than the control chart described in Figure 6.2a are used to control processes. Some of these are associated with the total quality management approaches taken by many firms. Chaos theory provides a fresh view of these charts and, in some cases, suggests new uses for them. Consider the cause-and-effect chart, or Ishikawa diagram, used to identify contributing elements of a process that cause a failure in a production process. The chart resembles a fishbone or tree diagram in which all the elements of a process that contribute to a final product are identified. The process is educational in itself; it aids in identifying all the activities processes that contribute to a production process. All the major contributing elements are considered; they include the general classifications of personnel, equipment, policies, materials, and procedures.

Most of the processes identified on a cause-and-effect chart are periodic processes. For example, ordering of raw materials and stamping of a printed-circuit board are common elements in the production of any electronic device, and these processes are clearly periodic with a low-order stability. However, just as sequential production or distribution processes contribute to the creation of a complex nonlinear system, so do the elements of a process contribute to the behavior pattern of the final process. Put simply, we can use chaos theory in combination with a cause-and-effect chart to determine the level of stability and sources of instability in a process. In doing so we will probably discover that errors in the final product are the result of a dynamic interaction between two or more processes—an interaction that occasionally causes instabilities. It may be that occasionally late inventory shipments require operating the printed circuit stamping machine at a production level that causes errors. To stabilize the system, one needs to either increase the capacity of the stamping process, increase the level of raw materials safety stock, or improve the timing of raw material shipments.

Pareto charts are used to identify the primary causes of a condition. They represent a way of decomposing the contributing elements into those that are most important and those that are not. For example, assume that preparing a budget involves the following activities: (1) collecting data, (2) creating electronic spreadsheets, (3) making estimates, (4) conferring with management, (5) printing the budget, and (6) distributing or reporting the budget to department heads. A delay in getting the budget distributed can result from a delay in any of these contributing activities. A Pareto analysis would call for identifying the number of times each activity caused a delay. One might discover that collecting data and printing the budget often were delayed and that the other activities were typically completed on time. Knowing that, changes could be made in how the data was collected and printed to ensure timely delivery of the budget. Pareto analysis points to the most important activities to control in a larger process to control behavior of that process.

Similarly, the nonlinear behavior of some processes is more important than others. If one decomposes the limit cycle of final production by examining the trajectories of the primary contributing activities, one will find various levels of disorder among those activities. Some will mirror the final production cycle, whereas others will differ from it considerably. Those that most closely resemble final production can be considered more important to manage than those that differ; these processes *drive* the final production limit cycle. Often they are the dominant activities in the production process, and their behavior dominates other activities. For example, highly chaotic processes in the production of raw materials are smoothed out when those materials are shipped and received. Disorder in producing a subassembly is smoothed out by stocking supplies of that component as it waits for final assembly. Although disorder anywhere in the production process is undesirable, its influence varies, and can be identified by comparing limit cycle patterns with those of final assembly. Just as one can "Pareto" the causes of failure, one can "Pareto" the causes of instability in a production process.

A histogram is a particularly common method of describing the behavior of data. It summarizes data by describing the frequency with which certain values are observed. For example, a production worker may be asked to collect data by accurately measuring the pressure of a containment vessel. The data would provide a distribution about a mean value and would have a particular statistical variance. The mean and variance could be used to determine certain confidence limits for the process that may have to comply with specified quality standards. The data also could be used to develop a histogram—a bar chart—that supposedly describes the behavior of the data. Figure 6.4a provides a histogram of pressure data for our example.

The failure of the histogram is in its disregard for the evolving state of the system it describes. One cannot tell which observation came first, which came next, and which came last. There is no reporting of the chronological pattern of the data, which may be vitally important. Consider the trajectories in figures 6.4b and 6.4c. These trajectories are based on the *same data* used for the histogram. The two limit cycles differ only in the order in which the data was received. In Figure 6.4b observations were collected alternately, working from the two tails of the normal distribution; in Figure 6.4c the trajectory was developed by collecting observations starting at the left tail of the normal distribution and progressing to the right tail.

Figure 6.4
Conventional and Nonlinear Images of the Same Data Set

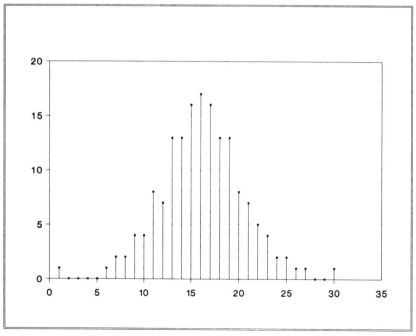

a

Figure 6.4 (Continued)

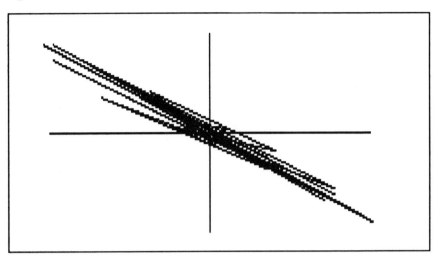

b

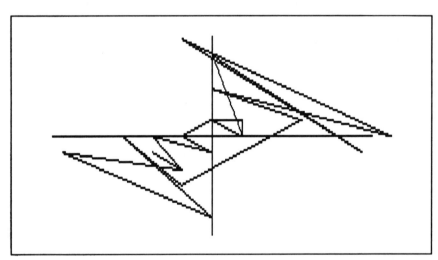

c

From a view of conventional statistics, all three images in Figure 6.4 have the same mean, mode, variance, and standard error. They are statistically identical but fundamentally different when one considers the patterns that evolve over time.

Histograms are clearly inappropriate for any data that have a time orientation. They mask important patterns of behavior that may be necessary to control the system they describe.

Scatter diagrams suffer the same failing. They relate the value of one measure to that of another. They form the basis for regression analysis, in which one tries to fit a line (or curve) to the pattern of dots that relate paired observations of the two measures. However, any chronological pattern in the data is entirely excluded, and because system behaviors evolve from one observation to the next, such charts also are inappropriate for any data that describe a continuous or periodic process.

Sampling

Chaos theory makes us reconsider sampling. It suggests that processes should be *continuously* measured to adequately describe their behavior. One hundred percent sampling is considered too costly and unnecessary, and this surely can be the case. Sampling, however, does not necessarily imply that we must use conventional statistical approaches, which make estimates of a population based on the sample. A sample is not something separate and apart from the entire population of observations; it is part of the population. A sample does not *approximate* the behavior of a system; it *is* a direct artifact of the system.

When the National Aeronautics and Space Administration (NASA) transmits images of our solar system back to earth from their venturing spaceships, they digitize the image. Not all of reality comes through, as not all of it is captured and the resolution of the image is limited by the amount of data that can be efficiently transferred; on early missions the resolution was quite poor by today's standards. These images, although they were only partial collections of reality, were not considered samples; they were simply incomplete pictures of what was actually there. In the same way, samples of production activities should not be extended by statistics into speculative estimates of reality. NASA now has improved imaging techniques that are largely the result of advanced technologies. Business also has those technologies, and it is time to discard the simplifying procedures of the past. We can now use every data point we can get. We should focus on reducing the cost of sampling and spend less on statistical manipulation of the data we collect. With time, our images on phase planes will come closer to describing reality.

Chaos theory causes us to see the production process differently. It causes us to see the process as a series of nonlinear relationships. It suggests new approaches to controlling production volume, cost, and quality, and it offers a new perspective of the process with its phase planes trajectories. Chaos theory exposes the inadequacy of some traditional statistical charting and causes us to question some of the most fundamental assumptions of classic statistics.

7

Chaos Theory and Human Resource Issues

Goals and objectives are the products of linear thinking, whereas human behavior is unequivocally nonlinear. The science of biology has been transformed by chaos theory. However, biologists focus on the behavior of nonhuman species—rats, rabbits, bacteria—while managers deal with the attitudes, opinions, and motivations of employees. What biologists study has little to do with human resources on the job; human resources are the concern of any manager who hires, trains, evaluates, promotes, compensates, or negotiates with employees. Human resource management is, by necessity, a practical activity that touches the personal lives of people. Personnel policies are expected to be uniform yet accommodating, consistent yet adaptive. Personnel programs and policies are structured, whereas personal opinions, needs, and attitudes are decidedly dynamic.

Human resource management includes the broad academic areas of organizational theory and organizational behavior. It deals with selection and placement, compensation, motivation, training and development, leadership, and other related topics. Academic texts provide a collection of well-accepted concepts that constitute the most common denominators in the field; they contain those things that most academicians recognize and accept. What is in the academic texts, however, is *not* what is being discussed in corporate offices; the current hot management topics in industry are found on the back shelves of commercial bookstores. On those shelves one finds a collection of unconventional, highly effective approaches to management, sold by consultants and practiced by some. That is where one finds the real innovations in human resource management.

The difference between what is taught and what is practiced is probably greater today than at any time during the past twenty years. Some academic texts still spend pages describing management by objectives as an ideal model for planning and controlling activities within an organization.

Table 7.1
Some Major Management Concepts

Concept	Approximate Year
Scientific Management	1912
Human Relations Movement	1927
Bureaucratic Management	1947
Fayol's Principles of Management	1949
Management By Objectives	1965
System Theory	1960
Intrapreneurship	1985
Empowerment	1990
Total Quality Management	1991

(The concept can be traced to Peter Drucker, who coined the term in the 1950s.) Businesses have changed over the past forty years, and so have the people they employ. It's not that management by objectives never worked; it did. It's simply that new approaches are more appropriate to the conditions of today. People's attitudes change, and human resource management must change to remain effective.

It is at this level we should begin to discuss human issues in organizations—at a level where we can appreciate transitions in concepts over time, where we can see the waves of concept popularity come and go. Table 7.1 provides a partial list of some major concepts that have influenced management since 1900. Many other ideas are not included in the table, but the list provides some appreciation for the dynamic nature of management; every few years a new idea emerges, becomes popular, becomes more or less effective, and gets replaced by a new concept. Often these transitions can be related to other major events of the times. For example, the concept of *systems theory*—that organizations consist of interactive subsystems and interface with an external environment—emerged during the turbulent 1960s when many organizations first realized the importance of the external environment. In the sixties that environment was filled with vocal constituencies (protestors), national issues (civil rights), and international events (Vietnam). Those years presented an excellent opportunity to realize that an organization must be responsive to its environment.

Similarly, *intrapreneurship*—the idea of an entrepreneurial spirit *within* a large organization—emerged as an inviable idea as companies grew out of the recession of 1979–1980 and struggled to incorporate new technologies being developed by smaller firms. *Empowerment* and *total quality management* are continuations of the intrapreneurship theme—empowerment being the vesting of substantial decision-making authority in employees and total quality management being a philosophy and management system that calls for personnel participation with a focus on continuous improvements in quality. Total quality management requires empowerment; empowerment is an attempt to capture intrapreneurship quality in personnel. The acceptance of new ideas depends on experience with older ones. Old ideas are modified to create new ones. The history of management is a trail of ever-changing concepts and practices.

Yet some concepts have survived the years. Recognition of the need to "staff," "organize," and "direct" can be traced to 1300 B.C. The concept of "span of management" is described in the Bible. The fundamentals of management haven't changed. What has changed are the specific programs and concepts we use; those change to reflect the continually evolving conditions of our day. We cannot expect constancy; we must expect change. We cannot manage to maintain current programs; we must manage to change them.

Human resource management is probably the most dynamic of all management activities. The changing attitude of employees, combined with their changing demographic characteristics, and the ever-increasing stack of federal, state, and local compliance issues make it a particularly turbulent and challenging topic. Let's see how our understanding of these activities changes when we view some of the more common concepts in the field from a nonlinear perspective.

DECISION-MAKING AUTHORITY

Decision-making authority within an organization can typically be described on a continuum from fully centralized to fully decentralized. When firms are centralized, decision-making authority is vested in a limited number of people who communicate directives to employees through midmanagement levels. When significant decision-making authority is distributed throughout the organization, the firm is said to be decentralized. This basic idea has been used by many as firms adopt the concept of empowerment and move toward greater decentralization. But decentralizing decision-making is not that simple. Besides the difficulties of actually delegating responsibilities and authorities to lower levels in a firm, management typically has serious concerns about control. How will decisions be coordinated with others in the firm? How do we ensure compliance with company policies?

Decentralization often is accompanied by creation of some form of work teams. Hence decision-making in a firm is better described as a combination of centralization versus decentralization and individual versus group approaches. Consider the recent trends in management based on these two interactive continua. The movement toward empowerment, employee involvement, quality-control circles, and work teams has pushed us toward a decentralized-group combination. The decision-making style is clearly more of a team approach than that taken in previous years. Consider the alternatives. Instead of being vested in a decentralized group, decision-making could be (1) decentralized to individuals, (2) centralized in an individual, or (3) centralized in a group. These latter two combinations represent the more classic, historical approaches to decision-making in organizations. The first alternative—decentralization to individuals—is a common approach to decision-making without the use of teams.

One cannot define any one of these approaches as preferred, since their effectiveness is contingent on the specific conditions of the firm and its environment. However, there has been an obvious trend in recent years toward a more decentralized, team-oriented approach. The important point here is that the concept of decision-making is dynamic and dependent on environmental conditions, the needs of the organization, and the attitudes and expectations of employees. There is an evolving pattern of change in how we handle decision-making within a firm; there is a pattern at the macro level, within industries, and within each individual firm. How to handle decision-making in a firm is an issue of great concern for management, particularly today, as firms see others decentralize and hear the merits of team approaches. Yet the decision about how to recast decision-making in a firm is one that is typically made based on *what is being done now* and *what apparently is needed*. In fact, the decision is only another step in a continuing journey of changing decision-making relationships. It is probably only part of a pattern that has been emerging over time like that suggested in Figure 7.1a. The trajectory exists because there are powerful underlying forces that drive the management style.

We can extend the notion of decision-making to include a concept of organizational structure. Two terms, span of management and span of control, are useful. Span of management is defined as simply the number of subordinates to a supervisor. If a supervisor has five direct subordinates, then the span of management for the supervisor's position is five. There is an average span of management for each level within a traditional hierarchial organization and an average span for the entire organization. Span of management, although a simple concept, has major implications for an organization. If the span is relatively small, subordinates are more closely supervised and typically have less decision-making authority. Conversely, a supervisor with several subordinates must delegate more decision-making because each cannot be as closely supervised. Organizations with large spans of management tend to be "flatter," with fewer supervisory levels, whereas those with small spans of management are "tall," hierarchial structures.

Span of control is a more conceptual notion. It relates to the number of subordinates a supervisor can effectively manage. Span of control, therefore, is more difficult to measure and varies according to the person in the supervisory position. (It also is affected by the type of subordinates being

Figure 7.1
Nonlinear Models of Decision-Making Styles

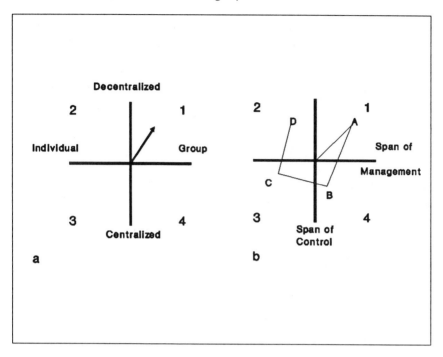

supervised and the nature of the work they are doing, along with other factors.) There should be congruence between these concepts. Again, the relation is a dynamic one influenced by changes in the organizational structure, the abilities of supervisors, and the abilities and cooperation of subordinates.

Consider the implications of the various positions in Figure 7.1b. At position A on the 45-degree axis both span of management and span of control are increasing proportionately. That would be acceptable, reflecting a flattening of the organization (span of management) and improved effectiveness in the supervisor–subordinate relationship (span of control). The off-axis positions B and D represent incongruent positions. At B the number of subordinates per supervisor is being increased while the ability of the supervisor to control subordinates declines. The result is an inefficiency through lack of control. It also calls for intervention by training the supervisor or restructuring the supervisor–subordinate relationship. At D the opposite is true. Although supervisors have improved spans of control, the number of subordinates they supervise is being reduced. Inefficiency results from the increasing oversupervision. Accordingly, position C in quadrant 3 reflects declining values in both measures. It should be apparent that the desirable position on Figure 7.1b would be some point in quadrant 1.

Proposition 21: Organizational theory concepts such as centralization-decentralization and span of management trace trajectories in phase space reflecting forces in the external environment and within the organization.

These two phase planes are more conceptual ideas than practical ones. However, they demonstrate how conventional management concepts take on a new dimension when viewed from the perspective of nonlinear systems theory. Organizational concepts, even at this macro level, lend themselves to study as trajectories that emerge from the past influenced by current decisions. Even if such trajectories cannot be generated, there are practical implications here for management. What are the forces, internal or external to the firm, that drive either of the trajectories in Figure 7.1? How quickly can the relations be changed? What happens when top management "earthquakes" the organization with major changes in management style or organizational structure? These are valid questions for management; they come from a recognition that organizational concepts, such as these related to decision-making, must not only be consistent with current demands on the organization, but must also be consistent to a pattern that has been developing over time.

MANAGEMENT STYLES

Management literature is rich with classification schemes for management styles. Fortunately, there are two common denominators that characterize most of the proposals. Management styles typically include some address toward *concern for people* and *concern for task*. Often the classification scheme addresses the extent to which management emphasizes one of these dimensions or the other. For example, a manager who is only concerned with getting the job done (concern for task) and has little or no concern for relationships with employees (concern for people) is typically considered an autocrat. A manager who is able to blend an emphasis on the job with a concern for people is considered most effective. The classifications are inevitably static, however; management style seldom is viewed as a dynamic phenomenon changing over time.

A concept called *contingency theory* recognizes that appropriate management styles depend on the specific type of work being done and the quality of the relationship between the manager and employees. Some contingency management models prescribe appropriate management styles for various conditions. The styles, however, typically relate to the balance between emphasis on the job and emphasis on relations with people.

What if the balance between these two fundamental dimensions of leadership is viewed as a dynamic one in which a manager changes style over time as a result of his or her effectiveness in previous situations? The approach seems more descriptive than a static model, which views a manager as eternally consistent in style. If we place *changes in concern for job* on the horizontal axis and *changes in concern for people* on the vertical axis, we obtain a phase plane that can trace changes in management style over time. The quadrant descriptions would be as follows: (1) increased ability to integrate, (2) exchange of job for people, (3) decreased ability to integrate, and (4) exchange of people for job. This approach suggests that management might continually vary its style based on the apparent effectiveness of the current style and in response to changing conditions in the workplace. Management style is, therefore, seen as time-dependent, evolving in response to perceived effectiveness in previous situations. Imagine the trajectories that would emerge as one tracked the results of a management training program.

Proposition 22: Management can be viewed as an evolving form of behavior that is part of the system being managed. Management style can be expected to change in response to perceived effectiveness, previous experiences, and changes in the system; the evolving style will trace a trajectory on a phase plane.

This interpretation is quite different from the traditional view of management as a static pattern of behavior. Given the increasing rate of changes in the workplace, it seems appropriate to direct our attention to a model that can capture corresponding changes in management style.

MOTIVATION

There are two approaches commonly taken when focusing on motivation of employees. One approach views motivation from an organizational perspective. Organizational attributes are said to create a climate or conditions that either encourage employee motivation or destroy it. Such conditions may have to do with appropriate degrees of delegated responsibility or authority, or they may identify characteristics of the job, such as the level of status, the suitability of the company benefit package, or supervisory and subordinate interrelationships. These attribute models are practical and useful, and from the perspective of chaos theory, there seems to be nothing fundamentally wrong with the approach as long as it acknowledges the continually changing nature of the contributing attributes and the changing value systems of employees.

A second approach to motivation takes a more individual view. Motivation is seen as the product of certain beliefs of the individual. Consider the following equation in which each of the variables is quantified as a subjective measure of belief.

Motivation (M) = Ability × Fairness × Goal Orientations

The terms can be further defined in this way. *Motivation* is the strength of one's motivation toward any particular act. *Ability* is the strength of the person's belief that if he attempts a particular task, he will be successful at accomplishing it. *Fairness* reflects the person's belief that the organization is able to recognize able performance and will distribute rewards (i.e., promotion, compensation) accordingly. Finally, *goal orientation* measures the degree of emphasis the person places on achieving some specified set of objectives. Admittedly, these concepts are difficult to measure, but the approach represents the basic idea taken by many that motivation can be viewed as the quantitative product of a collection of perceived conditions.

However, this model of motivation fails to acknowledge any form of feedback. There is no recognition in the model that motivation tomorrow may be affected by the degree of motivation exhibited today. Computing a "point" solution for motivation seems awfully naive for something so dynamic. Consider the revised equation below that provides for some recognition of changing motivation levels.

$$M_t = \text{Ability} \times \text{Fairness} \times \text{Goal Orientations} \times (1 - M_{t-1})$$

The additional term provides for the fact that motivation levels for any given person tend to adhere to some relatively constant level. For example, if the level of motivation on day $t-1$ is particularly high, a person may be less motivated on the subsequent day. The model is still quite naive, but at least it now provides for more than a point solution. Instead, it provides for a series of solutions, the behavior of which will depend greatly on the initial values for *Ability, Fairness, Goal Orientation,* and the person's initial level of motivation. Depending on the values of these variables, the solution to the equation—the motivation—will exhibit any of the nonlinear behaviors described in Chapter 1. Motivation is a nonlinear phenomenon.

Although the equation above is not intended to be a valid description of motivation, it stands as a surrogate for those many quantitative theories of individual motivation. It would be interesting to include a nonlinear term in any proposed theory and iterate the equation to view its solutions. Do motivation levels sometimes decline to zero? Do they sometimes oscillate periodically? Do the motivations of some people vary at unpredictable levels? Surely these possibilities are at least as plausible as the belief that motivation has a constant level described by a point solution.

Proposition 23: Motivation can be studied as a nonlinear phenomenon that may be highly sensitive to initial conditions and may exhibit constancy, decline, acceleration, oscillation, or erratic levels over time.

Figure 7.2
Compensation Models

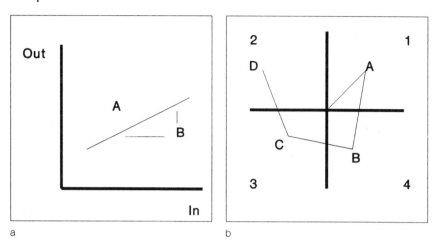

a   b

Proposition 23 provides a challenge to those interested in motivation or organizational behavior. Can a person's future motivation level toward a certain action be anticipated by determining certain current perceptions and iterating the motivation model to derive future solutions? Can we improve our current motivation models by testing their components in this way? Consider the implications of models that could estimate future tendencies toward depression, success, or criminal activity. Are there medical implications here? Although the success of such initiatives seems remote, the fact remains that there are no apparent *dynamic* models of motivation—the approach simply has not been tried.

COMPENSATION

Impartiality is a primary objective of most compensation programs. Employee review and evaluation are fairly standard means of judging employees, and form the basis for decisions on merit pay and bonuses. However, before addressing pay directly, consider some of the fundamental assumptions of compensation in the workplace.

Note the diagram in Figure 7.2a. The horizontal axis labeled "In" represents all those things one puts into a job. It includes time, education, previous experience, opportunity costs, and any other real or perceived contribution to the job. The axis labeled "Out" is used to measure all those things one receives from a job. It includes compensation, benefits, education, experience, social benefits, security, and any other such real or perceived values. Now one can see the implications of the diagonal line on the diagram. The fact that it intercepts the vertical axis above the origin suggests that one can receive something from employment in an organization even if not contributing. Perhaps this is actually possible, given the nature of some benefit packages and labor agreements. More important, the line is upward-sloping, suggesting that as one contributes more to an organization, one will receive additional benefits consistent with those contributions. The line reflects an underlying concept of compensation theory, that compensation should be commensurate with the level of contribution to the firm. Consider the implications of changing the slope of the line in Figure 7.2a. If it is more upward-sloping, it suggests a firm that readily recognizes and rewards additional efforts by employees. If it is more flat, it suggests just the opposite—that pay remains relatively constant regardless of the level of effort on the job. It may be that the line isn't always straight; it may increase in slope, allowing disproportionately greater rewards for those that make marginally greater contributions to the firm.

Regardless of the shape of the line, it traces what is perceived to be "fair compensation" for the employees in the firm. It is widely believed that employees evaluate the fairness of their compensation by comparing their pay (openly or otherwise) with that of their fellow employees. Positions A and B on Figure 7.2a describe the situation if a person believes he/she is not being rewarded at the same relative level as others in the firm. There are major implications when one is not on this "fair compensation" line. At position A one feels overpaid; the level of compensation is disproportionately high considering the amount put into the job. One can only imagine what action, if any, an employee would take under this condition. It is thought that the employee will reestablish, at a higher level, the perceived value of his/her contribution or reestablish his/her belief of other employees' compensation. In either case, the employee will no longer be off the "fair compensation" line.

The implications of position B are more interesting and provide some understanding of many employee behaviors. At B the employee feels underpaid. The solution is to seek higher compensation or to contribute less to the organization. If a pay increase is not given, the employee may decide to "self-compensate" by stealing, or contribute less by absenteeism, tardiness, extended breaks, and other such common behaviors.

Although the concept described in Figure 7.2a is strictly theoretical, it does provide an excellent basis for compensation. We can't expect compensation programs to be sensitive enough to recognize all the contributions an employee might make, but we can attempt to provide fairness by attempting to measure employees' true benefaction to the firm. Likewise, the model reminds us to include all forms of employee compensation—pay and benefits—when computing total compensation.

If we consider compensation from a nonlinear perspective, some additional issues come to light. One begins to focus on the rates of change in pay rather than simply the actual amount of pay. Surely one is pleased to learn that his or her latest pay increase is greater than that of other employees, even if total pay is still perceived as somewhat too low. A disproportionately greater pay increase carries with it concepts of recognition and achievement, which are considered powerful motivational factors. *Changes* in pay are probably very important. The nonlinear perspective also causes one to consider changes in pay relative to previous changes. Perhaps the issue is not simply "how much was the pay increase relative to others"; it probably also includes "how much was the pay increase relative to last year."

Figure 7.2b provides a phase plane diagram that captures these two dimensions of compensation. The horizontal axis measures changes in pay *relative to the change in pay during the previous period*. The vertical axis represents changes in pay *relative to the average changes in pay of other employees*.[1]

Now consider the implications of the various positions on the phase plane. A "fair compensation" line would be the X axis. To the right it would represent an accelerating increase in pay that is greater than the increase of the previous year, but proportional to the average pay increase. To the left on the X axis one has decreases relative to last year; however, these, too, are proportional to those received by other employees (i.e., the average). We can trace the trajectory in Figure 7.2b to consider other conditions. At A pay increases are greater than those of last year and greater than those received by the average of all others. At B one receives a pay increase greater than that of last year but not as great as that received by others. At C both the chronological pay change and the pay change relative to others are less. At D the chronological pay change is lower, although it is greater than that of other employees.

Consider how counseling with employees differs based on these four conditions. An employee in quadrant 1 should be congratulated for his or her success and told how much of the increase is chronological (i.e., cost of living) and how much is based on merit relative to other employees. An employee in quadrant 2 should likewise be congratulated for merit and notified that much of the increase is merit, not cost of living. An employee in quadrant 3 should be told that the pay change is down as a result of a decrease both chronologically and relative to other employees. Discussion should focus on activities needed to increase merit. Finally, an employee who finds his or her pay change in quadrant 4 should be told that although the increase is greater than during the last period, there is a need to improve relative to others, as the pay increase is not as great as that received by other employees.

Proposition 24: Changes in compensation relative to previous periods and relative to pay changes of other employees can be sensitively monitored as a trajectory on a phase plane with these dimensions. The approach suggests a way to create more consistent and effective compensation programs and provides information useful when counseling with employees.

It is doubtful whether anyone ever examines pay changes over time as sensitively as possible with a technique like that described in Figure 7.2b. What would be the trajectory of an employee's pay change over the past several years? Is there any consistency over time? Does management council with employees in as much detail as would be possible if pay changes were viewed from this perspective? The consistency of compensation would no doubt be increased if traced in this way. Although one surely cannot ignore total compensation, it is obvious that one should clearly not fail to consider the importance of change in compensation, since that is what must often be explained to employees in detail.

ORGANIZATIONAL STRESS AND MORE

Perhaps the most exciting application of chaos theory in the human resource domain has to do with descriptive studies of employees as a group. Employees—as an integral part of the organizational system—are bound by certain constraints and subject to certain forces. They exhibit patterns of behavior and patterns of opinion that have specific structural characteristics. One can view limit cycles that suggest underlying attractors that bind the patterns of behavior for employees as a group.

In this section we focus on studies of organizational stress. However, the following methodology can easily be applied to any other collection of data on employees. Here we also break with our pattern of using *time* as the basis of our limit cycle trajectories and demonstrate an approach to capturing the interaction of three variables on a single two-dimensional phase plane.

Concern over stress in the workplace has provided a rich arena for research, consulting, and training. A number of "stress diagnostic surveys" are available to aid researchers in identifying important stressors. Typical questions may ask employees to indicate the extent to which they agree with statements like "Supervisors don't trust subordinates" or "Quality standards are unrealistic." There may be sixty or more such questions on a typical survey. Clearly, considerable thought has been put into the issues that are included, and in many cases attempts have been made to validate the survey instrument. A recent application of one such survey at a major telecommunications company provided the set of stress factors listed in Table 7.2.[2]

One should note that the labels given to the factors are provided by the researchers, based on the questions that became associated with the factor.[3]

This traditional statistical analysis of survey data provides us with some

Table 7.2
Factors Associated with Organizational Stress

Factor Title	Mean Score
1. Lack of Supervisor Trust and Respect	9.979
2. Too much work / Too little time	8.051
3. Politics	10.119
4. Inability to do Job	5.724
5. Help Disincentives (misdirected credit)	10.017
6. Job Boredom	7.780
7. Job Performance-Reward Conflict	10.186
8. Non-Challenging Work	8.966
9. Unreasonable Work Assignments	8.695
10. Job Communication	10.241
11. Supervisor Inaction/Action	10.000
12. Leadership Issues (Confusion)	7.915
13. Time Pressure	7.525
14. Organizational Issues (Restrictive Policies)	9.362
15. Job Non-Performance (No Control over Job)	10.966

basic information regarding stressors important to this group of employees. First, the factor analysis identifies which questions are most closely associated with which others. It provides a means for grouping the questions together according to those that vary, independent of all other questions. The fact that fifteen significant factors could be extracted is a credit to this particular survey instrument.[4]

We also know which factors are most important by examining the mean scores for each factor. In this case factors 3, 5, 7, 10, 11, and 15 all have means of 10 or higher, suggesting that they are the most important stressors to this group of employees. Although this is important information to know, it still provides only a static view of stress within the organization. It provides a linear perspective of what we know must be a nonlinear phenomenon. Surely stress levels vary over time; they probably vary in response to a wide range of changing conditions within the organization. We need a dynamic picture that can begin to reveal the complex patterns of the stress phenomenon—not point measures, which we know are inadequate.

If we had survey data from previous years, we could take an approach similar to that used in the other applications that have been described. In this case, as in many similar cases, we do not have chronological data; we have only one set of measurements from only one slice in time. We can, however, still capture the dynamics of the stress relationships by creating a trajectory that varies with any other dimension other than time.

Proposition 25: Limit cycles typically report the evolving dynamic response of a system over time. However, they are not limited to using time as their third dimension; any other variable may be substituted to provide a descriptive image of a system's response to the chosen variable.

Consider the implications of Proposition 25. A combination of any three variables will trace a trajectory on a phase plane, and the resulting trajectory will reflect the state of that system for any combination of values. The traditional statistical approach would be to regress any two of the variables against the third; further, the assumptions of regression analysis call for each of the independent variables to be autonomous (i.e., not correlated with each other). This approach recognizes the interdependent nature of all variables in the system. The values any one variable assumes are entirely dependent on the values of the two (or more) other variables in the system. Collectively, the state of the system is described by the combination of variables, and that description of the system takes on a structural shape traced by the limit cycle. Implied by the limit cycle is an underlying attractor that binds the system to its pattern of behavior. Chaos theory offers us a much richer picture of organizational dynamics than that provided by conventional statistics—even the more advanced statistics of multiple regression, analysis of variance, or factor analysis. And it provides its new view with rather unsophisticated analysis; one can use simple frequency counts and other forms of raw data to generate the intricate trajectories on a phase plane.

For our study of organizational stress we are interested in how these various stressors relate to one another. Factor analysis separates the various questions into groups based on the combined variance of each factor. Typically, we interpret the factor analysis result as a set of autonomous concepts. But intuitively, one would suspect that there are still some underlying patterns. For example, how can boredom (factor 6) not be related in some way to time pressure (factor 13). There must be other underlying patterns among the supposedly independent concepts. What, if any, patterns would emerge if we look at the rates of change for these factors?

Consider factors 12, 13, and 14, which are leadership issues, time pressure, and organizational issues, respectively. Although they are not the most

Figure 7.3
Limit Cycles of Stress Determinants

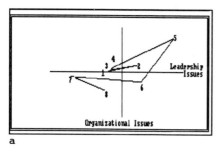 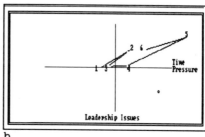

a   b

important factors identified in the study, they seem to capture rather global concepts. How would these stressors respond interactively to changes in other conditions? For example, how would the importance of leadership issues and time pressure change in response to increasing work load (factor 2)? We can investigate patterns of interaction between these supposedly independent concepts by tracing the trajectory of factor 2, titled "Too Much Work / Too Little Time." Put simply, we can use factor 2 as a scale of work load and see whether there is any structural pattern that describes how the other two factors respond to increases in work load.

Figure 7.3 provides phase plane diagrams that relate these variables. The trajectory on each phase plane traces increasing values of factor 2, describing "Too Much Work / Too Little Time." The axis in Figure 7.3a combines factor 12 (leadership issues) with factor 13 (organizational issues). Any point on the phase plane in Figure 7.3a describes the state of the system, combining these three variables. The numbers on the plane trace the direction of the trajectory as perceived work load increases. Note that as work load increases from its lowest level, there is little change in the importance of either leadership or organizational issues. Organizational issues are particularly unaffected, as demonstrated by the fact that the trajectory moves only horizontally close to the center of the phase plane. As work load continues to increase, there is a major increase in the importance of both of these factors, as demonstrated by the trajectory's movement to position 5 in Figure 7.3a. At still higher levels of work load leadership issues continue to increase in importance while organizational issues decline in importance (as noted by position 6). Thereafter, both issues apparently become less important. It is unknown what other issue, if any, emerges to become important at these high levels of work load (such a factor would enter quadrant 1 later in its trajectory).

Similarly, Figure 7.3b combines factor 12 (leadership issues) with factor 13 (time pressure); it also traces the relationship between these two variables in response to increases in perceived work load.[5] Again we see some pattern to the behavior of these factors. As work load increases, survey respondents cited increased time pressure as a stressor. At some threshold level, however, the importance of leadership issues emerged, and combined with increases in the importance of time pressure, the trajectory ventured deep into quadrant 1 at position 5. Both factors continued to increase in importance at position 6, although the rate of increase for each was somewhat less.

At higher levels of work load each of the trajectories in Figure 7.3 becomes much more disordered. The patterns seen here are associated only with mild increases in work load from a very low level. At higher levels the relationships are far less stable, far more chaotic.

This application suggests that phase plane trajectories can be generated for any system, using one or more measures of that system, even if chronological data are not available. In this case subjective data was used as the basis of the analysis. Consider the possible implications of the approach. Similar phase planes could be generated for any combination of the stress factors identified in Table 7.2. In this case the results suggest that stress is a concept that has certain structural characteristics that are determined by organizational issues, leadership issues, and various other factors. That has significant implications on its own. However, for any study the approach offers a new way to visualize the interaction of data describing a system. Just as certain thresholds became apparent in this stress study, one will no doubt find complex relationships and thresholds in relationships between most any variables describing a system. Systems are stable only within certain parameters; when one of those parameters varies too much, one can expect the system to become unstable. For this reason a nonlinear analysis is an appropriate extension of any traditional statistical study.

OTHER HUMAN RESOURCE APPLICATIONS

The possible applications of chaos theory to human resource issues are limitless. Here we have examined possibilities in organizational decision-making, management styles, motivation, compensation, and stress in the workplace. One can easily see the applications in other common human resource activities. Consider employee turnover activities, for example. The employee turnover ratio (typically computed as number of terminations divided by average employment level) is a common measure of transitions in the employment group, and it could easily be converted to a phase plane diagram. The horizontal axis can represent changes in the average employment level and the vertical axis can represent the changes in the number of terminations. Proportional turnover rates would appear as movement on the 45-degree axis. Any movement into quadrant 2 would suggest excessive turnover (while average employment levels decrease); a movement into quadrant 4 would suggest a substantial reduction in the turnover rate resulting from increases in the average employment level while the number of terminations decline. Because turnover rate is a ratio, just as any of the financial ratios discussed in Chapter 4, it has the same misleading disadvantages; its true behavior can be better understood on the phase plane. Imagine the insight available by viewing a trajectory of turnover rates over several years.

In a similar approach one could examine the balance of voluntary to involuntary terminations. Often this is an important factor in management training programs. A phase plane of these two variables would quickly illustrate the pattern of behavior for this costly activity. Likewise, the analysis could be extended to examine patterns of absenteeism.

Consider the implications here for health care costs. What are the changes in any of the many categories of treatment? What patterns of association exist between conditions on the job and various types of treatment—patterns that are not evident at a statistical level, but are clearly evident as recent changes in the overall medical cost figures?

What of job satisfaction? What structural relationships exist between perceived level of satisfaction and job characteristics?

Consider applying the technique for assessing training and development activities. It would be useful for identifying the effect of training programs, using any preferred measures of job performance.

Although these approaches may appear very "applied," they are, instead, deeply rooted in the foundation of nonlinearity. A nonlinear view is simply a recognition that systems evolve incrementally, that they tend to adhere to an underlying attractor that controls their behavior. Sometimes nonlinear systems are highly sensitive to changes; hence changes in a system are important to monitor. Biological activity fits these descriptions precisely; it is inherently nonlinear. If nonlinear approaches seem particularly applied here, it is only because they are particularly at home in studies of human behavior.

NOTES

1. Specifically, the horizontal axis and the vertical axis in Figure 7.2b measure change in pay relative to change in pay of the previous period (X) and relative to the change in average pay (Y) as follows:

$$X = (Pay_t - Pay_{t-1}) - (Pay_{t-1} - Pay_{t-2})$$
$$Y = (Pay_t - Pay_{t-1}) - (Average\ Pay_{t-1} - Average\ Pay_{t-2}),$$

where t, $t-1$, and $t-2$ reference the pay period, and Average Pay is average pay for all employees.

2. The specific questionnaire used had sixty questions and a sample of 100 employees was taken. For this study the sample included only male employees aged thirty-five to fifty. The data set was factor-analyzed, and the fifteen factors listed

in Table 7.2 were identified. The mean value represents the average rating given to the three questions that best represented each factor. The mean value can be viewed as the importance placed on that factor as a stressor.

3. This discussion is based on research conducted by Jack Davis. It was reported in a conference paper titled "Predicting and Preventing Organizational Stress," which was presented at the International Association of Business Forecasting at Baltimore, 1990.

4. The questionnaire used was a version of the Stress Diagnostic Survey by Ivancevich and Matteson, 1980.

5. The specific procedure for constructing these phase planes may not be readily apparent from the general discussion. The procedure is as follows.

Cross tabulations of factors 12, 13, and 14 *by factor 2* were generated from the original data set to obtain the data for each variable. In these cross tabulations the columns represented increasing values of factor 2 (work load) and the rows represented increasing values of one of the other factors.

A measure of the importance at each level of factor 2 (i.e., in each column) was obtained by totaling the products of the frequency counts and their corresponding values on each row. The variable being plotted represents a "total score" that includes both the number of people who responded and the degree of importance each placed on the particular factor at each level of factor 2.

The "total scores" derived in this way from two factors (i.e., leadership issues and organizational issues) provided the raw data used to develop the phase plane trajectory, according to the procedure described in Chapter 2.

PART III

NONLINEAR DECISION-MAKING

8

Forecasting and Visioning

What can chaos theory tell us about the future? The immediate response of many when hearing chaos theory described is to assume that it is a tool for forecasting. Accordingly, chaos theory is a hot topic in journals on forecasting and at conferences of forecasters. However, chaos theory doesn't simply offer a new technique or procedure for forecasting; its contribution is more profound than that. It forces us to reconsider the very act of forecasting, and it suggests that there are merits in a notion that we can call *visioning*. In this chapter we examine the precepts of forecasting and consider the merits of various common forecasting techniques. We then describe visioning as a specific procedure with important implications for planning within an organization.

What, precisely, is a forecast? We all know it as a projection—an estimate of sales, a quantity somewhere beyond the present. It may be a single point, or more likely it is a range of expected future performance. A sales forecast is one of the essential ingredients of profitability. When compared with on-hand inventory information, it drives production and purchasing functions. Through production it contributes to establishing employment levels and shipping schedules. The forecast provides us the time to configure our organization for the coming period; it anticipates the future so we can manage through that future.

WHAT IS A FORECAST?

But what, precisely, is a forecast? What is the underlying rationale that says that this number or that will be the future?

Consider the job of a meteorologist. Each day he studies the weather— its temperature, its wind speed and direction, its pressure and humidity. He studies the advancing fronts and cloud formations, and from this information, from this pattern of the past and the present, he forecasts the future. It doesn't matter that the forecast is for continued drought or impending disastrous winds; these things do not affect the forecast. He reports what he believes will be, knowing that no one can influence what actually happens.

The meteorologist's forecast is a *prediction*. Is this what we do in business? Do we simply forecast the future from the patterns of the past with no regard for future action? Clearly not. Sometimes management announces promotional plans or plant closings. Sometimes they add sales representatives and sometimes they close regional offices. Managers have a free will that allows them to decide whether or not to take action and what kind of action to take. They help decide the future. We are not like the meteorologist, who has no one who can influence the future of the weather.

Consider an athlete who is committed to running a mile in six minutes. Each day she takes a morning jog. She adjusts her diet to build strength and lose weight. She joins a health club near work so she has a place to exercise during lunch each day. She talks about running with others who run. She buys new running shoes. She challenges herself by entering local charity events in which she runs with hundreds of others. Eventually—and perhaps quite soon—she reaches and surpasses her goal of running the mile in six minutes. If you knew of her commitment, how would you forecast her performance? Is it determined in any way by her previous performance? Would extrapolating the past into the future give you an accurate forecast of that future? No. In her case the future is defined by her and her willingness to make all the changes necessary to attain a goal. She had a *vision* of how she wanted the future to be; your best forecast would be her vision. The runner's forecast is a goal, a vision.

To the extent that management envisions the future and is willing to make the changes to create that vision, our forecast is like a forecast for the runner. What management wants may be all that matters; management may be willing to do everything necessary to attain an envisioned level of performance.

To the extent that management fails to vision the future, fails in the will to make changes to create that future, or fails to understand how to create that future, we are like the meteorologist. The performance of our firm will emerge from the patterns of the past if we fail to exercise the free will to make it different.

As we have demonstrated, organizations have a variety of structural characteristics that help define their patterns of performance. These structural characteristics include their methods of purchasing, producing, marketing, and managing; their manner of financing; and the nature of their contracts with suppliers and customers. These characteristics relate to how the organizations are managed, where they operate, and when they promote. A firm's structural characteristics define the firm. It may be rigid or adaptive. It may be resilient to shortages of raw material, or it may be brittle to any interruption in supply. It may have an established means of reducing excess inventory, or excess inventory may cause severe cash flow and production problems. The performance of the firm is a reflection of these structural characteristics.

Management determines the structural characteristics of the firm. Managers make the decisions that cause a firm to be adaptive, responsive, resilient, or rigid. When these structural characteristics interact with patterns in the environment, a specific level of performance emerges. Actual performance emerges naturally from the interaction of the firm and its environment.

So, what is a forecast? Is it only a prediction like that of the meteorologist? Is it a goal like that of a runner? Is it a combination of both? Is it neither? In the presence of free will, how can one forecast the future when it hasn't occurred? How can one anticipate the future if we have the ability to change the future? These are some of the fundamental questions that chaos theory forces us to ask.

APPROACHES TO FORECASTING

Forget, for a while, everything you know about forecasting. Let's take a fresh look at the need for a forecast and the process of forecasting. Let's begin with a definition: Forecasting is the process of predicting, projecting, or calculating an estimate of conditions in the future, as in "The meteorologist *forecasts* the weather." This definition presents forecasting as a process that extends historical or current information into a projection of the future. Forecasting, by this definition, is a practical activity when one has no control over a system. For example, it is what we do if we need an estimate of national health care costs for automobile-related injuries or an approximation of the trade volume between two countries five years from now. In these cases we have little control of the forces at work, so we extend the past into the future and cite some estimate of the future value. We cannot expect to change conditions substantially enough to influence the behavior of the process appreciably. At the same time, we know of no way to accurately compute the future values for either of these systems because they are so complex.

A lack of control over a system does not imply that we must *forecast*. When a system is simple enough, we can compute its future. We no longer forecast lunar eclipses. We understand the dynamics of this solar system well enough to compute precisely when they will occur. Even though the onset of the eclipse varies according to the longitude and latitude of the observer, we know how to take these factors into account. We understand the behavior of the system. Interestingly, we can compute the time of an eclipse, but we must forecast our ability to see it because of the nature of Earth's weather system (remember Lorenz). Both systems, the solar system and Earth's weather system, are dynamic: one is understandable, low-order chaos and the other has high-order chaotic behavior. One is considered reliable and deterministic; the other must be "forecasted."[1] We no longer need any historical data to determine the time of the next eclipse; we can compute the next event using only the current relative position of the moon and our equations of celestial dynamics. For the weather we must continuously study the past to estimate only a short distance into the future.

In many cases, however, the future is more than a simple extrapolation of the past. If humans are involved, there is the force of free will that changes the present, dramatically or subtly, to change the trajectory into the future.[2] It seems that there is more than one possible future but that we select only one with every action or inaction. If this is true, then forecasting, as defined above, may have gained more attention than it deserves in business. Sifting and sorting historical data ever more quickly and accurately will tell us little more about the future. There is no new technique that can be applied to historical data to significantly improve its ability to represent the future. One cannot simply *forecast* the future because we have not chosen it yet.

Proposition 26: Forecasting, the process of using historical data exclusively to make estimates of the future, fails to acknowledge the presence of free will. Such approaches are naive for any system in which humans participate.

Consider the approaches we take to forecasting. When we use regression analysis, time series analysis, moving averages, or exponential smoothing, we are simply studying the past and then making the assumption that the patterns of the past will continue into the future. When we make that assumption, we discard any hope of being right.

Although one can categorically attack any statistical procedure that uses historical data exclusively to estimate the future, such approaches are the only practical ones in cases where many approximations about the future must be made. If we sell 650,000 items and we need production estimates by next week, our only hope is to use some statistical procedure that will forecast demand by extending the patterns of the past into the future to provide the needed information. That is pure forecasting—it is a *statistical projection*.

What we often do in business is first *forecast* and then *estimate*. We develop a statistical projection based on historical data and then we adjust that projected value, using additional information. We *estimate* a future value. This is a very different thing from a forecast (as defined above), although it often is referred to as a forecast (perhaps another term should be coined). It is not simply a statistical projection, and it is not simply an estimate with no statistical basis. It is a blend of the two approaches. But what is the underlying rationale for such a method? Are we saying that the future will be a combination of patterns from the past and events that may occur (will occur) in the future? What does the past have to do with it? Further, why do we feel that we cannot control future events adequately enough to select, with precision, the future that we want? We are bound to the idea that the past is important and the future is unpredictable, but those ideas simply may not be true. The past was not important; in fact, it was misleading for the runner described earlier.[3] And the future is not unpredictable with regard to the next lunar eclipse. If a blend of statistical projection and estimation is not consistent with the realities of the systems we manage, what approach should we take?

VISIONING

Visioning is synonymous with discernment, foresight, insight, imagination, and dreaming. It is the process of defining the future. The concept flows from an understanding that the state of a system in the past, at the present, and in the future is deterministically defined by its initial condition and the forces that act on it.

Consider this. The final position of a cue ball is defined by its initial position before the opening break and all the forces that act on it during the game of pool. To forecast the cue ball's final position is unthinkable. One would have to consider not only the force of the opening break, but also the force and direction of every stroke of the game. One would have to estimate with absolute precision the deflection of every bumper and the momentum of every collision on the table. One would even have to project the order in which each ball would be played. One simply cannot forecast the final resting place of the cue ball.

But one can vision it. You simply would have to decide where you want it to be at the end of the game—"corner pocket, that end"—and you could put it there. Or if you don't have control of the ball at the end of the game, your partner could put it there. If your competitor has control of the ball, you may be able to show how it is to his or her advantage to put it there. The ability to know the future greatly increases when we vision it.

Proposition 27: Rather than trying to estimate all the forces that act on a system in order to forecast the future behavior of that system, we can vision the future and then act on the forces to create the visioned condition.

Examine the image in Figure 8.1. It demonstrates a visioning feature that is built into the Chaos System Software used to create the images in this book.[4] It provides a full-screen view of the phase plane and the statis-

Figure 8.1
Visioning with the Chaos System Software

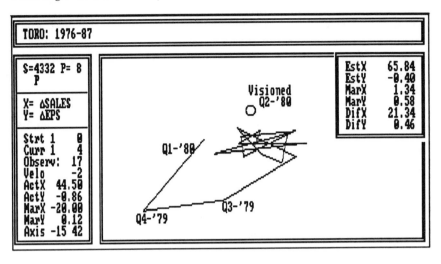

tics associated with The Toro Company's situation as of quarter 1, 1980. Recall that Toro was described earlier as having been shocked into a chaotic state by decreased snowfalls, which devastated their snowthrower sales in late 1979. Toro provides a suitable example here because it is, at this stage, in a highly chaotic state. No traditional forecasting technique that relied on data before 1979 could be applied to forecast performance after 1979. Further, forecasting would be even more difficult during 1980 and 1981, which are years at the height of transition for the company.

Recall that in this image the horizontal axis represents changes in sales and the vertical axis represents quarterly changes in profits expressed as earnings per share. Also remember that this pattern represents a behavior in the rates of change for sales and profits. Let's examine some of the items reported on the screen. The last four quadrant positions of the trajectory, the trajectory *sequence,* are reported on the upper left as S = 4332. Note that the current position of the trajectory is in quadrant 2 (the upper left quadrant) and that the previous three quadrant positions of the trajectory were 4, 3, and 3. The current period of the limit cycle is reported as P = 8, indicating that these latest four quadrant positions do not correspond with any Period 1–, Period 2–, or Period 4–type behavior. Period 8, therefore, is assigned to any trajectory considered to be in high-order chaos.

Additional information about the current position of the trajectory is reported in the column on the left. The variables displayed as ActX = 44.5 and ActY = −.86 report the actual quarterly sales ($44.5 million) and earnings per share (a loss of $.86 per share) for quarter 1, 1980, which is the latest position of the trajectory. The variables displayed as MarX =

−20.00 and MarY = .12 report the marginal values—the changes—from the previous quarter. Note that their position is plotted relative to the center of the phase plane. Here they indicate that sales have dropped by $20 million (note that the trajectory at Q1-'80 is left of the center of the phase plane). The marginal value of earnings (Y) is .12, which places the trajectory above the center of the phase plane. (Recall that when the value of X is negative and the value of Y is positive, the trajectory must be in quadrant 2.)

As the trajectory traces its way about the phase plane, these values change to reflect its current position. The entire phase plane is mapped, therefore, with interactive positions, any of which could be visited by the trajectory. One might think of the trajectory as a description of *what has been* and all the positions on the phase plane as *what could be*.

The software allows one to visit any of these potential future realities. It allows one to drive a circular *visioning curser* about on the screen. In Figure 8.1 the visioning curser is positioned above the center of the phase plane and is labeled "Visioned Q2-'80." Associated with the curser are the variables reported in the box on the upper right. There the coordinates of the curser are reported. Its current position corresponds with an "estimated" sales volume (EstX) of $65.84 million and an "estimated" earnings per share value (EstY) of −.40. The marginal values shown in the box (MarX = 1.34 and MarY = .58) reflect the change required to attain the visioned position relative to the average rate of change for the system.[5]

The last two variables, DifX = 21.35 and DifY = .46, have particular importance. They report the *difference* between the current position of the trajectory and the center of the visioning curser. Interpreting them is quite simple; to attain the position designated by the visioning curser, sales must increase by $21.35 million and earnings per share must increase by $.46.

How did I choose the position identified by the visioning curser? I pressed the right and left arrow keys and watched as an almost infinite number of other possible sales volumes went by. I hardly glanced at *EstX* as it spun through the other possible future realities with unreadable rapidity. Then I pressed the up arrow key and moved to a vertical position without regard for the changing values of *EstY*. I chose a position that simply looked right—it looked appropriate given the pattern on the screen. It looked consistent and reasonable, in keeping with the pattern of things. My proposed Q2-'80 seemed to be a position from which I could begin to exert control over the renegade trajectory; I hoped to call it in by offering a position that was compatible with both its past and my desire. I *visioned* it.

I *visioned* it. Is that O.K.? Can we not simply decide what is wanted and then control the forces to get there? Are we not able to create any reality if we make the proper incremental changes that lead to that reality?

It seems important that the proposed Q2-'80 position was chosen without regard to the numbers. It is not a quantitative goal or an objective; it is a future condition that seems consistent with the current state of the system and the apparent forces that control the behavior of the system. It is a sort of "management by pattern recognition"; a visual, perceptual way of decision-making.

The complexity of forces that influence the trajectory of Toro at this stage are even more complex than those in a pool game. But, like the pool game, we don't need to forecast those forces. We can decide what we want and then change the system in an incremental or spontaneous way to ensure its arrival there.

This is not forecasting. It is not projecting and estimating. It is the process of choosing and creating a future. It is a technique of planning that emerges from an understanding that all that is important is the current state of the system and the way in which it evolves incrementally. Control over the current state, combined with control over the system's evolution, allows us to take it anywhere.

Don't degrade this concept as simply another form of goal-setting. This is a nonquantitative approach (although it has specific quantitative measures) based on a new understanding of dynamic systems. The limit cycles provided by chaos theory show us patterns of behavior we have not seen before—patterns in the rates of change—and those new patterns provide enough information to permit us to visualize their behavior.

If we knew the underlying equations that describe the observed system, as we do with the solar system, we could simply compute the future behavior for the system. (In Chapter 1 we demonstrated how complex patterns of behavior can be generated by incrementing a simple nonlinear equation.) However, there seems to be no *precise* way of determining the generating equation. Further, intervention with free will allows us to change the behavior of the system; therefore, visioning is more important to our future than any method that would reveal an underlying equation.

Visioning also is a way to test the appropriateness of traditional forecasts. We can gauge whether they are consistent with apparent patterns of system behavior.[6] Perhaps the reason forecasts are wrong is because they target levels that are simply inconsistent with the forces that control changes in the system. Forecasts based on aggregate values, such as those using regression analysis, fail to acknowledge patterns in the rate of changes and are, therefore, likely to be in error.

Visioning provides a way to relate short-term and long-term decisions. One can see how each position leads incrementally into the future. In our Toro company example we selected sales of $65.84 million and losses of $.40 per share as an appropriate level of performance for the next quarter. That decision seems far more defendable because of the way we made the decision; we selected that position because it was consistent with both the past and the future we intended to create.

Figure 8.2
Linear versus Nonlinear Forecasting

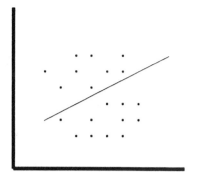

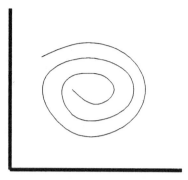

a. Linear   b. Nonlinear

HIDDEN STRUCTURES

Consider the images in Figure 8.2, which provide examples of two so-lutions for the same set of data. Imagine that the independent variable is housing starts and the dependent variable is furniture sales. Figure 8.2a provides a representative linear solution. An attempt to fit a regression line to the data is quite unsuccessful, leading to the conclusion that there is only a limited, perhaps "insignificant" association between housing starts and furniture sales. Even if we improved the fit of our regression model by introducing some polynomial functions, we would not improve it substan-tially. We may be led to include other variables, making it a multiple regression model, in an attempt to explain the random-appearing data set.

Figure 8.2b provides the nonlinear fit to the same data set, which reveals a profoundly consistent pattern of development in the data. In this ideal-ized example every data point is struck by the trajectory as it spirals (either inwardly or outwardly), bound to some underlying attractor. How many such patterns have we overlooked? How many forecasts have been built on linear models fitted to nonlinear relations?

Although the data and relationships depicted in Figure 8.2 are hypo-thetical, it is quite likely that there are many undiscovered intricate pat-terns of interaction in the data we collect. The systematic processes of a system can combine in ways that conventional statistics cannot discover. Let's take some specific data to demonstrate the point.

Imagine you are director of the McDonald Observatory, which, as part of its responsibility, collects and records data on pulsars, those rapidly spinning starlike objects that are light years from us at the edge of our universe. Pulsars are of particular interest to astronomers because they emit almost clocklike pulses of energy that can be monitored here on Earth.

Table 8.1
Values of X and Y

Frequency (X) (cycles per second)

16	37	64	96	134	176	220	264	306	344	377	405
428	446	459	469	478	488	500	516	536	556	576	602
628	654	684	714	746	774	804	834	866			

Luminosity (Y) (candlepower x 1000)

11	19	25	33	45	61	83	112	146	185	227	270
312	352	388	418	443	463	478	489	509	537	561	585
613	633	653	677	701	725	749	769	789			

Note: Observations are listed by rows

You have been asked to train the observatory's telescope onto one particular object that has demonstrated increasing luminosity and increasing frequency of pulsations over the past few days. The first of that data was collected last night, and a sample of it is provided in Table 8.1. Look over the data closely. What patterns do you see?

Along with the data is a note from one of the astronomers with the following statistics:

	Frequency (X)	Luminosity (Y)
Arithmetic means	460.515	395.788
Median	478.000	443.000
Maximum	866.000	789.000
Minimum	16.000	11.000
Range	850.000	778.000
Standard Deviation	235.819	253.473
Variance	55610.676	64248.477

It is apparent that both the luminosity and the frequency are increasing, so you generate a graphic plot of these two measures to see what patterns there might exist in the data. (See Figure 8.3.)

Seeing that the two variables are increasing at similar rates, you suspect that there must be some association between them. To measure the degree of association, you compute a correlation coefficient and find it to be +.983. The corresponding coefficient of determination is .966, meaning that fully 96.6 percent of the variation in luminosity can be explained by the increasing frequency of emission from the object. You suspect that there is some serial correlation, so you compute the correlation between the first set of differences of X and of Y but find it to be insignificant at only .059.

Figure 8.3
Graphic Plot of Observed Luminosity and Frequency

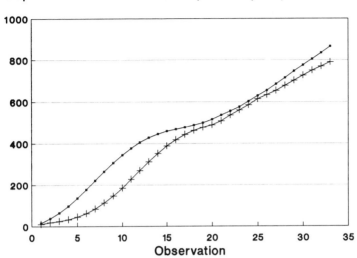

You call another associate to discuss the peculiar findings, and she joins you to continue the analysis.

Together you compute various statistics to test the significance of the relationship between the two variables. You find an F-ratio of 887.795 (significant at the .01 level) and a t-score for the X variable of 29.796 (also significant at the .01 level). You determine the equation that relates the two variables. Estimates of Y can be determined by the following equation:

$$Y = -90.780 + 1.057(X)$$

One can use this equation to predict luminosity given any measure of frequency.

You and your associate spend the rest of the afternoon speculating about the meaning of these observations. Perhaps the pulsar is destined to explode. Can we use the equation above to forecast when its centrifugal force will cause it to fly apart? Maybe the related increase in the two measures is due to some other underlying force. Perhaps there are chemical processes involved that are causing the radius of the object to decrease, thereby accelerating the frequency of rotation. You go home that night pondering the prospects. Continued observations that night reveal that the pattern has changed, and thereafter, as apparently random measures are received, you and your colleges lose interest in the object and go on to other, more interesting things.

Additional statistical studies would have provided little additional infor-

Figure 8.4
The Nonlinear Analysis of Luminosity and Frequency

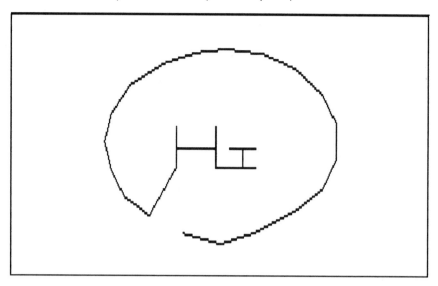

mation about the observed phenomenon. Additional precision in measurement would not have helped. Collecting data over a longer period to obtain a larger sample size would not have helped. Not even confirming the observations with another observatory would have helped to explain the phenomenon. Given the data collected and the methods of analysis used, we are left with a lack of understanding, and we can only theorize as to the forces that have caused the observed phenomenon.

Figure 8.4 provides a nonlinear perspective of the same phenomenon. Specifically, it shows the trajectory of the data in Table 8.1. It shows the two variables to be related in a very systematic way, one with considerable implications. One has to wonder what similar images were imbedded in the continued stream of "random numbers" that were subsequently emitted after we turned our attention elsewhere.

The phase plane in Figure 8.4 has changes in the frequency variable (X) on the horizontal axis and changes in the luminosity variable (Y) on the vertical axis. The trajectory was plotted in precisely the same way as those presented before; however, in this case there has been an obvious effort to control the trajectory to provide us with an *extraterrestrial* greeting.

This somewhat facetious example is meant to stress that there can be structural relationships in the behavior of data that are simply not captured by traditional statistical approaches. Knowing the structure of the interactions in data can greatly improve our understanding of the system and improves our ability to forecast. In this example traditional approaches would lead us to conclude that both variables would continue to increase with a high degree of association; nonlinear analysis leads us to look for another word.

This example should force us to question the merit of conventional statistics. How can such universally accepted computations be so utterly unsuccessful at explaining the data? What good are any of the conventional statistics that were provided? They mean nothing compared with the image in Figure 8.4. Conventional statistical approaches are based on a paradigm; they are the results of methods that were born over Two hundred years ago, matured during wartime, and elevated to a level of revered authority by the sophisticated machinations of modern computers. If the paradigm is wrong—that paradigm that is two hundred years old—or if it is inappropriate for the system being studied, then all the statistics become meaningless.

Surely we have learned something about system behavior since conventional statistical methods were developed; let's give ourselves credit for that. And classic statistical approaches were proposed at a time when it was believed that we should simplify observed behavior to understand it. Only a few people originally conceived that we should compute the mean, mode, and variance; the rest of us have simply followed the piper who taught our college statistics classes. With our new understanding that systems evolve incrementally, why should we not trace their evolution as a trajectory over time? With our number-crunching prowess today, why not consider every observation?

An improvement in classic statistics is analogous to a refinement in the terracentric theory of the universe; it is a refinement, but it contributes nothing to our understanding of the truth. Just as we have acknowledged that Earth is not the center of the universe, we must now acknowledge that we live in a nonlinear world. We should throw away our old models and find new, nonlinear ones.

COMMON DATA BEHAVIORS

There are three common types of behavior found in data that are of particular interest for forecasters. Often the suitability of a forecasting technique is judged by its ability to detect these types of behavior and adjust to accommodate them. Specifically, forecasters are interested in ramps, steps, and spikes. The concepts relate to changes in the values of a single variable. A *ramp* is a more or less steady increase in the value of a variable. For example, a ramp in annual sales data is a steady increase in sales over some period.

A *step* is a spontaneous increase in the value of a variable to another plateau; the data then remain fairly constant at that new level. The addi-

Figure 8.5
The Trajectory of Ramps, Steps, and Spikes

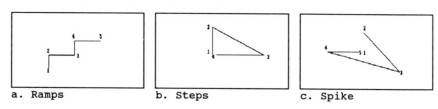

a. Ramps   b. Steps   c. Spike

tion of a single major customer account will cause a step in the sales volume of a small supplier.

A *spike* is a spontaneous increase that is not sustained. The variable returns to its previous level after the spike. For example, a sizable short-term sales contract will cause a spike in the supplier's sales volume.

It is interesting to view these phenomena as phase plane trajectories. To generate the images we'll use the technique presented earlier for displaying the behavior of single variables. Specifically, we will plot changes in the variable at time *t* on the vertical axis and changes in the variable at time *t-1* on the horizontal axis. Consider for a moment how these trajectories will appear and then examine the trajectories in Figure 8.5.

A ramp trajectory is displayed in Figure 8.5a (note that it *looks* like a set of steps). The trajectory maintains a constant position at 1 until it begins to ramp. When any increase in the variable appears, the trajectory moves to position 2. Immediately after visiting position 2 the trajectory will move to position 3, reflecting the subsequent increase in value of the horizontal variable (*t-1*). During the next observation the trajectory will move to position 4 as the vertical variable (*t*) continues to increase. It subsequently moves to position 5 as *t-1* comes in. A ramp, therefore, appears as a distinctive pattern of steplike increases. In fact, that is a fair reflection of what a ramp is; it is a series of sequential steps that raise the value of the aggregate variable to a higher level.

A step, however, presents a different pattern because it is not continuous. Figure 8.5b provides the trajectory of a step, which, like a ramp, begins by moving upward from position 1 to position 2. During the next observation the trajectory moves out to a position to the right on the horizontal axis. Consider why this is true. It is because the vertical measure (*t*) is now constant when the horizontal measure (*t-1*) increases; recall that a step goes up and *stays* up. After both measures have increased, they then remain constant; this constancy is reflected by the trajectory's move back to the origin at position 4.

What must be the behavior of a spike trajectory? Figure 8.5c provides the answer. A spike initially copies a ramp and step as it moves upward from position 1 to position 2, reflecting an increase in the variable. During the subsequent observation, however, both variables change. The vertical variable (*t*) changes downward, pushing the trajectory below the origin, and the horizontal variable (*t-1*) increases, pushing the trajectory to the right. The result is a movement into quadrant 4 at position 3. Subsequent to that *t* remains constant while *t-1* decreases, resulting in a position left of the origin on the horizontal axis. Finally, after both variables have reflected the spike, the trajectory stabilizes back at the origin (position 5).

These patterns provide signatures of common phenomenon in data. Their surprising and characteristic shapes suggest that many other patterns of behavior may become recognizable when viewed as changes on a phase plane. They provide "fingerprints" of activity in the data that probably go unrecognized by traditional approaches.

OTHER IMPLICATIONS FOR FORECASTERS

Although chaos theory doesn't threaten to undermine most existing statistical techniques, it does provide new insight into the challenge of forecasting future performance. At a minimum, forecasters need a sufficient understanding of this new science to reexamine their methods and ensure that their approaches are not inconsistent with nonlinear approaches. Below are some axioms of chaos theory and a discussion of implications for forecasters.

Axiom 1: The future is completely determined by the evolving state of the system; there is no natural randomness.

Iteration of relatively simple equations can generate sequences of data that appear random. More complex systems of equations can generate performance patterns that are profoundly complex, albeit entirely deterministic. Experiments with random processes reveal that systematic patterns of performance often underlie the apparent randomness. Forecasters should question the use of statistical processes that discard error as randomness. If there is no natural randomness, shouldn't our analytic techniques use all available data? Given our advanced ability to manipulate data, why should we continue to use techniques that were designed to simplify data by developing approximations.?

Axiom 2: The future performance of a system emerges incrementally from its current state; therefore, more accurate and complete information about the present is more important than information about the past.

Chaos theory illustrates that if you understand a system with precision and you know the current state of the system, you can forecast the future with accuracy. We are limited by not being able to understand business systems with precision, and hence even a knowledge of chaos theory may not significantly change our ability to forecast the future (using the original definition of the word *forecast*). Even so, the theory may suggest that we put more emphasis on current measurement and recent observations rather than try to determine future performance from a long history of observations.

Axiom 3: Although the future is determined by the system, it is not predetermined; changes to the structural characteristics can permit future performance at any level.

A system that is deterministic is not predetermined. The action of a lever or other mechanical device may be deterministic, but how it performs and when it performs are controlled by the free will of the person who operates it. We can make structural changes to a system and thereby change the performance characteristic of the system. We can, therefore, achieve any level of performance, given sufficient amount of structural change.

Axiom 4: The limit cycle describes the performance of the system as a balance between forces and constraints within the system.

Limit cycles on phase planes offer a new approach to viewing the performance pattern of a system without discarding any data. Even complex behaviors often reveal some constraint or periodicity. Changing the behavior of a system to attain new levels of performance should be equally as possible by removing constraints as by adding force. Because the limit cycle provides information as to when the system is constrained, it should be useful for determining appropriate timing of any intervention.

Axiom 5: A system can be highly sensitive or highly resilient to changes. Similarly, a system may require precise measurement or be insensitive to measurement error.

Although sensitivity to initial conditions is a fundamental attribute of nonlinear systems, it is also true that sometimes systems are robust to perturbations. If the basin of attraction about a system's limit cycle is quite large, it may permit considerable error in measurement (or error in management judgment) with no significant effect. It also is true, however, that a system can be sensitive to change and quick to escape even with minor perturbations. Information about the sensitivity of a business system usually is unknown and would be valuable when planning to make changes.

Axiom 6: Many statistical measures take the form of a ratio of other measures, which constitutes a simplification that masks the true behavior of the initial variables.

Traditional statistics is an exercise in combining variables in some mathematical way. However, every time two variables are combined by division, they create a ratio and thereby discard half of the available information about the movement of the variables. From simple t-scores to F-ratios to eigenvalues, there is information about the realities of the data being left behind as we construct our mathematical models that are supposed to describe reality. A "chaotician" has ample leverage to attack any traditional approach to massaging data. He can construct different data sets that provide identical statistics. He can supply you with a series of values, which linear forecasting models can only approximate, and then show that any value can be computed with precision from a simple nonlinear equation.

Axiom 7: Traditional statistical approaches often can fail to reveal intricate patterns of change in a system. These interactive patterns can only be identified by tracing the evolving trajectory on a phase plane.

Traditional forecasting techniques use approaches that either decompose time series data into different components (i.e., trend, slope, seasonality) or attempt to explain the behavior of one variable with one or more other variables (i.e., regression, manova). It has been demonstrated here that these traditional statistical techniques may be inappropriate at a fundamental level. If the systems being observed are nonlinear—and business systems are—then the approaches taken should be able to capture the nonlinear behavior.

THE FORECASTER'S JOB

The implications of nonlinearity for forecasters are similar, but not identical, to those in meteorology. Long-term business forecasting is apparently impossible because business forecasters, like meteorologists, can never know with precision the forces that drive a system. It seems that they will not be able to forecast business into the distant future, just as meteorologists cannot forecast specific weather conditions of the distant future. Both the business forecaster and the meteorologist are dealing with nonlinear systems that are capable of chaotic behavior.

For the meteorologist the realization that long-term forecasts are impossible changes the job. Rather than direct ever greater time and resources toward improved prediction, effort can be directed at more rapid recognition of weather conditions. For example, one may choose to fund a more capable weather satellite rather than direct funding toward research on long-term weather forecasting. Additionally, effort can be made toward establishing procedures to better inform the public of threatening conditions. Universal guidelines and definitions can be established to aid local meteorologists. Although efforts at long-term forecasting should continue, knowledge that the weather ultimately is unpredictable causes the job of the forecaster to be fundamentally different.

Similarly, knowing that an accurate business forecast *does not exist* in any historical data changes the job of the business forecaster. It seems that the focus of the forecaster's job should not be primarily on continued analytical refinement. Although there is always room for some improvement in method, the future ultimately is unpredictable for business. If emphasis should not be on improving methods, where should it be?

There are important differences between the weather and business. The weather is evidently more chaotic than business, as quite consistent, low-order patterns of behavior have been found in business cycles. Cycles of weather patterns are typically far less consistent. More important, however, is the fact that business involves people, and that suggests control through free will. Put simply, in business we have an opportunity to intervene and change the future; we can *vision* it. We have no such option with the weather.[7]

Proposition 28: The job of a forecaster within an organization changes to one that is actively involved in decision-making. Like cardiologists, forecasters should recommend actions that stabilize or improve the health of the nonlinear systems they monitor.

The forecaster's job should include participation in the decision-making that decides about the future. Business forecasting cannot be separated from decision-making. Most businesses recognize this, but only from the perspective that the forecaster needs to know what actions management is planning so as to allow for the effect of those actions. However, the relationship runs both ways. A forecaster can now offer management something more than a simple extrapolation of data from the past; he or she can offer a view of what is *reasonable, appropriate,* and *consistent* with the state of the system. Just as a cardiologist can make recommendations to a patient based on analysis of that patient's electrocardiogram, a forecaster should provide recommendations for maintaining stability and control by analyzing the nonlinear behavior of various organizational systems. Cardiologists don't just observe; they intervene to change things. Similarly, forecasters—perhaps more appropriately titled "organizational systems analysts"—should learn to observe, diagnose, and recommend interventions that will stabilize and improve the health of their organizations.

Significant improvements in the accuracy of forecasts will not come from improved statistical procedures. In fact, highly advanced analytic techniques often are not accepted in business settings because practicing managers don't understand them. Successful forecasters are those who use relatively simple techniques but actively involve other organizational personnel in establishing the forecast. Imagine what would happen if estimates about the future were based on the sensitive measures of change captured in a nonlinear analysis. Imagine what would happen if the forecaster worked with those same personnel to *vision* the future and then go about creating it.

NOTES

1. Recent discoveries that some high order chaos does exist in celestial orbits has some concerned about the disastrous effects—however remote—of a departure from the attractor that binds the current orbits.

2. Although it sounds pretty philosophical, the issues of free will raises the question of whether there are any other forces of free will at work that help to change the future.

3. The past is important because the current state of the system emerged from it. An understanding of the past is important because it helps one understand the current state of the system. The line in the text addresses the fact that events of the past are not necessarily repeated. Just because something has occurred is no mandate that it will ever occur again.

4. The Chaos System Software is a set of microcomputer programs developed by the author.

5. Rather than use 0,0 as the origin, the software uses the mean of changes in X and the mean of changes in Y as the center of the phase plane (computed as summing all the marginal values of each variable and dividing by the number of marginal values, which is one less than the number of actual observations). The mean changes are used simply to center the trajectory on the plane; it amounts to adding or subtracting a constant from all the change values. For this reason the marginal values of MarX $= 1.34$ and MarY $= .58$ position the visioning curser above and slightly to the right of the center of the phase plane.

6. Interestingly, studies of Value Line forecasts show that the trajectory based on Value Line's forecasted data often is radically different from limit cycle patterns of the past.

7. There is ample evidence that human activities are influencing the weather in detrimental ways (the ozone hole is the obvious example). Although this influence is viewed as destructive and negative, it demonstrates that humans can exert control over the entire atmospheric system of Earth. We are probably better off having that control than not having it. Recent efforts to improve conditions constitute the first attempts to deliberately change *(vision?)* the planetary conditions rather than simply forecast them.

9

Strategic Decision-Making

What happens when two limit cycles collide, as in a merger? Strategic management addresses competitive strategies and strategies of corporate growth. It is a field dominated by a "strategic planning model" that attempts to identify "strengths," "weaknesses," "opportunities," and "threats." Strategic management is an attempt to understand and control organizations on the macro level. It focuses on conditions in the environment and the way in which the firm interacts with that environment. Strategic management calls for establishing a mission, positioning relative to competitors, selecting strategies, and implementing them throughout an organization. It is an attempt to identify strategic advantages and strategic competencies. It is that field of management that attempts to create and manage a portfolio of business activities that allow the organization to survive and grow. What can chaos theory tell us about these strategic issues?

STRATEGIC PLANNING MODEL

Strategic planning is dominated by an almost universal strategic planning model that provides a framework for assessing an organization and defining its future. To discuss strategic issues we must consider that model and explore any new perspectives that might be offered from a nonlinear view.

Developed by industry during the 1970s, the strategic planning model was initially perceived as a tool of top management.[1] The classic strategic planning approach called for a thorough inquiry into topics shown in Table 9.1. Collectively, these topics constitute sequential steps in the analysis, which was to be conducted at least annually.

There has recently been a greater recognition that lower levels of man-

Table 9.1
Generic Strategic Planning Model

1.	Corporate Mission	An examination of the primary purpose or "reason for being" of the organization.
2.	External Analysis	A search for opportunities and threats in factors outside the firm such as changes in technology or stakeholder attitudes.
3.	Internal Analysis	A search for strengths and weaknesses within the functional activities of the firm. Prescriptions are typically written to address any weaknesses.
4.	Strategic Issues	Recognition of the primary strategic issue(s) of the firm (i.e., growth, risk reduction, competitiveness).
5.	Strategic Alternatives	Identification of the options available to address the major issue.
6.	Decision	Use of a systematic procedure for selecting among the various strategic alternatives.
7.	Implementation	Development of plans, programs, and budget allocations to implement the selected strategy.

agement within the organization should be actively involved in the strategic planning process. Some theorists have suggested that strategic planning should be a continuous process rather than an annual or periodic one; however, it is questionable whether the original model lends itself to continuous assessment.

Our appreciation of organizations as nonlinear systems can provide a fresh assessment of the strategic planning process. It seems, for example, that the frequency of strategic planning efforts should somehow relate to the degree of stability of the firm. Instability suggests interaction of more complex forces, which requires frequent assessment. Stability suggests continuance of current conditions, which may require little, if any, intervention. Any transition from stability to higher-order disorder should be examined for both its opportunities and its risks.

The model in Table 9.1 is a rather simplistic view of organizational analysis. It suggests that one can understand the state of the system by assessing current conditions, when in fact an understanding of evolving conditions is important. Further, like every other traditional management tool, it suffers by focusing on actual values rather than identifying patterns in the rate of change.

The concept of establishing a "mission" for the firm has some interesting implications. Typically the mission statement of a firm designates the purpose or reason a firm exists. It probably provides a definition of the firm's industry and the market the firm attempts to serve. It may identify the type of technology used (although there are some dangers in doing this). A mission statement helps to focus attention on the firm; it serves as a guiding principle for decision-making, and it helps to ensure nonconflicting initiatives by the firm. Mission statements often are stated in two forms: broad and narrow. The broad statement tends to describe philosophical or ethical tenets of the firm, whereas the narrow statement tends to identify specific markets, tactics, or technologies. Providing both broad and narrow mission statements seems preferable to providing a single statement because the broad and narrow statements permit greater generality and greater detail than any single statement can accomplish. Undoubtedly a mission statement and the by-products of working to define a mission are valuable to a firm.

A corporate mission statement, therefore, defines what an organization strives to do and how it intends to do it. However, it is not a goal: Goals are considered subordinate to the mission; goals (and to a greater extent objectives) are considered shorter-term concepts that are meant to challenge operational personnel. But something seems to be missing in this process. Where is there an accommodation for *visioning?* Mission statements are not statements of vision; they provide only broadly termed purposes. Goals and objectives are not visions; they are only threshold performance levels stated for the purpose of motivating personnel or facilitating efficient budgeting. Where is there a *vision statement?*

The order of items in Table 9.1 is consistent with most business policy or strategic management textbooks. However, there are variations in the order worth recognizing. Some strategists proclaim that the mission statement should be placed after item 3, "Internal Analysis." Those who argue this approach say that one can only assess the suitability of the current mission statement after having reexamined both the external and the internal environments. Those who place the mission statement first apparently believe that the mission of a firm—its purpose—should not be subject to frequent reexamination and questioning.

Perhaps this dilemma exists because all missions are somewhat attainable. For example, if an organization strives to "become a dominant supplier of consumer products for infants and children," this goal is always somewhat accomplished. In the absence of any quantitative measures how can one say *what* is "dominant"? With this approach the firm *always* accomplishes its mission, more or less. Why are we so afraid to quantify a mission statement? Is it because that makes it a *goal?* Perhaps this is the role of a vision statement. Perhaps we need to vision future conditions at this macro level. What is wrong with defining the desired future state of an organization?

A privately funded hospital in a major southwestern U.S. city closed its door to the low-income population it had served for years. The closing meant that emergency medical facilities were no longer available to a large part of the city. The City Hospital District (a public entity) immediately began an investigation into how to purchase and finance the hospital so as to put it back into business. What would be the mission of the hospital? Its *purpose* would be the same as before: to provide quality medical services to the population in its district. What would be different about it? Its *vision*. As part of the district it must be less costly to operate and more self-sustaining. Perhaps it should be expanded and upgraded. These things are not nonquantifiable, nor are they simple goals. Visions are specifically stated "states of the system" with specified times for attainment. Here's a simple example to clarify the difference:

A Mission: To provide quality medical care to the population in the district

A Vision: To attain a bed capacity of 300 and a budgeting surplus of $100,000 by June 30, 1996

Goals: To remodel the East Wing within eighteen months
              To reduce utility costs by 15 percent this year

Proposition 29: Visioning, which identifies a specific future state of a system, can be integrated into the strategic planning process to quantify a broad mission statement. Visions differ from goals or objectives because they are multidimensional.

Visions describe a combined set of conditions, and they state when those conditions are to exist. They define the state of the system at some future date. That is more than what a single goal does, and it adds substance to a mission statement. Mission statements direct us but only generally; vision statements can help us to define the future we want. Call it "management by visioning."

In a similar way one can enrich and expand each of the other items in the strategic planning model. Consider the external analysis. How can one look at the current state of environmental conditions and extract any kind of threat or opportunity? The current state of the environment results in precisely the current state of the organization. The organization is integral to its environment; they are part of the same system, and so current conditions are already reflected in current performance. If a competitor has a large market share, that is not a threat; that is a fact, and the current state of your organization has already adapted to that condition. However, if a competitor's share is expected to increase, that is a threat. Again, the importance is in the anticipated changes to the system. What are the probable changes in legislation, taxation, labor regulations, and competition? How are the demands of customers, creditors, stockholders, and society changing? We should monitor these trends on the margin and look for patterns in their rates of change that can help us better understand their behavior.

An internal analysis typically attempts to identify the unique strengths and weaknesses of the firm. We do this to develop the strengths into a competitive advantage for the firm. For example, if our firm has particularly advanced research and design ability, we may want to use that strength to rapidly respond to changing demands in the market or to produce more innovative products for the market. A collection of strengths become strategic advantages if we use them. The internal analysis also identifies weaknesses in need of correction. For example, if order specifications are being poorly communicated from marketing to production, the cause of the problem will be identified and a correction prescribed.

However, strengths and weaknesses are relative things; they are relative to our previous abilities or relative to our competition. It is the change in the strength or weakness that is important.

For example, if we have been successful at shortening our time from design to production and our competitor has not, that is a strength, even if our competitor is still beating us to market. Viewed on the margin, we are encouraged to develop and increase our strengths; viewed traditionally, we are encouraged to leave our strengths alone (until they become weaknesses).

Proposition 30: An internal analysis based on changes in organizational conditions identifies a different set of strengths and weaknesses than one would identify traditionally. Recognizing factors with marginal improvements encourages development of those abilities, ultimately making them strategic advantages, and permits intervention for those factors with declining ability before they constitute strategic disadvantages.

Consider the implications this proposition has for the common strategic planning model. We tend to identify current strengths and to use them as strategic advantages even though their relative strength may be declining. The current model directs us to allocate toward our weaknesses rather than fund those factors that have shown some incremental improvement.

The external and internal components of the strategic planning model constitute the assessment stages. Thereafter, the model takes on a rather classic decision-making style: What is the issue? What are the choices? How do we choose? How do we implement?

If vision statements are defined, the strategic issues would seem to relate simply to attainment of the visions. They would address the structural changes necessary to attain the desired vision. For example, if we have established a vision of having 300 beds, then the strategic issue focuses on how we are to attain that increased capacity. Strategic issues, it seems, simply identify the structural changes necessary to attain the vision.

The alternatives identify the possible choices. In our hospital example we may have the choice of remodeling the current facility, acquiring an adjoining facility, or building a new facility. When a decision is to be made, it should be made within the constraints offered by the vision statements. Which facility will provide the needed capacity *and* result in an accumulating surplus that will reach $100,000 per year? The vision statements define a future condition and force decision-making to comply with that future state.

The question is not "Which alternative might be consistent with some general mission statement and result in attainment of some lesser goals?" The question is "Which alternative will force the structural changes and result in a state of the system defined by the vision statements?" Vision statements can provide precision, balance, and clarity to an organization's mission. Because they are multidimensional and there can be any number of them, they define and restrict the future course of the firm to a specific trajectory that leads to the desired state. They allow us to create the future.

Proposition 31: One needs to know the trajectory of change in any business activity before attempting to implement a change to it. The activity may have stabilized at some desired or undesired state, or it may already be on a trajectory toward improvement or decline.

Implementation takes on a different character when organizations are viewed as dynamically evolving systems. Activities within a firm will follow any of several possible trajectories over time, and one needs to know the trajectory of the behavior before attempting any intervention. Why spend money to correct a problem that is already declining substantially in frequency? Why not spend money to correct a procedure before it constitutes a problem?

The effectiveness of any implementation will depend on the stability of the system being affected. Hence one may be able to gauge the degree of intervention needed to create a permanent change. Recall how some systems have an inherent stability that causes them to return to constancy even with substantial perturbation. Others are quite sensitive to any disturbance. These are facts one needs to know when planning an intervention. For example, if the trajectory describing milling errors is quite constant, the required intervention may be greater than if the trajectory depicts fairly high order chaos. Constancy suggests that the system has stabilized, so that changing its performance will require structural changes to the system (perhaps replacement of major equipment). Chaotic behavior is likely to be stabilized with minor interventions that provide timing to the system (i.e., a pacemaker).

WHEN CYCLES COLLIDE

What happens when two limit cycles become one, as in a merger? Which of two limit cycles will prevail when two firms are combined? As a general rule, the limit cycle that results from a combination of two others will reflect the higher-order chaos of the two. For example, if a Period 1 limit cycle and a Period 2 limit cycle are combined, the resulting cycle will be Period 2 in nature. Combining a Period 2 limit cycle and a Period 4 limit cycle will result in a Period 4 limit cycle. However, if a low-order cycle (Period 1, 2, or 4) is combined with a very high order cycle (Period 8), the result will probably resemble the lower-order cycle. That is, a low-order cycle tends to add order to a highly chaotic cycle.

The relative size of the firms being combined has much to do with the resulting trajectory. A large firm will tend to dominate a smaller one, causing the resulting cycle to closely resemble that of the larger firm.

We can create some artificial mergers to begin to understand combined limit cycles. By taking two separate firms and combining their quarterly sales and profits we can create a combination that reflects the two. Admittedly, this approach fails to recognize many conditions and effects that would result if the two firms actually merged, but the approach has certain advantages. It allows us to see the two cycles of both firms, with and without the merger, and it allows us to simulate any companies and any type of merger.

Let's begin by looking at a theoretic merger of a major supplier and its retail customer. The supplier in this case is Hasbro, Incorporated, the largest domestic toy manufacturer. Our retailer is Toys Я Us, the nation's largest toy retailer.[2] Hasbro has annual sales of about $1.5 billion. Toys Я Us has a significantly higher volume of about $5.5 billion. The limit cycle of each of these companies and their combined cycle are shown in Figure 9.1. In each of the figures the data represent ten years of quarterly performance dating from 1981 through quarter 3 of 1991. In these images and the ones that follow changes in quarterly sales (SALEQ) are on the horizontal axis and changes in quarterly net income (NIQ) are plotted vertically.

One can see that of the two companies, Hasbro has a far less stable quarterly limit cycle. Much of the disruption to the cycle is due to various acquisitions. Hasbro bought Glenco Infants Items in 1963 and Milton Bradley in 1984. It also purchased lines from Child Guidance in 1985 and Coleco in 1989.

Toys Я Us has pursued continuous horizontal expansion, opening virtually identical retail locations over the past ten years. The similarity in operations and the profound seasonality of the industry have resulted in an almost clocklike annual oscillation. The stability and size of Toys Я Us result in a similar Period 2 oscillation when the two companies are com-

Figure 9.1
Merger of Hasbro and Toys Я Us

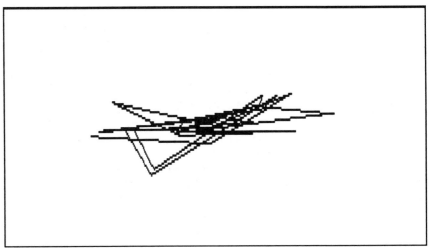

Hasbro, Inc.

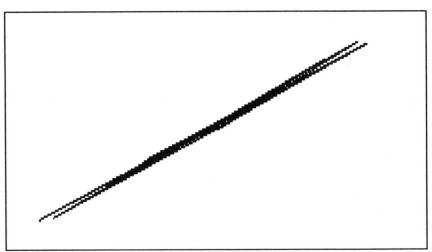

Toys Я Us

Figure 9.1 (Continued)

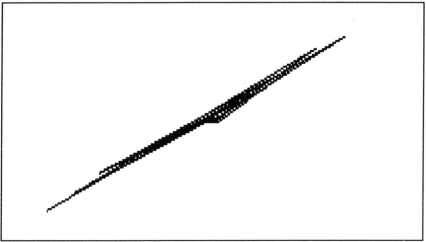

Combined

bined into one financial entity. Theoretically, a combination of Hasbro (with ticker symbol HAS) and Toys Я Us (with ticker symbol TOY) would result in a company (HASTOY?) with a quarterly pattern of performance much like that of the current Toys Я Us. Even with the many simplifying assumptions, it is unlikely that the commanding seasonal pattern of Toys Я Us would be significantly disturbed. It is possible to show that there are other companies that would disturb the Toys Я Us cycle. Disney, for example, is of sufficient size and has a distinctive countercyclical cycle that, when combined with Toys Я Us, results in a combined limit cycle that is more disordered than either of the two companies independently.

In this Hasbro–Toys Я Us example it is not surprising that the combined cycle resembles that of the larger firm. However, it seems possible for a larger firm to be stabilized by a smaller one. In the absence of any distinctive pattern the addition of any new pattern will dominate. Consider the hypothetical merger of Hughes Supply and Wolohan Lumber.

Hughes is a wholesale distributor of electrical, plumbing, and heating and air conditioning equipment in the Southeast. It has annual sales of about $590 million. Wolohan Lumber is about half that size, with sales of about $300 million. Wolohan is a retailer of building supplies operating a chain of more than fifty locations in the Midwest.

Rather than examine the limit cycles of these two firms, let's consider their velocity history charts first individually and then as a combined entity (see Figure 9.2).

Note the absence of any quarterly cycle for Hughes Supply and the dis-

Figure 9.2
Velocity Histories of Hughes Supply and Wolohan Lumber

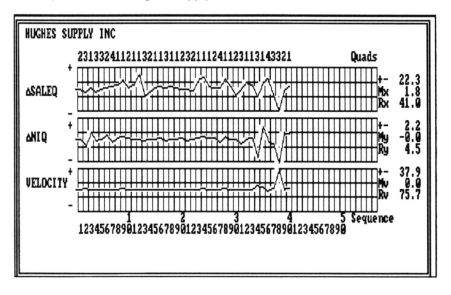

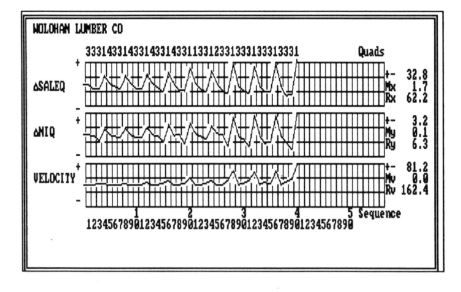

Figure 9.3
Hypothetical Merger of Hughes Supply and Wolohan Lumber

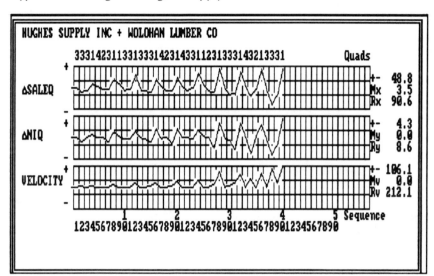

tinctive seasonal cycle of Wolohan resulting from the cycle of its retail business.

Figure 9.3 shows the velocity history charts for the two companies when combined. Note how the pattern becomes distinctly cyclical despite the fact that Wolohan is not the dominant company in terms of size. The fact that smaller companies can create pronounced patterns in larger ones has important implications for any management contemplating a merger or a divestiture. It suggests that the effect of the merger may cause new patterns of performance more significant than expected. In the case of a divestiture it may be that the division being sold offers significant stability (or instability) to the firm beyond what would be expected. At the risk of stretching the analogy too far, divesting a minor division may result in instability in much the same way as failure of a pacemaker can cause fibrillation. The size of the stimulus may not be as important as the timing it offers. Some divisions may act something like a metronome, setting the pace of performance for the entire organization. Others may only contribute to disorder because of the erratic performance patterns they possess.

Proposition 32: Mergers and acquisitions cause changes in organizational limit cycles that are not simple combinations of the two firms. The impact of such combinations can only be estimated by observing the behavior of the combined trajectory.

These theoretic mergers suggest that the patterns of change resulting from the combination of two firms are not necessarily mirrored by the patterns of actual behavior displayed by the combination. That is, although the actual figures may be additive, the resulting patterns of changes are not as readily apparent.

ACTUAL ACQUISITIONS AND DIVESTITURES

The impact of actual acquisitions and divestitures can be seen in the limit cycles and velocity histories of selected firms. Like the simulated mergers above, actual mergers or acquisitions can cause a fundamental change in the limit cycle trajectory of the parent firm. This should come as no surprise, since any major acquisition or divestiture changes the very character of the organization.

Sony Corporation enjoyed several years of highly stable performance until January of 1988, when they acquired CBS Records. The stability is evident in the limit cycle of Sony shown in Figure 9.4. The limit cycle from 1981 through 1987 remained tightly bound to a single point on the phase plane, indicating constant increases in both sales and profits. In January of 1988, however, Sony acquired CBS Records and that changed everything. Since then Sony has departed from its Period 1–type condition and has adopted a Period 2–type oscillation, depicted in the phase plane labeled 1988–1991. The impact also is apparent in the behavior of the velocity history charts. Stability was replaced with oscillation in both sales and profits. Study the tracing of the marginal net income and note its increasing irregularity. Without a doubt, management at Sony has a greater challenge than before; they have traded constancy, the lowest order of chaos, for something higher on the scale. As noted before, higher-order chaos brings increased opportunity, but it also brings increased risk.

Sometimes an acquisition simply doesn't work. The combination of the two companies results in a trajectory that is simply uncontrollable or unacceptable. Such is the case of Owens-Corning's acquisition of Aerospace and Strategic Materials Group.

Before September 18, 1985, Owens-Corning enjoyed considerable stability of performance, as depicted by the preacquisition pattern in Figure 9.5. Although sales volume oscillated regularly during the year, net profit performance remained relatively consistent, resulting in a trajectory that lay fairly flat on the horizontal axis.

Owens' experience with Aerospace and Strategic Materials Group provides us with an example of both an acquisition and a divestiture. Note the trajectory that resulted after the acquisition. The acquisition apparently took Owens-Corning away from its attractor—out of its basin of attraction.

Owens sold its new acquisition in 1987, having held it for less than two years. It subsequently returned to a stabler pattern of performance, as indicated by the postdivestiture pattern in Figure 9.5. One can see the impact

Figure 9.4
Sony's Acquisition of CBS Records

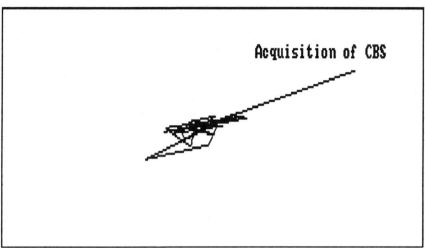

Acquisition of CBS

1981 through Q1,'88

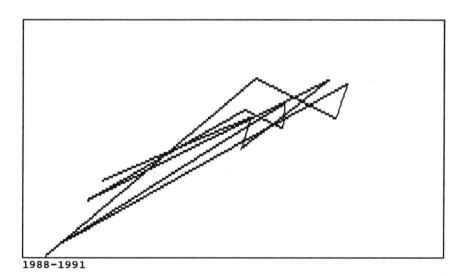

1988–1991

Figure 9.4 (Continued)

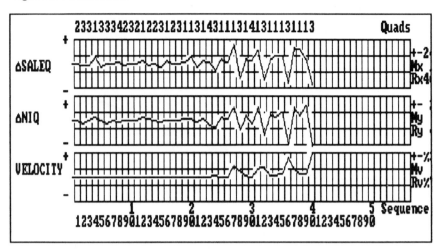

of the acquisition and divestiture in the marginal history charts extending from sequence 19 through sequence 25.

When corporate limit cycles collide, the result can be either accommodation or chaos. The new acquisition may reinforce the company's original cycle, or raise it to a higher level of disorder. In some cases there can be an increase in stability, if countercyclical forces are combined. In some cases the acquisition can shock the company into high-order chaos.

The simulated mergers can provide some suggestion of what might happen when two firms combine. However, there are various factors that control what will actually happen. The extent to which the two companies are integrated operationally will undoubtedly have an impact on the subsequent cycle. Even the extent of compatibility between the human resources of the two firms will probably have an impact. If we adopt the notion of visioning, we may be able to exert greater control over what the resulting cycle will be; we may be able to designate the pattern we want.

In these cases we have focused entirely on the trajectory of the quarterly net profit margin (sales versus profits). Every other operational measure, every other financial ratio, will reflect the impact of an acquisition or a divestiture. Perhaps an assessment of the expected cycles in these other areas may help to identify the quality of fit of two firms. Perhaps it would help focus attention on those relations that will need the greatest control. The limit cycles of firms, like the electrocardiograms of people, provide an extremely sensitive measurement of activity patterns. It is no wonder that these cycles are so profoundly affected by something so dramatic as an acquisition or a divestiture. Viewed from this perspective, it seems almost unthinkable to collide two organizations without considering the nonlinear

Figure 9.5
Owens-Corning Fiberglass' Acquisition and Subsequent Divestiture of
Aerospace and Strategic Materials Group

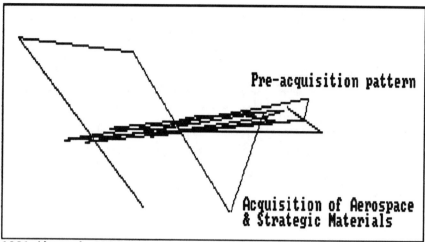

Pre-acquisition pattern

Acquisition of Aerospace
& Strategic Materials

1981 through 1986

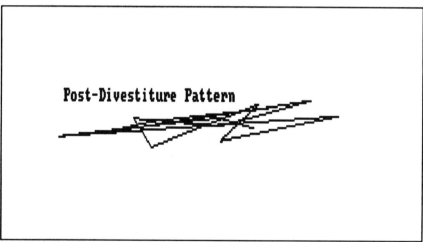

Post-Divestiture Pattern

1988 through 1991

Figure 9.5 (Continued)

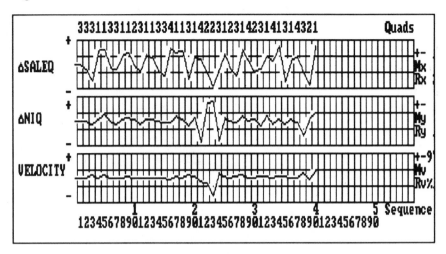

stability of the resulting organization. Similarly, it seems that one would surely want to examine the expected stability of an organization before divesting of some of its assets.

GROWTH STRATEGIES

Just as there exists a well-accepted model of strategic planning, so, too, there are generally accepted growth strategies for an organization. Although various authors may apply different names for these strategies, they usually are identified as (1) growth in the same industry, (2) growth in a related industry, (3) growth vertically (forward or backward), and (4) conglomerate growth or growth in an unrelated industry. Because these concepts are so fundamental to the field of strategic management, it is worth considering any new perspective a nonlinear view can offer.

Growth in the same industry is sometimes called horizontal growth. It is characterized by the addition of identical operations, such as another McDonald's or another K Mart. The primary advantage is considered to be the additional economies of scale increased size provides. It also is true that management can continue to apply what it already knows, focusing on what it knows best.

We have already seen the results of same-industry growth on an organization's limit cycle; the expansion of Toys Я Us provided a prime example. The limit cycle is reinforced with each new expansion because of the identical patterns of the additional operations. In the case of Toys Я Us the limit cycle is rather low order (Period 2). However, it is entirely possible that horizontal expansion could introduce higher orders of chaos if the business segment being expanded is high order. For example, a company with rather stable patterns of performance may find its stability declining if it expands that part of its current operations that is inherently unstable.

Related-industry growth also was demonstrated by the experience of the Toro Company. Toro's expansion from its original lawn equipment into snowthrowers and chainsaws is an ideal example of related-industry growth. The company was capitalizing on its high name recognition, its established reputation for quality, and its dealer network when it decided to expand into a related-industry segment that was countercyclical to its current market. From a strategic standpoint, the decision seemed flawless; it allowed the company to better utilize corporate assets and stabilize cash flow. It allowed the company to sell related products to its same customers with different needs at a different time.

Toro's decision was not a mistake, but their experience suffering through two snowless winters demonstrates the risks associated even with this conservative growth strategy. Related-industry growth, sometimes called circular growth, differs from same-industry growth in that it substantially changes the structural characteristics of the company. It is not inherently good or bad. Related-industry growth may allow a company to become stabler, or it may introduce instability, depending on the segment being exploited and its relation to the original business.

Vertical growth offers a different sort of nonlinear condition. Vertical growth is typically further defined into vertical growth forward and vertical growth backward. The notion of forward or backward relates to the marketing channel for the goods being manufactured or sold. A wholesaler that buys a retailer is an example of vertical growth forward; the company is expanding forward toward the market. A retailer that buys a supplier or manufacturer of the goods it sells is said to have expanded vertically backward. Either of these expansions is termed vertical integration because the company becomes more fully involved in manufacturing and distribution within the same industry.

Vertical expansion permits the nonlinearities of channel management to occur within the same company. In Chapter 4 on marketing we demonstrated how the relationships between manufacturer, wholesaler, and retailer can generate nonlinear changes in inventory. A firm that owns any vertically related participants in a market channel has both the risk of these inefficient behaviors and the opportunity to control the channel with greater precision. In practice, most vertical expansions occur so a company can stabilize its sources of essential supplies or to ensure access to market. Realizing the marginal profits that might be possible by eliminating the profits of a supplier is typically a secondary motive.

Vertical growth represents a greater commitment to a single market or industry. Whatever forces drive the trajectory at one level will be supplemented by forces at another level in the channel. One can see that the firm that expands vertically may find that its limit cycle becomes more stable, or as in our hypothetical merger of Toys Я Us and Hasbro, the limit cycle of one part of the business may dominate that of the other. Most important are the nonlinearities between the two businesses that represent both a risk and an opportunity.

Unrelated-industry growth, or conglomerate growth, offers considerable risk diversification, since it positions the firm in two independent markets. However, this strategy suffers from the absence of any operational economies of scale and a possible lack of management expertise. Further, the degree of risk diversification may be misleading. For example, a firm that manufactures kitchen cabinets may seek to diversify by opening automobile dealerships. Although the two industries seem entirely independent, both may suffer if interest rates increase. The phase plane diagrams suggested here may serve as useful tools for identifying hidden associations between apparently unrelated industries. They also suggest that the addition of relatively small business segments may cause instabilities or stability in a larger organization.

OTHER STRATEGIC MANAGEMENT ISSUES

There are other strategic management issues that can be reassessed from a nonlinear perspective. There are, for example, generic competitive strategies such as differentiation and low cost. A differentiation strategy calls for development, production, and marketing of products or services that differ in fundamental ways from those of competitors. The basis of the differentiation may be in reliability, quality, or design. The extent of the differentiation and the perceived value of that differentiation dictate the relative price of the product compared with the price of competitors' products. IBM produced and marketed personal computers that were differentiated from those of competitors. However, as the market evolves, the degree of differentiation and the value of it change. IBM initially perceived that quality allowed them to price their personal computer products above those of competitors. More recently the degree of that difference has declined, as personal computers have become almost generic. That changing relationship could, no doubt, be traced as an evolving trajectory over time. Similarly, low-cost pricing is relative to other products of similar design, and the changing relation in that strategy could be monitored on a phase plane diagram.

There are models of the environment that describe the forces of competition that bear on an industry. These, too, are dynamic forces that could be traced as trajectories on a phase plane. When do prices cause a nonlinear response in the marketplace? When do trade barriers become low enough to cause an explosion of exports? There is every reason to expect that market conditions and competitive forces are nonlinear. However, current strategic planning models of the environment simply serve to identify the forces. We should seek to understand the structural characteristics of that environment.

Perhaps the greatest contribution of chaos theory to strategic management is at a level above competition, growth, or even visioning. Perhaps it is at the level of survival, which often is cited as the prime objective of any business. In a dynamic environment one survives by adaptation. As markets evolve, so, too, should the types of products and services offered. Sometimes the market is quite constant, allowing a product to continue successfully filling the unchanging need. Sometimes the market is rapidly changing, forcing constant evolution; in these cases it is unreasonable to expect a product to remain successful indefinitely.

However, the qualities of a firm that make it successful may be more long-lived. The abilities to innovate, produce with quality, and market responsibly transcend any single product. These are competencies that allow survival. A firm can practice them continually, regardless of the markets it serves or the products it produces. Recognizing that organizations and their markets are nonlinear systems focuses our attention on the changes that occur in the interactive relationship of the two. Rather than seeing change as the producer of threats, opportunities, strengths, and weaknesses, we can see change as a continuing trajectory, one that can be managed by visioning and adapting.

NOTES

1. General Electric was a major contributor to the creation of a strategic planning model during the 1970s and remains a major innovator of strategic planning concepts.

2. The merger of Hasbro and Toys Я Us is unlikely for a variety of reasons; however, the prospects of such a merger are interesting, and the combination of their limit cycles provides a useful example.

10

The Center of Chaos

It is no wonder we have failed to give adequate attention to the nonlinearities in business. We have failed to develop the tools that would allow us to report dynamic relationships. We have stayed bound to the traditional approaches of the past—totaling sales, totaling profits, counting defects, plotting distributions, and computing ratios. Advancements in computer technology have only caused us to do more of the same with increased precision. It is time to break the paradigm of numbers. It is time to let go of the concepts of estimation and probability. We need to see patterns of business activity, trajectories of change, and structural limits as they are, not as some obscure estimated value. Organizations need a Center of Chaos to explore what they have been missing. They need to embark on a mission to find patterns of organizational activity that are currently hidden and undiscovered. They need to identify the sources of stability and instability in all that they do.

Businesses simply do not own the necessary tools for nonlinear analysis. Business information flows through an organization in quantitative form. It appears as periodic budgets and financial statements. It is reported on inventory control sheets, purchase orders, and production reports. We pump numbers in and get numbers out, showing perhaps a variance compared with budget, an "open-to-buy" quantity, an average cost, or a gross margin percentage. We think we have added meaning by computing percentages—sales are up 5.7 percent, costs are down 2.3 percent, payroll as a percentage of sales is 13.4 percent. Accounts receivable are down 1.8 percentage points below this time last year. Admit it. These are only glimpses of reality compared with the graceful limit cycles they represent. We have been bound to this numerical pattern of analysis long enough; it is time to escape it.

SOFTWARE DEFICIENCY

The propensity to analyze business with traditional financial or statistical measures is perpetuated by the software we use. Even in the intensely competitive market of spreadsheet software there is no product that will automatically make the simple computation and display a phase plane.

Proposition 33: Software developers have failed to provide for display of nonlinear relationships. Options for generating phase planes and velocity histories should be added to common spreadsheet programs and graphics software.

One would think that graphics software would allow one to display the trajectories displayed here, but popular business graphics programs, such as Harvard Graphics, won't permit it. Give any graphics program two variables and direct it to plot the relationship between the two and it will plot the points as a scattergram and discard any record of the sequential order. You get a disordered plot of points when there might have been an underlying trajectory to their evolution.

There are two messages here for business software developers. First, provisions for displaying nonlinear relationships should be included in many existing products, and second, developers should not be so myoptic about their product development; they should look beyond what is commonly acceptable to see what else is possible. Perhaps there will be a nonlinear response. Perhaps this one additional discussion of chaos theory will cause there to be a provision in your next spreadsheet that allows you to tag two columns and generate the associated phase plane of the data.

Fortunately, computation and display of phase planes are relatively simple matters, and any desktop computer can handle it with some clever programming. Our challenge will not be imaging the nonlinear patterns, but breaking away from our tendency to interpret and respond to the new images in traditional ways.

NEW QUESTIONS

What is needed is a deliberate search for nonlinear relationships. A business needs to examine the forces in its external environment and the patterns of behavior in the markets that it serves. It needs to identify relationships in the rates of change in marketing, finance, production, and human resources activities. There is an entire set of relationships in business that reflect the evolving transitions of an organization; these relationships are currently being masked by the information and methods we use.

The value of nonlinear information becomes evident only after one asks, "What are the implications?" Only then do we ponder how to react to the wandering, nonlinear trajectory. If that trajectory traces a slight drop in consumer satisfaction, we begin to identify recent changes that might have caused the decrease. It is then that we realize we have intercepted the problem before it is translated into an actual decrease in consumer satisfaction. We caught it on the margin. We managed it as it happened, controlling it and directing it. We might even push it beyond its current bounds—outside its attractor—to generate a nonlinear response in the marketplace.

We don't know the value of nonlinear information because we have never used it. We have always managed by the totals, discarding the trajectories. At best we compute a percentage change from the previous period, but we do that by habit; it actually tells us very little. It would be worthwhile to examine the business reports currently in use and look for any that reflect trajectories of change. It is not enough to have historical data or computation of a recent change; one needs a plot of the trajectory over time to understand its shape, its behavior, its stability.

Proposition 34: Businesses should examine the information they currently use and consider which measures should be examined as nonlinear relationships. They should then devise ways of regularly displaying those relationships.

Patterns of change raise new questions. A trajectory of sales and profits forces us to ask why sales are bounded. What is the restraining force that pulls the trajectory in as it pushes outward into quadrant 1? Is the business constrained by capacity, efficiency, or a lack of human resources? Why are we bound to the current pattern of behavior? Is it by deliberate or coincidental design? The answers will point to specific constraints that, when removed, release the trajectory to visit new levels of performance on the phase plane. We are constrained not by our capacity, but by our ability to change capacity. Our profits are limited not by what they are, but by our ability to change them. It is the constraints that restrain us; knowing them releases us.

A linear perspective leads us to believe that more is better until something goes wrong. If a little advertising is useful, a lot must be even better. If the quality of interior fixtures enhances sales in a retail establishment, then top-quality fixtures must be even better. If higher quality is better, then the highest quality is better still. These are the assumptions we live with if we adopt a linear view. But this is not a linear world. We readily acknowledge that there are diminishing returns to almost any investment. Nonlinear dynamics helps to explain why that is true. It demonstrates that there are limits beyond which we escape our current domain of operation. Sometimes that is desirable, sometimes it is not. For example, we may not want to position our retail outlet at the upper limit of quality. That may not be the market we hope to serve; that may not be the largest market or the most profitable one. We may want to adhere to our current domain,

Table 10.1
A Proposed Agenda for the Center of Chaos

Step 1: Establish a procedure to display phase planes and velocity history charts, providing some means for interacting with the charts for forecasting purposes.

Step 2: Identify common measures considered critical to the business' successes. They may be marketing-, cost control-, or human resource-related measures.

Step 3: Examine the nonlinearity of these critical measures and consider the implications of the patterns found.

Step 4: Produce a set of visioning statements as examples that could be used for planning.

Step 5: Explore ways in which nonlinear patterns of behavior can be regularly made available to decision-makers.

Step 6: Present concepts of nonlinearity and preliminary results to management.

---

and that domain has limits. Nonlinear questions ask, "How much? How often? How far?" They probe the limits of a system's stability.

AN AGENDA

A Center of Chaos could be charged with exploring nonlinear patterns of behavior for measures considered critical to the business. It can consider the agenda in Table 10.1 as its preliminary approach to a study of organizational dynamics.

Those assigned to work on such a project should include, in addition to a programmer, two or more representatives from any functional area being examined. It might also be wise to include another representative from one or more other functional areas. The patterns that emerge from this type of analysis typically present more questions than answers. It is only through considerable discussion that one discovers the implications of the patterns. The following questions may be helpful to those examining the newly found limit cycles. They are questions that should provide meaningful discussions of limit cycle behavior.

1. Why is the system under analysis considered nonlinear?
2. What changes in system parameters are most likely to cause it to escape its attractor?
3. What business activities are affected by the movement of the limit cycle?
4. What forces or constraints bind or restrict the limit cycle's behavior?
5. What specific conditions are associated with any given point on the trajectory?
6. What factors or conditions need to be controlled to control the behavior of the limit cycle?

Perhaps the most meaningful contributions a Center of Chaos can make relate to the educational process it could provide. The intricate patterns of behavior it can present demonstrate that the organization is a constantly changing, constantly evolving system with a future that can be defined. Managers will better understand the sources of stability and instability in the firm. They will be more aware of potential risk, and at best, they will adopt the notion of visioning as a way to control the organization.

Seeing the patterns of behavior in change causes one to ask why they exist. What causes them? How can such elaborate orbits be imbedded in such common activities of business? There is but one answer to that question. Patterns of organizational behavior exist because our patterns of behavior adhere to powerful attractors. Moment by moment we choose to follow repeated trajectories of behavior, thereby producing complex interactions that are revealed on the phase plane. The powerful attractors that bind our behavior cause us to be more or less predictable; they also avoid the catastrophic results of a truly chaotic society.

Managing chaos can be extended beyond managing behavior within a single organization. It can include issues of society or issues of individual behavior. Why do crowds sometimes become riotous? Why do we almost always take the same road home? These are issues for our final chapter, which will look at chaos at a personal level.

11

Managing the Chaos Within

Management is universal. It is something we all do to control the activities that constitute our lives. We manage our job and we manage our homes. If nonlinear systems can be found in the workplace, then surely they also can be found at home. Chaotic systems are not exclusive to physics, biology, or business; they seem to abide most anywhere as descriptions of natural behavior that have remained overlooked for too long.

Understanding chaotic or nonlinear systems casts the world into a different light. It is not like a new pair of glasses that make images clearer; it is more like seeing an x-ray film or a thermal image for the first time. Things simply look different; we see features about them that we did not see before.

In this chapter we carry our understanding of nonlinearity outside the organization to the common things in our lives. We'll see how it applies to the ordinary and mundane things about us. We'll look at how it pertains to our simplest behaviors, our relationships with others, and our acceptance of new ideas. This is the opportunity to see the nonlinearity that surrounds us.

There is motive here. Traditions in business die slowly. We still use the same terms, titles, and gold watches of 100 years ago. We still teach the same principles of management taught 100 years ago. How can one expect a notion as alien-sounding as chaos theory to have any impact on such tradition; management despises chaos and hates theory. Surely these views will have little impact. But that is all that is needed. All we need is for someone to apply one of the notions presented here. When one person acts on anything said here, that changes the world incrementally. Perhaps that is the attractor that draws me to write this book.

To make chaos theory unforgettable, it must be made visible in common things about you. It must be seen as a universal phenomenon.

THE CRITERIA

I have chosen to describe chaotic systems as nonlinear systems and vice versa. Some might object, preferring to reserve the word *chaos* to describe the apparent disorder that can emerge from a system. But who is to say what is disorder? As mentioned in the opening chapter, what is chaotic to my dog is not chaotic to my kids. What is chaotic for us today may be understandable tomorrow. To me chaos is a description of behavior ranging from low-order stability to high-order disorder. Nonlinearity describes a system that is able to occasionally provide a disproportional response to input. Seesaws are linear systems. Swings are nonlinear ones.

Nonlinear systems develop incrementally. Their future state is, at least in part, dependent on their current state. They evolve. Trees and seashells are nonlinear systems. Organisms, organizations, you, and I are nonlinear systems. Behavior is dependent on behavior. Ideas are dependent on ideas. Success is built on success. Failure breeds failure.

Nonlinear systems—chaotic systems—tend toward identifiable patterns of behavior. They stabilize, oscillate, or oscillate in complex ways. At still higher levels their behaviors become so complex that we cannot understand them; so we call them chaotic. We might be inclined to call such behavior *random*, but random suggests "without meaning," and chaotic behavior is entirely deterministic. We are struggling with the idea that anything random can emerge from anything deterministic.

Patterns of behavior are all about us. The swing is drawn to the bottom of its ropes if left alone. It oscillates when sufficient energy is put into it. It will oscillate even if that energy is constant, as it does in a steady breeze.

Nonlinear systems can be sensitive to initial conditions. Because chaotic systems evolve, their futures can be highly dependent on the state of the system when the behavior begins. The final resting place of a golf ball is highly dependent on its position on the tee relative to the golfer and the initial position of the club head before the swing begins. However, sensitivity to initial conditions is not a necessary condition of nonlinear systems. It is possible that a nonlinear system will converge to a designated state regardless of its initial position. This can occur because of some physical characteristic of the system (the swing ultimately returns to stability) or because of some behavioral control (Palmer's ball always ends up on the green).

These are the characteristics that form the basis of an entirely new science. These are the characteristics you should be sensitive to as you reexamine the common activities about you.

NONLINEAR BIRDS, FISH, AND TREES

Watch a flock of birds the next time you are outside. They glide collectively, maintaining the space between them with practiced precision. Their flight is not random; they travel together drawn to this tree or that pond. They are attracted to it. Sometimes, as the flock makes a turn, one bird will peel away from the rest. The one that breaks from the flock is not the one in the center of the flock, but, inevitably, the one on the edge. It is so close to the edge that it exits the basin of attraction and pursues a trajectory of its own.[1] Schools of fish exhibit the same nonlinear behavior. Does the bird that breaks from the flock do so by its free will? Does it *decide* to leave the flock? Those are questions for philosophers.

Trees, though, offer something extra. Unlike many systems that leave no evidence of their past behavior, trees provide a visual record of their "decisions." They stand like three-dimensional graphic plots of their own evolution. Their intricate pattern of growth is exposed to all and serves as vivid testimony to the patterns of behavior that can be produced by evolving, nonlinear systems.

A tree is interesting because it is proof of sequential time. When it branches here it forgoes the opportunity to branch there. It precludes the other options. Even without a decision it selects one course into the future and leaves behind all others. Its choice, whatever the basis, is irreversible, and it pushes on to the next branching and the next, closing out each yesterday and defining each tomorrow. Interacting with its environment, it creates its own future. Unlike us or the organizations we manage, it leaves a complete visual record of all its choices.

From the seashell to the ecosystem of Earth and beyond we live in a nonlinear world. I strongly suspect that even those systems that we define as linear are only tightly confined nonlinear systems. The seesaw may one day break in response to a little more rain and a little more weight. All systems evolve so all develop incrementally. All systems have limits that can be exceeded.

SO, WHAT ABOUT US?

Be thankful for stability. It allows you and me to do as we wish within limits. Although we are part of a larger system, we are bound to our own attractors, bound to our own patterns of behavior, and bound to our own patterns of decisions. We are part of the same, but the stability of our own attractors makes us autonomous. Occasionally the actions of one substantially change the characteristics of the systems of others to change behavior. For example, we are less influenced by the pleas of a president than by changes in the tax laws. We are less influenced by the pleas of a pastor than we are by the presence of acquired immunodeficiency syndrome. Changes to fundamental structural characteristics of our lives cause changes in behavior.

We are more bound to patterns of behavior than we can ever imagine. Our definition of innovation is restricted to a "new idea." How would you define innovation if we removed *all* the patterns that bind us? Can't innovation be a new language, a new country, a new life form? Can't innovation be a new approach to kindness, concern, and honesty? We follow a flock that considers it unruly behavior to go to another tree even if that tree is better for the flock. Our behaviors are extremely stable.

Be thankful for stability, but know that stability has its drawbacks. It preserves what is learned from the past, but it attacks new ideas. It provides order, but squelches creative approaches that might be born in disorder. Stability is at one end of the chaos continuum; disorder is at the other. Our lives are somewhere in between—not so close to stability that we do not change, not so close to disorder that we cannot live together.

Let's put our lives on a phase plane. Choose something common like our travel to work each day. Make the horizontal axis *change in distance* measured in miles from home. Make the vertical axis *change in time* measured in minutes from home. Make the origin your home.[2] Figure 11.1 provides a sample.

Now consider your pattern of behavior over the course of a week. You travel to work and home and then to work and home again. Occasionally you visit the gas station or the grocery store. Add any other possible stops, and you'll still find your behavior tightly confined to a pattern that oscillates regularly with the sun. Your trajectory is defined by the roads you travel, and the roads you choose to travel are defined by previous behavior. This regularity, this order, makes life predictable, makes cooperation possible, and stifles creativity. If your daily pattern is not followed closely enough, you will be unacceptable by others at work and at home. Followed too closely, you will never find new opportunities or new ideas beyond those that might be at work, at home, at the gas station, or at the grocery store.

Figure 11.1 is actually an illustration of behavior patterns; it describes where we choose to go. Doesn't the same apply to what we choose to believe? Are we not bound to beliefs in the same way?

It has been said that there are two great tragedies in life. One is when you fail to achieve your goals; the other is when you achieve your goals. In either case you must reassess your beliefs. Either case is disturbing because it positions you at a point that is out of the pattern; each is the end of a predictable trajectory.

Like our repeated patterns of movement, our repeated patterns of belief give us comfort, confidence, and predictability. But they also restrict us. Like our patterns of movement, our beliefs also are defined by other char-

Figure 11.1
Phase Plane of Weekly Travel

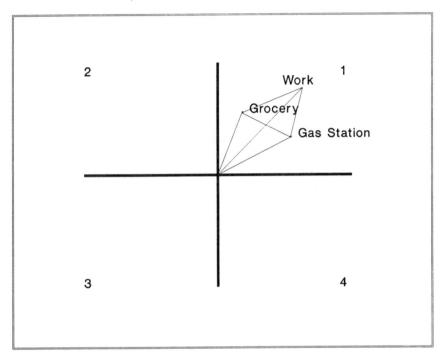

acteristics of the system. There are roads that guide us and there are lead-
ers to follow. We can choose to follow the same roads each day, or we
can choose to take different ones. Viewed this way, it is conceivable to
guide our own beliefs.

Chaos theory might help to explain why we, as a group, a market, or a
society, are fairly predictable, whereas individually we are not. In a real
sense we are not one; we are a set of autonomous islands bumping and
bending one another, adamantly adhering to our individual patterns of
belief. The resulting pressure is both good and bad. It pushes some so far
that they produce original ideas. It pushes others to adopt patterns of survival behavior that are costly to all of us.

HABITS

Habits offer the most identifiable patterns of behavior; they also demonstrate the power of an attractor. Although many habits are good (such
as fastening a seat belt), many, like smoking, drinking, and raiding the
kitchen at midnight, are considered undesirable. Their character is the same,
however. They are patterns of highly systematic behavior that are defined

by some underlying attractor. The only hope for breaking a habit is to attach to some other attractor. One needs to *vision* conditions without the habit and behavior without the habit and follow those alternate behaviors.

RELATIONSHIPS

Although nonlinearity in personal behavior may seem a bit too removed from the practical arena of business, the interaction of individuals is not. Business is a social process, and as demonstrated in Chapter 7, there are many human resource issues that can be explored with chaos theory. Here, though, it is worth examining personal relationships in greater detail. There are many occasions when we deal with only one or two other individuals, and in those situations we may shed some light on the evolving relationships between individuals.

If each person binds to certain beliefs, it is possible that a working relationship between people may be fundamentally impossible. Let's take it from a practical to an emotional level.

If two persons differ in their willingness to do a quality job, we will find one continually trying to correct the inaccuracies of the other. Each person may continue to do the same job he or she would otherwise; the quality and quantity of work produced may remain the same, as each binds to his or her intended pattern of behavior. However, the actions of one will affect the other, and one or both must compensate. If behaviors adhere to attractors, then these are logical extensions of nonlinearity in a relationship. Likewise, if behaviors are nonlinear, then we can expect that there is some limit, some threshold beyond which actions will become unpredictable. Is there one more word, one more mistake, or one more glance that causes one or the other to quit or causes verbal or physical violence between the two? Because unpredictable behavior emerges when a person leaves a behavioral attractor, we should all be asking how we measure the extent to which a person resides within his or her attractor of behavior.

Conflict can occur if two persons differ in the degree of generosity they generally offer. If one person possesses a demeanor of openness and benevolence and another demonstrates malice and selfishness, a relationship is possibly untenable. The interaction of the two behaviors may cause the benevolent one to feel "used." Perhaps the extent of the behavior is limited enough that it can accommodate. Perhaps it pushes one to the threshold where one more selfish action breaches the relationship.

Consider the job of a marriage counselor. The counselor not only attempts to understand the perspectives of the two clients, but he or she actually attempts to intervene in this complex network of behavioral patterns in an attempt to create a common ground. In doing this, however, the counselor actually becomes part of the relationship. It is no longer a relationship of two; it is a relationship of three. And it evolves over time, from session to session, until stability or failure ensues. What tools does the counselor have to track this weaving pattern of developing behavioral trajectories? At best, some notes and a good memory.

There are, however, many accepted survey instruments to measure feelings like *trust* and *responsibility*. But they, like so many other measurement tools commonly in use, provide only that single frame from the continuing movie. After all this discussion of nonlinear trajectories, it seems unthinkable that one would attempt to measure something as dynamic as the relationship between people with a singular instrument. The usefulness would increase manyfold if it were applied regularly and tracked as a dynamic trajectory. Instead of asking 100 questions once, ask 10 basic questions ten times. Consider the patterns of relationships that could be displayed with that data.

Figure 11.2 provides two tentative models for any counselor. In each image the behavioral quality being traced is "trust," however defined and measured. A conventional phase plane is presented in Figure 11.2a. On it the horizontal axis measures *changes in perceived trust* and reported by one person, whereas the vertical axis measures the same variable as perceived by the other person. Imagine that the numbers tracing the trajectory are session numbers that can be associated with specific dates at weekly intervals. Now follow the trajectory and consider the implications. Off-axis oscillations report a developing imbalance in which one person gains while the other loses. In quadrant 3 each person loses. Improvements in the relationship occur when the behavioral pattern pushes into quadrant 1.

Figure 11.2b provides for the counselor as part of the relationship. By converting the phase plane to phase space, making it three-dimensional, we can place the perceptions of the two persons on two of the axes and the perception of the counselor on the third. The moving trajectory is still time-oriented transiting from one session to the next (here labeled A, B, C, D, and E). Although the clients' dimensions may still measure *trust*, the counselor's dimension may measure some other intervention measure.

Consider this proposal at a practical level. With only ten questions asked of each client one can generate ten sets of interactive patterns, not counting interactions across different concepts (i.e., does increased generosity by one lead to increased trust by the other). In only five sessions some type of trajectory will probably emerge. It may reflect constancy, thereby indicating that the intervention sessions have had no result, or it may indicate movement by only one of the people involved. It may begin to show one person less stable than the other.

Perhaps we fail to attempt this level of understanding in relationships because our statistical tools are simply too crude. The statistician would prefer to wait for thirty observations and would then draw some conclusion based on the averages over thirty weeks (7½ months) of counseling.

Figure 11.2
Phase Plane for Counseling Relationships

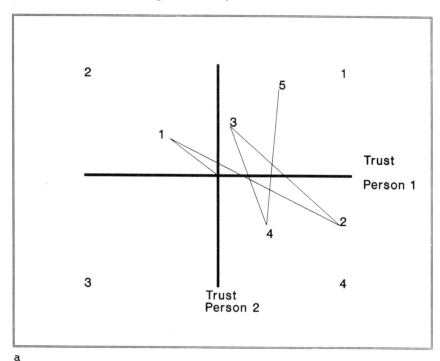

a

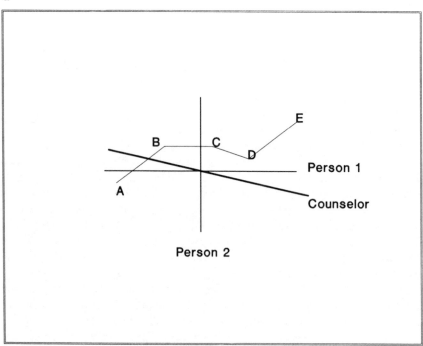

b

Chaos theory presents the data as it is without any assumptions of confidence limits or probabilities. Because it treats each observation with such importance, it can present an intricate picture that would never emerge from traditional statistics.

And the phase plane is not all that is reported. One can generate velocity histories showing the developing patterns of opinion for each person. Just as a physician demands an electrocardiogram on cardiac patients to gauge their health, so should a counselor demand a marginal history chart before beginning treatment. Both are dealing with nonlinear systems.

We should expect to find stability, oscillations, complex limit cycles, and disorderly chaos in the trajectories generated by these relationships. Although constancy is probably not the goal, one would expect that some degree of stability is preferred to chaos. Recall that it is the stability of our behavior that makes us predictable and cooperative. It is the instability in our behavior that makes us creative and perhaps interesting.

When during a counseling session should one collect the data? At the beginning? At the end? Perhaps, like a physician, it can be collected immediately before the session, processed, and delivered to the counselor before the session begins. It seems that this would greatly influence the action the counselor takes.

How should such information be used? Should it be shared with the clients? Would that assist them in controlling their attitudes and behavior, or would it erode its usefulness? Can clients *vision* new positions on the phase plane, thereby controlling it, managing it? Those are questions that must remain unanswered for now.

In what other situations can this same model be applied? Imagine the possibilities. Could it be applied to a single person for drug counseling? Does it have an application to any relationships created and managed in your organization?

ASSOCIATIONS

Relationships can be examined at a different level. Rather than focusing on individuals, we can focus on the proliferation and interaction of groups. We have become a segmented society by propagating professional associations. From animal rights groups to zero gravity clubs, we have formed associations to further causes, whatever they may be. Sometimes the association is mandatory to do our job, such as in the case of the American Bar Association or the American Medical Association. And most such associations serve real purposes by qualifying or authorizing members or by advocating their cause. The issue is not the merit of their existence; the issue is our reason for joining. We can view associations as attractors that draw us to join. But why do we join in such record numbers?

In some cases the need to join an association is so great that the attraction cannot be denied; such is the case when membership is mandatory for a specific line of work. In many, however, we are drawn to join for other reasons. Perhaps the association offers position or rank within one's profession. Perhaps it is seen as a way to enhance the possibilities of promotion. Because the costs frequently are low and the benefits, real or imagined, are high, we find ourselves drawn to join when one other employee says, "Haven't you joined our professional association?" How can one resist?

For those who promote associations the implications are clear. You need to make your association as essential as possible or, without that, make membership as desirable as possible, and you need to open the channels—identify the trajectories—through which nonmembers can join. Make the membership procedure clear, obvious, if not unobstructed. Those ideas are nothing new.

But the multiplication of associations reflects other conditions of our society and other human qualities. We are able to communicate inexpensively. We live in a world so rapidly changing that we need one another to keep up with whatever is new. We live in a world so complex that we need one another's involvement to be successful. We need a collective focus because we too often lack one of our own. As we bind to associations we give away a little autonomy. No doubt the trade-off usually is worth it, but joining does move one closer to stability, and too much stability stifles creativity.

One should question the validity and benefit of associations. One should never step too near them, as it is probably more difficult to leave than it is to enter. Whether that attractor is the National Geographic Society or the National Rifle Association, one is inclined to stay joined once joined.

The topic of chaos theory is wide-ranging. It touches the philosophical questions of free will and challenges the mathematician. It is at the same time applicable to soft sciences and hard ones. We can examine machines, behaviors, and beliefs using the same words and the same tools. To make it work, however, we must see it at work. We must see it in the jobs we do.

AMUSEMENT GAMES

Consider the job of the amusement game operator. Imagine you are the person who buys commercial amusement game equipment from any of several manufacturers, and places that equipment in bars, bowling alleys, or your own arcade. If the equipment is placed in a business owned by someone else, it is called a route location and you pay to that owner about 40 or 50 percent of the collections. If the equipment is placed in a company-owned arcade, then you keep the collected revenue but you have to cover the greater costs associated with the arcade. You probably own about

500 machines valued at $1,500 each. What can this chaos stuff do for you?

Plenty. The key to making a profit in this industry is rotating equipment from one location to another and buying new equipment frequently enough to keep your customers coming back. If you don't buy often enough, your sales volume will fall. If you buy too often, your costs (primarily depreciation) will consume any profits. But the job is not that simple. You can also "tweek" the equipment—you can adjust it, making it give out more free games. You can make it easier or harder to play. You can make the crane more able or less able to pick up the little pink bunny.

Week in, week out those 500 pieces of equipment pump out their quarters. When one seems to be less productive than it should be, you "tweek" it or move it to another location. If it doesn't recover, you replace it. But imagine how crude the information is that forms the basis of these essential decisions. Even with the best systems now available for tracking game performance, you are still only looking at total revenue or total plays over the past several weeks. You probably have a cumulative measure of each machine's collections for whatever purpose that serves.

Imagine a phase plane of each machine's changing collections over time. If it is stable, it remains in the center. Perhaps it oscillates weekly, corresponding to pay day. You can see the effect of any adjustment. You can see the effect of any rotation from one site to another. Your job becomes one of managing trajectories of change rather than counting quarters. You learn to read velocity history charts and you learn to identify dysrhythmia. You learn how to intervene in those patterns of behavior and you know when to trade in one of those "pacemakers" for another. Imagine it. Every major amusement game business in the United States may one day have its resident chaotician.

If it applies to the amusement operator's business, it applies to yours. The amusement operator's job is quite universal. It involves the management of multiple businesses that have changing relationships to their markets. In this case the businesses are machines, but they could just as easily be retail locations, different products, or individual sales representatives. In all of these cases there is simply a need to measure the changing dynamic relationship before it becomes unstable or unprofitable.

RETAIL

Consider the job of operations director for a chain of retail stores. The performance of each store, each department, and each product line can be tracked on the margin. The levels of nonlinear analysis are no different than we might use for traditional financial analysis. In fact, the data might be the same. The information derived, however, is different.

Is there a preferred pattern of behavior for our retail stores? Can we take the ten best performing ones, study their limit cycles of inventory turnover or payroll costs in detail, and then merge the data to create a corporate standard? It would be something like establishing a healthy heartbeat to use for comparison. We could overlay each other store's phase plane onto the healthy one; we could compare their marginal history charts. Most important, we can intervene before the incremental changes accumulate to such magnitude that they become apparent in the aggregate data.

There would be distinctive patterns for many common operations. The obvious financial ones were presented in Chapter 5. The human resource ones, like employee turnover, were presented in Chapter 7. We might develop software that monitors the patterns of change in product sales and flags us when there is a deviation from normal patterns. Let's not concern ourselves with when things change; let's concern ourselves with when things change differently than expected.

SALES MANAGERS

Any sales manager can use these ideas. He or she can use them to describe the behavior patterns of his or her sales representatives. Sales personnel interact in a dynamic relationship between supplier and customer. A little extra push closes the sale. A little too much push causes it to not close. The evolving condition of the representative is particularly evident if there is a commission on sales. The feedback of positive reinforcement encourages greater and greater performance, whereas a lack of compensation resulting from poor performance encourages avoidance. Incrementally, each representative steps farther down a trajectory of success or a trajectory of failure. One can imagine, in the extreme, that success or failure on the first call might dictate the ultimate success or failure of the representative.

If nonlinear systems remain faithful to their behavior, we would expect some representatives to hire on and report sales that decline steadily until they leave the organization by their own accord or with help. These are the ones who failed to attain a fixed point of stability and, instead, slid down the path of attrition. We would expect others to quickly reach a stable sales volume and turn it in regularly. If their volume is a bit low one week, it will probably be a bit higher the next and vice versa. They are bound to a stable attractor.

Some representatives may exhibit an oscillating sales volume; they are up one week and then down in diphasic reflection. On the average they are as good as the rest. On a weekly basis their performance may seem unpredictable.

We would expect some representatives whose performances are ascending. Each week's production is better than the week before; incrementally, they seem to be destined to infinity. Finally, there are those who deliver entirely disordered sales performances. They are truly unpredictable, sometimes turning in record volume, sometimes taking off for two weeks unannounced. These may be the same ones who occasionally cost the organization in excessive expenses. They are chaotic.

Many will agree with these characterizations. Unfortunately, it is difficult to provide precise recommendations for managing each type. Recall that the behavior of a nonlinear system is determined (at least in part) by the conditions of its environment. Remember how we demonstrated all these types of behavior by changing a single parameter in a nonlinear equation (Chapter 1). It follows that the behaviors of sales representatives are likewise determined to some extent by the environment—the firm. Those representatives who slide down a trajectory of failure probably need greater intervention than others. Perhaps more training. Perhaps there is a way to make the job more important, more meaningful. Perhaps they need to define a vision for themselves. Chaos theory seems to suggest that the potential for success is in these people, given a sufficient injection of "environmental influence."

There are only two ways to deal with those representatives who reach a stable state. One can either leave them alone and permit them to deliver steady production, or one can intervene, exposing the fact that they have bound to an arbitrary attractor. It might be particularly valuable to those in a stable state to explore the concept of visioning. They may realize the artificial nature of the forces that bind them and be able to move to higher performance levels. However, exiting a stable attractor has its risks, as behavior then becomes unpredictable. It does seem, however, that one could always return to the original stable-performance attractor.

A prescription for representatives with oscillating performance patterns is much more difficult. Perhaps they can be stabilized to a fixed performance pattern. Perhaps they can be pushed forward to an ascending pattern. Perhaps there is nothing fundamentally wrong with their pattern of sales production. It is a natural artifact of the person and of the market being served. Maybe it is simply a characteristic of the system.

Ascending performance suggests a need for intervention. It produces burnout, as the person works ever harder for ever higher levels of production. If a limit is reached, it is probably caused by a restriction, a barrier independent of the person. This type of performance is easily recognized; perhaps a better understanding of it will help to manage it.

Finally, our chaotic sales representative is probably one we do not need. The inefficiencies associated with such erratic behavior will make the person costly to the organization. Perhaps there is a way to stabilize the performance by adding structure to the behavior patterns.

One could probably classify sales representatives by observing their performance patterns in phase space. The behaviors described above would probably become evident, and the necessary interventions, if any, will come from an understanding of the business.

ATTORNEYS IN CHAOS

What shred of evidence tipped the scale and caused the jury to vote guilty? The legal profession presents, as its symbol, a scale that balances one way or the other, sometimes tipping this way and then that before cascading downward on one side or the other. Tipping the scale from center is the hard part; once it starts to go it is easy to pour on the evidence.

The scale, however symbolic, is a long way from descriptive of modern legal practice. There are, though, some thoughts for those in the trade.

People bind to attractors, as we have already discussed. Their beliefs constitute a collection of cohesive nonconflicting ideas that are difficult to change. Once bound to a set of ideas, they are comfortable with it and uneasy with leaving those beliefs behind. However, two attractors can be attached by a single trajectory, a single course or path that leads from one side to the other. Nonlinear systems, and perhaps beliefs, can remain in an orbit in a given domain for extended periods and then exit, almost inexplicably, to another domain, where they visit for another extended, unspecified time. When handling conflict, one should be aware of the underlying attractors of either side and know the paths that connect them.

At a practical level, it is obvious that litigation is nonlinear. A case is born of conflict that emerged because of misunderstanding or deliberate attempts by one to exploit another. It takes an accumulation of forces and finally one additional push to call the lawyer. That choice, that trajectory, leads to the filing of the suit, which ultimately leads to some disposition. There is a trajectory that defines the life of the case; theoretically, it can be managed and controlled. In fact, it is the attorney's job to guide the case to a preferred solution. I wonder, however, how well attorneys see that trajectory. Because of the protracted nature of legal activities and the mixing of other case loads, it seems that sometimes the evolution of the case gets lost.

Admittedly, the attorney may review the file completely before proceeding to the next step, and that adds consistency and perspective. But legal decisions often seem to hang on a balance of little things that make all the difference.

An investigation follows a trajectory, each step building on the last. It is that first step, that initial inquiry and how it is handled, that seems to be of particular importance.

Similarly, the path toward final resolution is started with a first step, a first interview, and a first deposition. It begins with a first review of existing case law, and final resolution may hinge on that extra incremental minute of additional effort put forth by a law clerk to check one more source. The message is the same. The little things are important, and collectively, they contribute to creating a trajectory that leads to some specific conclusion. Perhaps, like anything else, that conclusion can be visioned and created with sufficient effort. There are important issues regarding statistical evidence that may be of interest to attorneys as well.

STATISTICIANS

It is often said that you can make statistics say anything. That really isn't true. You can make statistical calculations so poorly or you can deliberately violate some of the proper procedures of statistical analysis to make the numbers support any idea; you can reverse engineer statistics to support your case. But any good statistician can reveal your tactics. In fact, a really good statistician can find flaws with any study. Statistical procedures have become so standardized that they are subject to such high levels of scrutiny.

Statistical analysis is but one way to search for "truth." It is but one way to measure and understand the world. There are other approaches. Many people prefer to interpret events and make decisions based on faith. Some guide their lives with astrology. Although you and I may refuse to acknowledge these approaches as equal to decision-making based on the scientific method, they are valid approaches for those who use them.

Now our scientific method has revealed something new. It has exposed a peculiar behavior of systems that shows them capable of generating random-appearing numbers that can be computed directly. Chaos theory has shown us that what we thought was random may not be; that beneath those numbers there can be a relatively simple iterating process that generates the apparent randomness. That fact strikes at the heart of traditional statistics, which were built on acceptance of randomness as a natural law of the universe (witness the assumptions of the normal distribution). How many statistical analyses start with the statement "Assume X is a randomly distributed variable with a mean of *mu* and a variance of *sigma*"? It now seems that that is a *major* assumption.

All the precision of a statistical computation becomes laughable when it fails to fit the solutions to a simple nonlinear equation (recall our "HI" example in Chapter 8). The gross inefficiency of something so common as a histogram is a direct assault on classic statistics.

The statisticians who read this will fall back on their time series analysis as a means of explaining the phenomenon described here. If they do that, they have failed to capture all the implications offered by nonlinearity. Chaos says systems are deterministic and that what we see as random is only that which we do not understand. Discard the notion of randomness and restart by observing the actual behavior of the system. Use the computational prowess of today to capture all the data points and use the information in each one. Quit throwing out outliers; quit averaging numbers; quit speaking of probabilities. This is not a world of chance; it is a world of choices.

Those who are obsessed with numbers can dive deeply into nonlinear dynamics. There they will find plenty of calculus and lots of manifolds to study. They can go in search of the underlying, iterating equations that create the patterns of data we observe. Progress will come by accepting a new set of assumptions, not by trying to explain it with conventional tools.

I am reminded of a B-rated sci-fi movie in which New York gets destroyed (again) by another atomic bomb and the last man on Earth (probably Charleton Heston) survives in a submarine. Hearing a lonely, coded radio message from the center of the city, he pursues the source only to find a window shade tripping a telegraph key. The message wasn't intelligent, but it also wasn't random. How many messages do we receive and interpret as either randomness or intelligence. If those are our only two paradigms, then we must classify everything as one or the other. If we redefine randomness as a phenomenon of nonlinear systems, we are inclined to continue our inquiry and attain greater understanding. In the movie Heston became convinced that the message wasn't random, so he concluded it must be intelligent. That decision led him to know reality.

Statisticians should explore nonlinearity, if for no other reason than to be prepared; there is another dimension to data behavior that is not being captured by traditional statistical approaches. Nonlinearity is an Achilles' heel in conventional statistics, and one is wise to know his or her vulnerabilities. Those of us who use statistics also should be warned; we may not be seeing the true behavior of the systems we manage. Academicians at conferences better beware the chaotician, who will attack their work on its assumptions of randomness. They should cringe at the thought that someone might reveal an intricate nonlinear trajectory in a data set just reported to be uncorrelated. Heaven help the expert witness who speaks of probabilities when the chaotician says, "Let me show you the patterns that actually developed and caused this event."

TEACHERS

This is the stuff teachers live for. They like new ideas, fresh perspectives, and new rules to explain. Chaos theory inspires interest, and if that term is too sensational, one can always claim to be into nonlinear dynamics. Whatever you call it, this newly emerging field of science will impact our view of virtually every subject from physics to history. Search the data bases for any combination of the terms nonlinear and chaos and key words for your field of study. You'll find that someone has already pushed in an article. It may be in an obscure journal, but it will be there. Read about chaos; get some working definitions of terms. Don't shrink from the mathematics. Write a program for limit cycles.

Students probably develop according to nonlinear paths. Perhaps we can help them *vision* their future performance. Perhaps we can help them vision the future. As educators we are in the thick of it; we work within nonlinear organizations, we deal with nonlinear behaviors and relationships, and we can teach nonlinearity. We are obligated to understand it.

From the organizational level to the personal one, chaos theory provides a new set of tools to help us understand. If we can see it in our own actions, we are more likely to see it everywhere. That has been the purpose of this chapter. To make nonlinearity something that is evident all around us.

NOTES

1. The flight of birds has been described by others as a nonlinear system.

2. We have effectively centered the phase plane from your place of birth. Otherwise, your current home would constitute a position in quadrant 1.

12

Some Closing Thoughts

This seems to be the age of new paradigms. There are new paradigms of management, new paradigms of control, and new theories in physics, astronomy, behavior, and government. There are even paradigms to explain the evolution of new paradigms. Out with the old, try something new—a different approach, a different philosophy. Paradigms are not necessarily trends. In fact, they are typically founded on some rather substantial new discovery that cannot be denied. Total quality management is a modern management paradigm. Although its popularity will probably fade, its impact will not. We will learn to accommodate continuous quality control in our ways of production, and we will transform the ideas it offers into other approaches that are built on it.

Similarly, chaos theory is a new paradigm. It is based on fundamental truths about system behavior. We can demonstrate chaos on our own home computers and in our own kitchens. It will not go away.

It is tempting to call chaos a trend, and perhaps the term will become so overused that one will shrink from using it. But nonlinear dynamics have been here a long time and will continue to describe system behavior. What chaos theory has done is popularize the obscure equations of mathematicians. Many of those mathematicians don't like us to be playing with their toys, but we have hold of them now and we're going to see what they can do. Mathematicians don't want us to treat their ideas crudely, with a lack of sensitivity to every nuance in the equations. I suggest that the popularity of chaos theory is an opportunity for mathematicians to demonstrate the practicality of what they do. We can use them now in business.

There are old and new attractors and old and new paradigms; perhaps the ideas are synonymous. We leave old ideas and venture to new ones, and the unfamiliarity of the new domain makes it interesting; constancy is comfortable but boring. It makes one wonder if there is a pattern to this incremental development of ideas, a manageable trajectory.

Here we have focused on old and new ideas of management. We used chaos theory as a tool to force open some hardened concepts of marketing, finance, production, and human resource management. We used chaos theory to give forecasters a much bigger job, and we offered strategists the opportunity to become practical visionaries. Perhaps it is time to rename chaos theory, as it is clearly no longer only a theory.

Although the issue of free will has already been addressed, it is an issue of particular importance here. Also of continued interest is the notion of incremental choice. By every action we take, or even by our inaction, we select a future condition that changes the state of the system. Our next action is based on that one. Our next thought is based on this one. We chose whether to move, speak, smile, or frown, and that choice is irreversible. Without vision we tend to repeat known patterns of behavior. With vision and *will* we can chose to push away from those patterns to move to different conditions.

The other day I put a pencil to a blank piece of paper and asked my son, "Where will it go?"

He said, "Anywhere."

I moved the pencil to trace a line to another position on the paper and stopped.

I asked, "Why did I move it to there?"

He said, "Because you wanted to."

I asked, "Could you predict it?"

"No," he answered.

"Who, if anybody, can predict where it will go?" I asked.

"You, because you have the pencil," he answered.

The future is not set if we have free will. The priests will assure you of at least two things regarding the free will issue. First, humans do have free will. Second, nothing else does. Without accepting the presence of free will one must believe that I had no choice about where to draw the line on the paper. I was inclined by past experiences to do it as I did. In the absence of free will we have predetermination, and that is a detestable idea.

I moved the pencil again, continuing the line to another position on the paper.

I asked, "Where didn't I go?"

"Everywhere else," he said.

He is right. When we choose one trajectory, we close out forever any other. We choose and then create each new reality. If there are alternate ones, they are down paths never taken.

This doesn't mean that we can't recreate conditions similar to those in the past. We can move the line on our paper to a position very near one we have visited before. A system can be periodic, returning to its same condition repeatedly. That is what causes periodic behavior; that is what creates stability and oscillation.

I drew a circle on the paper and handed my son the pencil. He extended the line from where I had stopped before to the center of the circle. He didn't start from somewhere else; the current state of the system was evident by the endpoint of the previous trajectory. It was from there that he started. The circle defined an alternate state of the system, a vision of what could be. It served as an attractor drawing in the trajectory. Had there been alternate positions identified on the page the decision might have been more difficult and the outcome less predictable. They would have offered more choice, and it was his decision, not mine, as to where things were going.

That simple paper and pencil exercise had meaning even though there was not meaning attached to any position on the paper. It provided insight because it described characteristics of natural systems. It provided discussions of conditions and choices and futures and time and transitions and alternate realities. These are the substances of systems. They are the framework to which we can attach any description. We can describe the population of rabbits that way. We can describe market share and financial performance that way. We can describe any management activity that way, even those dealing with behavioral and perceptual issues.

There are many organizational issues that have not been addressed here. We never mentioned ethics or research and development. We avoided the stock market and stayed out of the darkest corners of accounting. We didn't deal with crime directly.

I hope that what we did do together was to touch enough topics, define enough paths, and provide enough examples to prompt new ideas. I hope I kept the topic practical, yet general enough to allow one to extend it in one's own way.

It is now for the reader to consider the implications, to look around the room and find the closest nonlinear system. It is your chance to develop a phase plane diagram of your travels to work or plot the trajectory of your changing financial condition. Discover the patterns of nonlinear behavior in any system and then ask what you can do to manage the trajectory. Look for them in any of the functional areas addressed here. Look for them from where you are sitting. Look for them in what you believe. See the patterns of change; see them repeating themselves or following a wandering trajectory. Take one and control it. Vision a future and then create it.

Appendix: The Propositions

Throughout this book various propositions have been put forth to capture the central thoughts and considerations of the discussion. These are offered as a set of contentions for others to ponder. They are proposed as a framework for practitioners hoping to exploit nonlinearity in business. They are provided as tentative hypotheses to those interested in researching organizations.

The propositions are collected in this appendix for ease of use. They are titled below and then repeated as they appear in the text.

Marketing Management
1   Supply and Demand Relationships
2   Chaos Offers Opportunity and Risk
3   Distribution Channels Are Nonlinear Systems
4   Efficiency of a Distribution Channel Is Reflected in Its Cycles
5   Information Stabilizes a Distribution Channel
6   Products and Markets Trace Industry Cycles
7   Marketing Strategies Differ When Viewed from a Nonlinear Perspective

Financial Management
8   Financial Management Requires Understanding of Chronological Patterns
9   Intervention Strategies Can Be Related to Phase Plane Diagrams of Income Statement Relationships
10 Phase Planes Report More Information Than Common Financial Ratios

Production Management
11 Production Systems Can Be Managed as Nonlinear Systems
12 Phase Planes Reveal Inefficiency in Production Systems
13 Complex Production Processes Can Be Managed as "Black Boxes"
14 Chaos Theory Can Help to Relate Changes in Input to Changes in Production Output

Marketing Propositions

Proposition 1: Traditional supply-and-demand theory as we know it doesn't work. The sales of Coca-Cola sometimes go up when we raise the price.

Proposition 2: High-order chaos offers opportunity and risk. Low-order chaos offers predictability and constraint.

Proposition 3: A distribution channel constitutes a nonlinear system with an overall behavior resulting from the behavior and interaction of the channel participants.

Proposition 4: The efficiency of a distribution channel is evident in the limit cycles that reflect the channel's behavior.

Proposition 5: The source and type of information in a distribution channel greatly determine the ability of that information to stabilize the channel.

Proposition 6: Product and market evolution traces a trajectory defined by an interaction of forces. The trajectory's behavior over time is bound to and defined by an industry attractor.

Proposition 7: There are strategies for managing products when analyzed using conventional marketing matrices. However, when products and their markets are analyzed as nonlinear relations, the products get reclassified and these new classifications suggest strategies that can be completely contradictory to the conventional ones.

Financial Propositions

Proposition 8: Financial analysis requires more than simply a study of the current relationships between various financial measures. Understanding and prudent intervention require an awareness of the chronological patterns in the activities those measures represent.

Proposition 9: Phase plane diagrams provide a way to express the current state of an income statement's relationships. Because certain zones on the phase plane can be related to specific conditions, appropriate intervention strategies are prescribed directly by observing the current position of the limit cycle on the phase plane.

Proposition 10: Phase plane diagrams report financial information that is often used for ratio analysis in a way that much more effectively displays the behavior of the contributing measures.

Production Propositions

Proposition 11: Chaos theory is particularly appropriate as a monitoring system for production processes, since production typically involves periodic process and processes with many interrelationships. The process of production inevitably requires the management of a chaotic system.

Proposition 12: Study of production and distribution as a nonlinear process can reveal inefficiencies in the system.

Proposition 13: Sometimes highly complex production processes can be adequately controlled as a "black box" with nonlinear behavior.

Proposition 14: Chaos theory can be used to identify specific sources of instability or stabilizing effects by relating changes in input or changes in the production process to measures of subsequent output.

Proposition 15: Nonlinear behavior in production is not limited to simple quantities of production. The behavior includes attributes such as the quality and cost of the goods that are produced.

Proposition 16: The effectiveness of various costs and expenses can be determined by examining their association with total costs on a phase plane. Further, sources of instability in production costs can be identified by decomposing total production costs into a series of limit cycles that reflect the various cost components.

Proposition 17: Chaos theory offers a new level of control over production budgets. By relating changes in actual expenditures to changes in the budget, one can identify departures from budget sooner than with traditional approaches.

Proposition 18: Chaos theory offers a simple way to increase the precision and sophistication of quality control beyond those levels possible with statistical quality control. Because intervention always takes the form of a change to the system, changes in the system's behavior should be measured.

Proposition 19: Phase planes can be used to sensitively examine the behavior of a single measure over time, thereby offering a simple, more efficient substitute for traditional statistical quality-control charts.

Proposition 20: Phase plane diagrams can be used to reveal additional information about data beyond that provided by many common quality-control charts. They also suggest certain weaknesses of some conventional statistical charts.

Human Resource Propositions

Proposition 21: Organizational theory concepts such as centralization-decentralization and span of management trace trajectories in phase space reflecting forces in the external environment and within the organization.

Proposition 22: Management can be viewed as an evolving form of behavior that is part of the system being managed. Management style can be expected to change in response to perceived effectiveness, previous experiences, and changes in the system; the evolving style will trace a trajectory in phase space.

Proposition 23: Motivation can be studied as a nonlinear phenomenon that may be highly sensitive to initial conditions and may exhibit constancy, decline, acceleration, oscillation, or erratic levels over time.

Proposition 24: Changes in compensation relative to previous periods and relative to pay changes of other employees can be sensitively monitored as a trajectory on a phase plane with these dimensions. The approach suggests a way to create more consistent and effective compensation programs and provides information useful when counseling with employees.

Proposition 25: Limit cycles typically report the evolving dynamic response of a system over time. However, they are not limited to using time as their third dimension; any other variable may be substituted to provide a descriptive image of a system's response to the chosen variable.

Forecasting and Visioning

Proposition 26: Forecasting, the process of using historical data exclusively to make estimates of the future, fails to acknowledge the presence of free will. Such approaches are naive for any system in which humans participate.

Proposition 27: Rather than trying to estimate all the forces that act on a system in order to forecast the future behavior of that system, we can vision the future and then act on the forces to create the visioned condition.

Proposition 28: The job of a forecaster within an organization changes to one that is actively involved in decision-making. Like cardiologists, forecasters should recommend actions that stabilize or improve the health of the nonlinear system they monitor.

Strategic Management Propositions

Proposition 29: Visioning, which identifies a specific future state of a system, can be integrated into the strategic planning process to quantify a broad mission statement. Visions differ from goals or objectives because they are multidimensional.

Proposition 30: An internal analysis based on changes in organizational conditions identifies a different set of strengths and weaknesses than one would identify traditionally. Recognizing factors with marginal improvements encourages development of those abilities, ultimately making them strategic advantages, and permits intervention for those factors with declining ability before they constitute strategic disadvantages.

Proposition 31: One needs to know the trajectory of change in any business activity before attempting to implement a change to it. The activity may have stabilized at some desired or undesired state, or it may already be on a trajectory toward improvement or decline.

Proposition 32: Mergers and acquisitions cause changes in organizational limit cycles that are not simple combinations of the two firms. The impact of such combinations can only be estimated by observing the behavior of the combined trajectory.

The Center of Chaos

Proposition 33: Software developers have failed to provide for display of nonlinear relationships. Options for generating phase planes and velocity histories should be added to common spreadsheet programs and graphics software.

Proposition 34: Businesses should examine the information they currently use and consider which measures should be examined as nonlinear relationships. They should then devise ways of regularly displaying those relationships.

Select Bibliography

Blatt, J. M., "On the Frisch Models of Business Cycles." *Oxford Economic Papers* 32 (1978): 467–479.

Butler, Alison, "A Methodological Approach to Chaos: Are Economists Missing the Point." *Federal Reserve Bank of St. Louis,* (1990), 48.

Chiang, Alpha C. *Fundamental Methods of Mathematical Economics.* New York: McGraw-Hill, 1984.

Churchill, Neil C., "The Entrepreneurship Paradigm (II): Chaos and Catastrophes Among Quantum Jumps?" *Entrepreneurship Theory and Practice* 14 (Winter 1989): 7–30.

Crichton, Michael. *Jurassic Park.* New York: Alfred A. Knopf, Inc., 1990.

Day, Richard H., "The Emergence of Chaos from Classical Economic Growth." *Quarterly Journal of Economics* (1983): 98, 201–213.

Day, Richard H., "Irregular Growth Cycles." *The American Economic Review* 72, no. 3 (June 1982): 406–414.

Deneckere, R., and Pelikan, S. "Competitive Chaos." *Journal of Economic Theory* 40 (1986): 13–25.

Feigenbaum, Mitchell J. "Universal Behavior in Nonlinear Systems." *Los Alamos Science* (Summer 1980): 4–7, 27.

Feigenbaum, Mitchell J. "The Universal Properties of Nonlinear Transformations." *Journal of Statistical Physics* 21, no. 6 (1979): 669–706.

Frank, Murray Z., and Stengos, Thanasis. "Some Evidence Concerning Macroeconomic Chaos." *Journal of Mathematical Economics* 22, no. 3 (1988): 423–438.

Freeman, Walter J., "The Physiology of Perception." *Scientific American* 264, no. 2 (1991): 78–85.

Glick, James. *Chaos: Making a New Science.* New York: Viking Press, 1988.

Gollub, J. P., and Swinney, H. L. "Onset of Turbulence in a Rotating Fluid." *Physical Review Letters* 35, no. 14 (1975): 927–930.

Grandmont, Jean-Michel. "On Endogenous Competitive Business Cycles." *Econometrica* 5 (1985): 995–1045.

Grandmont, Jean-Michel, and Pierre Malgrange. "Nonlinear Economic Dynamics: Introduction." *Journal of Economic Theory* 40 (1986): 3.

Granovetter, Mark, and Roland Soong, "Threshold Models of Interpersonal Effects in Consumer Demand." *Journal of Economic Behavior and Organization* (1986): 83–99.

Gross, Donald, and Harris, Carl M. *Fundamentals of Queueing Theory*. New York: John Wiley & Sons, 1974.

Hunt, Shelby D. *Modern Marketing Theory: Critical Issues in the Philosophy of Marketing Science*. Cincinnati: South-Western Publishing Co., 1991.

Jacoby, Jacob, "Consumer Research: A State of the Art Review." *Journal of Marketing* 42, no. 2 (1978): 87–96.

Kadanoff, Leo P. "Roads to Chaos." *Physics Today* 36, no. 12 (December 1983): 46–53.

Kelsey, David. "The Economics of Chaos or the Chaos of Economics." *Oxford Economic Papers* 40, no. 1 (1988): 1–31.

Levy, Paul. *Calcul des Probabilities*. Paris: Gauthier Villars, 1925.

Li, T. Y., and Yorke, J. A. "Period Three Implies Chaos." *American Mathematical Monthly* 82 (December 1975): 985–992.

Lorenz, E. N. "Deterministic Nonperiodic Flow." *Journal of Atmospheric Science* 20 (1963): 130–141.

Loye, David, and Eisler, Riane. "Chaos and Transformation: Implications of Non-equilibrium Theory for Social Science and Society." *Behavioral Science* 32, no. 1 (1987): 53–65.

MacKinnon, Greg. "Non-Linear Dynamics and Chaos." Working paper, (1991).

Mandelbrot, Benoit. "Statistical Methodology for Non-periodic Cycles." *Annals of Economic and Social Measurement* 1 (July 1972): 259–290.

Mandelbrot, Benoit. "Towards a Second Stage of Indeterminism in Science." *Interdisciplinary Science Reviews* 12 (1987): 117–127.

May, R. M. "Simple Mathematical Models with Very Complicated Dynamics." *Nature* 261 (1976): 459–467.

Mirowski, Philip. "From Mandelbrot to Chaos in Economic Theory." *Southern Economic Journal* 57, no. 2 (1990): 289–307.

Moon, Francis C. *Chaotic Vibrations: An Introduction for Applied Scientists and Engineers*. New York: John Wiley & Sons, 1987.

Penrose, Roger. *The Emperor's New Mind: Concerning Computers, Minds and the Laws of Physics*. London: Oxford University Press, 1990.

Peters, Edgar E. "Fractals Put Order in Chaos," *Pensions and Investment Age* 17, no. 7 (1989): 23–24.

Poincaré, Henri. *Les Methodes Nouvelles de la Mechanique Celecte I, II, III*. Paris: Gauthier-Villars, 1892.

Priesmeyer, H. Richard, and Baik, Kibok. "Discovering the Patterns of Chaos." *Planning Review* 17, no. 6 (1989): 14–21, 47.

Prigogine, Ilya, and Stengers, Isabelle. *Order Out of Chaos: Man's New Dialogue with Nature*. Toronto: Bantam New Age Books, 1984.

Rasmussen, Dan Rene, and Mosekilde, Erik. "Bifurcations and Chaos in a Generic Management Model." *European Journal of Operational Research* 35 (1988): 80–88.

Richards, Diana. "Is Strategic Decision Making Chaotic?" *Behavioral Science* 35 (1990): 219–232.

Ruelle, David, and Takens, Floris. "On the Nature of Turbulence." *Communications in Mathematical Physics* 20 (1971): 167–192.

Savit, Robert. "When Random Is Not Random: An Introduction to Chaos in Market Prices." *Journal of Futures Markets* 8, no. 3 (1988): 271–290.

Sayer, Chera L. "Diagnostic Tests for Nonlinearity in Time Series Data: An Application to the Work Stoppages Series." Preliminary results in an unpublished paper, February, 1988.

Scheinkman, Jose A., and LeBaron, Blake. "Nonlinear Dynamics and Stock Returns." *Journal of Business* 62, no. 3 (1989): 311–337.

Schewe, Phillip F., and Gollup, Jerry. *CHAOS: A Glossary.* New York: American Institute of Physics, Public Information Division, 1985, pp. 1, 5.

Stevenson, Howard, and Harmeling, Susan. "Entrepreneurial Management's Need for a More 'Chaotic' Theory." *Journal of Business Venturing* 5, no. 1 (1990): 1–14.

Vosti, Curtis. "Applications May Be Murky." *Pensions and Investment Age* 17, no. 15 (1989): 3, 45.

Index

About the Author

H. RICHARD PRIESMEYER is Professor of Management at St. Mary's University in San Antonio, Texas, where he is also Chairman of the Department of Management and Marketing. He is the author of several articles on chaos theory which have appeared in *The Journal of Business Forecasting Systems and Methods* and *Planning Review*. He also is the author of several software products.